About the Book

▲ ▲ ▲ ▲ ▲

So you have made up your mind. You are going to quit your job and start your own business. It can't be that hard, can it? All you have to do is come up with an idea, borrow some money, set up shop, and start raking in the bucks, right?

Well it may not be all that simple! Somewhere along the way—probably once you begin to think about quitting your job—you are going to run into a few problems. For instance, this idea of yours—whether it be a product or a service—needs a market. If a market exists, the question of money still looms large. Do you know what types of investors you need or how to approach them? And what about something as simple as your personality? Did you know not everyone has what it takes to become a successful entrepreneur?

Paul A. Brown, M.D., asked himself these same questions in 1967 and then turned a two-room business venture into MetPath Inc., which today is the largest medical testing laboratory in the world!

The trip was not, however, an easy one. Even the largest, most successful corporations are run by human beings who, like you and me, are capable of making mistakes. However, if you know what obstacles and mishaps await you beforehand, you should be able to avoid some of the costly and potentially devastating problems which Dr. Brown encountered on the way up.

What types of personal and financial risks play a role in any business? What sort of spending will help your business succeed—and what type of financial mismanagement will help it fail?

How can having too much money at the wrong time ruin your business? And how do you find—and keep—the best employees?

What do you do when a check for over one million dollars somehow winds up in the wastebasket, or three thousand addressed envelopes get mailed without the business flyers inside?

Whether you are just toying with the idea of starting a business or are ready to knock on that first investor's door, *Success in the Business Jungle: Secrets of an Entrepreneurial Animal* will provide you with a step-by-step guide to a prosperous and rewarding entrepreneurship. Take Brown's hard-earned advice, learn from his mistakes, and your journey to achievement and financial success will be a much smoother ride. He's already paved the way; the rest is up to you!

Success
in the
Business Jungle

Secrets of an
Entrepreneurial Animal

Success in the Business Jungle

Secrets of an Entrepreneurial Animal

by

Paul A. Brown, M.D.
as told to
Richard D. Hoffmann

DORRANCE PUBLISHING CO., INC.
PITTSBURGH, PENNSYLVANIA 15222

The opinions expressed herein
are not necessarily those of the publisher.

ISBN # 0-8059-4336-6
Printed in the United States of America

First Printing

For information or to order additional books, please write:
Dorrance Publishing Co., Inc.
643 Smithfield Street
Pittsburgh, Pennsylvania 15222
U.S.A.

Cover and chapter artwork: S. Neil Fujita

Dedication

▲ ▲ ▲ ▲ ▲

*Without a wife who was always
supportive of my "delusions of grandeur," I
would have stayed a pathologist
for the rest of my life.
Thanks "Charlie!"*

Contents

▲ ▲ ▲ ▲ ▲

Prologue

▲ ▲ ▲ ▲ ▲

This book is full of *secrets.*

It is also full of *mistakes.*

That's right, mistakes ... errors in judgment, wrong decisions, false starts, poor choices. In short, just about every mistake an entrepreneur can make, at every level of business life, is contained within these pages.

Such mistakes are the 'secrets' that most entrepreneurs would rather forget than talk about. But the real secret is in how to *overcome* those mistakes, which is exactly what this book is designed to help you do. The idea is that you can learn from someone else's mistakes, rather than from your own. What you will find on the other side of these lessons is exactly what you're looking for—the secrets to business survival and success, principles proven in not just one but *two* major entrepreneurial ventures that together have spanned nearly three decades and are still going strong.

The spirit, if not the letter of such entrepreneurial success, it turns out, is perfectly captured in the instinctual behavior of the denizens of the natural world. Our animal friends' secret is that they are all experts at surviving in their dangerous and unforgiving natural habitats—and many of their characteristic traits are exactly what an entrepreneur needs to successfully negotiate *The Business Jungle.* We believe that the profiles of our feathered, furred, and scaly friends, and the entrepreneurial parallels they provide make the business lessons more enjoyable and a lot more memorable.

Certainly, there is no other book currently on the market that is anything like *Success in the Business Jungle.* We know. We looked. This volume was conceived expressly to share the *principles of business success* with entrepreneurs just starting out, those already starting up—and even those starting to wonder why they ever set out to start up a business in the first place. It came into existence out of the honest desire to tell a good story to anyone willing to listen and to learn. *Success in the Business Jungle* hopes to *educate, entertain* and *enlighten* serious people about the exciting personal and professional adventure that is entrepreneurship.

Our 'business plan,' so to speak, was to capture the heart, mind, and soul of an entrepreneur, as well as to accurately document, define and describe the entrepreneurial experience ... all with substance and style. Ambitious, yes, but we believed we were up to the task. We knew what we wanted to do and were confident of success!

Sound familiar?

We soon found out that writing this book was much like an entrepreneurial venture and, like most entrepreneurs, we hardly knew what we had let ourselves in for. Instead of the year or two we envisioned to complete this book, *Success* was ten years in the writing. It took us two years merely to agree on the title! But in the end, we believe we accomplished our goals. Along the way, we learned that anything, be it a business or a book, takes time and effort to do well.

As the chapters unfolded, we also discovered that the book had become just like a successful entrepreneur—a little bit of everything!

Success, for example, certainly is a *business* book, but it's not like one you've ever seen before. This book is definitely not a self-congratulatory tale written primarily for the benefit of the author and the publisher. Instead, *Success* is an honest effort to illuminate not only the why but the how of entrepreneurship, complete with a liberal dose of the who, what, where and when, at every level of business building. But it is, for all of that, a consciously entertaining book that has been woven and rewoven with care and attention to detail, covering every aspect of entrepreneurial activity—all delivered with good (often *very* good) humor.

Success also might be considered a *textbook*, although it is hardly one in the traditional sense. Yet we believe, along with several early reviewers of the manuscript, that this book should be read by every business school student interested in the reality as well as the theory of entrepreneurship. We must add that we have not seen any academic tome on entrepreneurship better suited to an educator's needs in the classroom than the practical volume you hold in your hands.

One might even consider *Success* an *inspirational* book, but only if you are an entrepreneur or a would-be entrepreneur interested in finding out the stuff of which you and your success might be made. If building a big business and making a lot of money are thoughts that excite you, then read on! Our hope is that the true-to-life anecdotes and down-to-earth insights will inspire and enlighten you on your road to success.

Now you know all the secrets behind this book. What lies ahead is *The Business Jungle*, full of pitfalls, adventure, and intrigue. If you *read* the rest of this book, you may survive and build a successful business. Your business idea might bring you wealth and fulfillment. But *learn* ...

The *$ecret$ of the Entrepreneurial Animal.*

Paul A. Brown, M.D.

Richard D. Hoffmann

February 1998

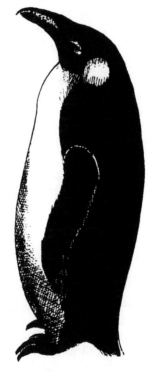

Knowing Your Limitations

Chapter One
The Penguin: Knowing Your Limits

▲ ▲ ▲ ▲ ▲

Penguins (family Spheniscidae) cannot fly, from the largest Emperors and Kings to the smallest Rock-hoppers and Adelies. All fourteen species' short wings lack quills and do not flex the right way to carry their heavy bodies aloft. Earthbound, they move in an antic, waddling parody of human gait, although capable of other, more imaginative motivation. They often slide on their bellies, pushing themselves along with their stubby, webbed feet, or hitchhike rides on ice floes. It is fish-like they move the best, though; and their characteristic black-and-white feathers even look a little like fish scales. Their swimming prowess often saves them from sea leopards and they survive well in the icy oceans of Antarctica . . . .

*　　*　　*　　*　　*

The snow started suddenly.

He had not expected it and that brought a sense of urgency to his mission. So he trudged along, propelled across the slippery surface as much by a kind of hunger as by his short, skinny legs. Navigating downhill among the already icy mounds heaped left and right along his path, he rushed because he was worried the fresh snowfall would ruin his search. The sun seemed to agree, looking in its own rapid descent like a frowning orange eye, now peeking distantly between the white line of the horizon and a low, miles-long ceiling of mackerel-scale clouds.

The boy scarcely had banged the front door shut on his parents' suburban home when the snow began falling. Perhaps most eight-year-olds in the affluent neighborhood would be catching snowflakes on their tongues, making snow angels, impatiently building snow forts and hoarding snowballs. But not Mark. He was heading downtown. Anyone watching the heavily muffled, booted and pea-capped child might have wondered what urgent errand sent him scurrying the three-quarters-of-a-mile distance at such a rapid pace, close as it was to dinner time. They might well have wondered, too, about the small yellow beach pail and little green shovel grasped in his mittened fingers. After all, they seemed a little out of place in the dead of winter.

The allure of Ridgewood's town center was not Mark's favorite candy store or ice cream shop, or even some poorly lit video game room that his mother had forbidden him to frequent. No, it was... parking meters! Mark Brown, son of Cynthia and Paul A. Brown, M.D., owners of the ten-acre estate he had just departed in the snow, had a thing about parking meters. Well, it was not the parking meters, actually. It was the money in them or, more precisely, the money that was *not* in them.

Now, before you get the idea that my adorable, gamin-faced, red-headed son was some kid-sized version of Cool Hand Luke who jimmied parking meters with his green, metal beach shovel and filled his little yellow pail with their contents, I had better explain. Mark had noticed that, after the first heavy snowfall a day or two earlier, the streets had been plowed by heavy machinery, piling up the white stuff high along the roadsides. Downtown, that meant mounds of snow covered the curbs and often half the side-walk, including the bases of the parking meters and a few cars as well (a time-honored practice in northern climes). If someone drove into town after the snowstorm and parked their vehicle at a meter, he or she would have to stretch and lean over a fair-sized snowbank to insert a coin into the parking meter's tiny, silver-rimmed slot.

Mark's coin-consciousness began to be expanded when he saw a man rushing out of a doorway, balancing a package or two and trying to stuff a quarter into a parking meter with a gloved hand. His clumsy effort quickly sent the coin into the relative vastness of that snowbank. Mark stifled a giggle as the man looked around hopelessly, shrugged and shot a frustrated glance heavenward, then put down his packages, took off a glove, reached into his pocket for another coin and finally managed its transfer to the parking meter.

Just then, a car pulled into a parking spot right next to Mark and an elderly lady got out, smiling at him as she gingerly minced her way onto the sidewalk. He smiled back, waiting to see what would happen. And sure enough, even her ungloved hands quick-ly sent a quarter disappearing into the dirty-looking pile of snow when she tried to pay her parking fee. As she fished in her pock-etbook to fetch another coin for a second try, Mark ran to where the quarter had dropped, dug around for a few seconds and came up with it. When Mark scrambled up the small snow-slope to put the cold coin in the meter for her, she was grateful and gave him a warmer quarter from her purse.

Suffused by his good fortune, Mark held his reward tightly. And as he followed the woman's retreating figure with his eight-year-old eyes, his vision all of a sudden was filled with a sight that promised even greater reward: *All those other parking meters!* As far as he could see, lining both sides of the street, the gray, metal faces stared back at him and all of them were similarly snow-bound. In that moment my son Mark, a genetically determined entrepreneur, had found a business to start.

But not right then. Already the shadows were lengthening and he knew his mother would be waiting with supper. Besides, he still had to dig out that other quarter. As he headed home, his young mind raced with the possibilities. If two people had dropped coins at the meters within five minutes and there were lots and lots of meters, there must be hundreds—no, thousands!—of dollars under all that snow. He would be back, and soon!

The fledgling businessman's foray the next evening over the frozen wastes of northern New Jersey was accompanied by such grand thoughts, even though he had seriously overestimated his market. He was spurred, too, by his concern that the money would be harder to locate and dig out with his little metal shovel if there was another snowfall. But he did not have to worry; the storm petered out quickly and he arrived back home a couple of hours later with about fifteen dollars'-worth of coins in his little yellow bucket. Not bad for two hours of digging in the snow! Only trouble was, besides overestimating his market, he had failed to consider one other very important facet of the operation. He returned home to a very worried mother that night who had no idea where he had been for all that time. She was decidedly less than thrilled with her offspring's success in his first venture and grounded him and his very cold little can and shovel, immediately!

Although his coming-out as a businessman was not quite the unqualified success he had expected, Mark was indeed an entrepreneur. An entrepreneur, by the way, as defined by *Webster's New Collegiate Dictionary*, is "one who organizes, manages and assumes the risks of a business or enterprise." The scale of his operation did not matter: He got the business organized, managed his time and took risks. Among other things, he also invested time and equipment, did some market research, identified a target market and was willing to work hard to get results.

Mark also made some mistakes in the beginning, including overestimating the potential size of the market, underestimating the risks, and not managing his time too well. But he stuck to his vision even when it turned out that there were not thousands or even hundreds of dollars out there; only tens. He scaled back his expectations and was satisfied with the four dollars or so that he was able to retrieve on his weekly outings. He kept at it and over the space of several winters Mark eventually made a fair amount of money. It just took longer than he thought. Much sooner, he earned a proud pat on the back from his father. And by watching the clock on his subsequent trips downtown, making sure to advise his mother exactly where he was going and when he planned to return, he even got one of her warm, loving hugs every time he came home.

All of these things, including the family adulation, are common to start-up businesses of any size or description. The traits Mark exhibited are typical of successful entrepreneurs, likewise of any size or description. That he did not make as much as he thought he would and missed on a couple of other points is hardly unusual for any first-time business person, either. Even there, he turned negatives into positives, a most necessary entrepreneurial skill. Mark is still intrigued with a business career even though he has first chosen medicine as a career. But who knows? So did his father. Mark may yet follow in Dad's footsteps.

But what was it that made him first venture out on that cold, snowy night? That question brings us to a consideration of the first of several earmarks that identify a successful entrepreneur. Without them, I believe an entrepreneur has about the same chance of being successful in the business jungle as a penguin has of taking off and flying with his short little wings.

You may look like a bird but, unless you have the right equipment, you will never get off the ground.

*　　*　　*　　*　　*

The term "penguin" was first applied to the now-extinct great auk (Pinguinnis impennis). Once the largest of the family Alcidae, that goose-sized bird of the North Atlantic was hunted to extinction by seamen in 1844. A few skins, skeletons, and eggs of the hapless birds have been preserved in museums. Although most people think the three-letter answer to the ubiquitous crossword-puzzle clue "large flightless bird" refers exclusively to the great auk, the word "auk" also names all of the remaining twenty-two species of Alcidae inhabiting the North Pacific, North Atlantic, and Arctic Oceans.

*   *   *   *   *

1. *Motivation*

What motivated Mark is what pushes most entrepreneurs and it has many names: the promise of profit; the lure of wealth; the excitement of gain; the promise of financial rewards; making a living. In a word, **money**. Cold, hard cash—rather literally—motivated Mark, as it to one degree or another motivates me and who knows how many millions of other business men and women who have started up companies throughout time. There are two other chief motivators in human affairs (if I remember my business school lessons correctly) which can also motivate the business person; namely, **personal achievement** and **power**. More about all three, presently, but first, let me confront a couple of myths about money and business people that bear heavily on the topic of motivation. They need some "exploding" to clear the way for our discussion.

MYTHIC MONSTERS

Myth # 1: *Need and greed drive business.*

Myth # 2: *Money is "bad," somehow.*

The first myth is the most distressing, unfair and misanthropic of all the unfortunate labels visited upon any community of individuals. Perhaps my sensitivity to such a facile generalization is heightened by the fact that I am a businessman who views himself as no more needy or greedy than the next person, so you can take my umbrage any way you want. Some businessmen may be needy and greedy or may become so, but so may ministers, politicians, or any person in any pursuit. More often, it is people without any pursuit at all that are needy and greedy. It seems grossly unfair that most people think that business people are more needy and greedy than most other people just because business people happen to be money-motivated. But, number one, not just business people are money-motivated and, number two, people can get needy and greedy about a hundred other things, too, like attention, sex, or companionship.

The "need and greed" model is closely linked to the idea that money is somehow "bad." Maybe it is a mental device that some people use to feel morally or ethically superior to other people, allowing them to justify or ignore their own shortcomings in their own lives and pursuits. Perhaps it is a way of excusing one's own failure to make enough money to satisfy one's self or some significant other. Perhaps it is born of some extreme form of altruism that most recently surfaced in the 1960s (apparently only to be replaced by its opposite mindset of rampant avarice in the 1980s). I don't know. I am a pathologist, not a psychiatrist.

Neither am I an historian, but I suspect such attitudes have plagued business people at least since medieval times, when merchants and craftsmen began to emerge as a wealthy middle class. *Noveau riche* business people were haughtily viewed by titled royalty and landed gentry as somehow less than acceptable, a rather hypocritical view that has persisted over the centuries. It was eloquently and most haughtily expressed by Samuel Johnson who, according to the diarist Boswell in 1775, said: "There are few ways in which a man can be more innocently employed than in getting money," although Johnson was quick to add that "the sons and daughters of alleys," as he described those involved in commercial pursuits, might be "innocent" but hardly "admirable."

Meanwhile, on the other side of the social spectrum, there was likewise a strange ambivalence. Although the "working poor" (which made up the bulk of society back then—and probably throughout history right up until today!) might admire those in business, they were also jealous and mistrustful, perhaps sometimes with good reason. But business forged a new image as enterprises and institutions grew larger, giving people work and generally advancing the standard of living. Eventually they gained enough power and collective wealth to weather "the slings and arrows of outrageous persecution."

Unfortunately, the old disease of the attitudes of rich and poor alike concerning money was never really cured. Attitudes, it should be noted, are the result of habitual thinking patterns, often colored by emotional issues. Much as the common cold, the idea that money is somehow "bad" or "wrong" persisted, particularly among those greedy souls who wanted to keep all the wealth to themselves and those needy, envious hearts who felt that they should be the ones with all the money.

But if anything is "bad," it is just such attitudes. The worst of it is that they keep whole groups of people down, denying them access to their highest and best purpose. Individually, if they could accept money as their motivation, they might even become happy and useful individuals with a sense of purpose. The point is that money is not "bad" or "good," and having some—even a lot of it—is not "right" or "wrong." **Money just is, that's all.** How we go about getting it and what we do with it provides good fodder for sermons and psychoanalysts. But the naked "money is bad" attitude is at least an irrational aberration, having something to do with temporary insanity or the lack of a sense of responsibility. But to a successful entrepreneur—and I said successful, not just rich—money is just money and making it is rewarding, worthwhile, and quite conducive to mental health!

It sure can make you feel good about yourself and the more, the healthier! Presuming that you are not a "bad" person—take note, all of you now-middle-aged former hippies and yippies, you young yuppies, you seniors, and any among you of any age and circumstance fortunate enough to have avoided a media label—making money can be exhilarating. Trust me, it's okay! Making money is good for you, as long as you do not get greedy or need it overmuch. I have made enough of it to be able to state that unequivocally.

My son Mark's experience serves to explode the "need and greed" supposition about the motivation of business people, at least to my satisfaction, and I have been a successful businessman who has started up numerous ventures over the past several decades. But I expect a story about an eight-year-old entrepreneur might not be enough to get the point across, so I will also tell you about another entrepreneur, aged eleven years: Me. I started up and ran a couple of businesses in quick succession in and around the Boston area during the years 1949 and 1950. The first was a distributorship for what at the time was a brand new product: stretch socks.

The stretch sock business involved selling door-to-door in the Boston suburb of Newton, Massachusetts. I covered a lot of feet by the time that fad ended and I had to find another business. I soon began building and selling birdhouses made out of scrap lumber from the new homes being constructed in the neighborhood, which unfortunately was dispossessing the avian population at the same time. Like my son Mark, I wanted to make money, even though we both got an allowance, lived in relative comfort, and had been given one pair each of attentive, supportive and sometimes-too-indulgent parents.

Need did not motivate Mark to go digging in the snow at the foot of parking meter after parking meter on cold afternoons in all kinds of weather, nor did greed. His great expectations did not pan out, but he did not give up because there was not enough there to satisfy him. That was not important to him; he was just interested in making money, that's all. Mark worked hard, kept digging, and managed to supplement his allowance rather nicely. I did not need to go selling socks and birdhouses door-to-door either and greed would be a tough one to pin on me as well. I was, after all, building birdhouses and selling them to homeowners in the winter to help the birds! Aggressive, maybe even opportunistic, but hardly greedy.

So, if not need and greed, what motivates a successful entrepreneur? What moves a business person to build a company, like the one you want to create? As I said before, the primary and perfectly acceptable motivator for entrepreneurs is *money*, no matter what the size, scope or subject of the business—and for my money, *money* is the only motivation that an entrepreneur starting out needs. I would hate for anyone to miss this, so allow me to state it even more categorically: **Money is the best motivator for a brand new business, the only one an entrepreneur who organizes, manages and assumes the risks should have.**

A desire for personal achievement or power will not build a business, although they may come into play later in the life of a business or a business person. Anyone lacking the motivation toward making money is unlikely to become an entrepreneur, at least not a successful one. Left to his or her own devices, someone who is primarily achievement or power motivated will do something else besides starting up a business. Those primarily motivated by power will probably become politicians and generals, to whom prestige and command are everything. The most obvious career choices of those primarily motivated by achievement (at least those committed to their professions and not just hiding out in some academic or governmental bureaucracy) are perhaps teachers and social workers.

One's primary motivation very well could be genetically predetermined. Not to become embroiled in the "nature or nurture" argument of the social psychologists, my own observations and instincts tell me that people are born with these things. Environment has little to do with whether or not you are motivated toward money, achievement, or power. My eldest son Richard, for example, was brought up in exactly the same environment as my son Mark, the entrepreneur. Both had the same parents, grew up in the same houses, and lived in the same states during their childhoods. They shared in the same family vacations, went to the same summer camps, and had all the same advantages. They went to the same high schools and both attended Harvard College.

But Richard is an international lawyer, not an entrepreneur. He learned to speak French and Chinese and chose to work in Taiwan for three years so he could gain enough experience to eventually land a job with a big multinational corporation. But he does not want to build that big multinational corporation, or even a small retail store. Although he has many of the entrepreneur's personal characteristics, a topic we will explore a little later in this chapter, he is not an entrepreneur and I do not think he will ever become an entrepreneur. And that is because he is primarily motivated by achievement and not by money.

If Richard's idea of personal achievement was to build the biggest or best company he could imagine, that would be a fine motivation for being an entrepreneur. Equally fine would be building a business for the power to make lives better for people or to change the way things are done in an industry. But he does not care to start up a business and I have known him long enough to assess the reason why: He is not motivated by money. He gets excited about the accomplishment of achieving fluency in foreign languages and in practicing international law. He will undoubtedly make a good deal of money in that pursuit, but it is not the pursuit of money that turns him on. Money, for him, runs a distant second to personal achievement.

It's also true that the money motivation can be hidden in a person and might not be readily discernible, even by the person himself. Dr. Michael Patipa, for example, had invented a hand-held instrument in 1985 for doing micro-surgical pigmentation. He wanted to form a company called Permark to manufacture the instrument and was looking for start-up capital. He and I met several times at my home, and each time he tried to convince me to invest in his company. When I asked him why he was starting up the company, he would give me any number of different reasons, some of them vague, some altruistic, others very personal.

Our discussions wore on but I declined from investing until one day I once more asked him, "Michael, tell me again why you want to start up this business."

"Well, I've got a lot of reasons, I guess," he replied, reflecting on the many answers he had already given me. "But to tell you the truth, one of the biggest reasons I have for wanting to start up the business is really to be able to buy the lot next to yours and have a home like this."

"Now you're talking! How much do you need?"

I simply would not invest in his company until I could see that he had a motivation to make money, which I believe is absolutely necessary for success in the business jungle. If you are about to start up a business, making money is a critical motivation. You must focus exclusively on getting that business started—and for that you need money as your prime motivator. Now, that is not to imply that entrepreneurs should forget completely about their other motivations. I certainly did not; I just delayed them.

When I started up Metropolitan Pathology Laboratory, Inc. in April, 1967, which later became MetPath, I had already realized that money was my main motivator. I could have just continued my residency at Columbia Presbyterian Hospital, gone into practice as a pathologist, and I would have had more than enough money. Following graduation from college, my three goals in life were to become a millionaire, to obtain a black belt in karate and to be able to speak French socially. But making money, a lot of money, appealed to me most at that point in my twenty-nine-year-old life, so I went and started a business. That business, at the time of this writing, has about $2 billion in annual revenues, a fact that is very satisfying to me. But to someone without a strong money motivation, it would not mean very much.

Today, I am still motivated by money but achievement has taken over first place. The latter is the primary motivator behind this book—as well as my second major business venture, HEARx, a hearing-care company. Maybe I am moving into a more permanent kind of achievement phase in my life. Each week I spend eight hours studying karate and now have a second-degree black belt. I have written this book because I believe I have something worthwhile to say. I may also make some money at it, but that is not the primary motivation. Yet I certainly never could have written it unless I made a lot of money first. Money still motivates me and—I'll say it again—it is the primary motivator for an entrepreneur starting a business. Your new business may never succeed without a personal desire for wealth.

If you are contemplating making a lot of money, I do not expect it will be from starting a coin-retrieval-from-snowbanks operation, a stretch sock distributorship or a birdhouse manufacturing and sales operation. But by now you probably have realized that whatever the business, the principles we are espousing here can be applied to any situation.

If you are thinking about starting up a company, it is time to get to know yourself, if you have not already.

Even penguins know that, if penguins can know anything at all. At least they have figured out that they cannot fly. Yet they also know that they can swim, slide, waddle and float.

Entrepreneurs need to know their strengths and limitations, too.

If they want to get somewhere.

*   *   *   *   *

*The most numerous of the family **Alcidae** are the razor-billed auks, the guillemots or murres, and the puffins. The most adept at survival are the puffins, also called sea parrots and bottlenoses—the latter for good reason: They can catch as many as ten fish in succession in their characteristically sharp, compressed, triangular beaks. Puffins are also noted for the punctuality of their return to breeding sites in the spring. Penguins,* *too, ensure their tomorrows in immense rookeries, often hiding their nesting areas in the most remote and inaccessible regions. The brooding instinct is so strong that some birds may try to brood lumps of ice. They will brood even when completely covered with snow. The young, requiring a long period of care and attention after hatching, are cared for communally...*

*   *   *   *   *

2. Personal Characteristics

Before we move into an examination of the personal characteristics of an entrepreneur, let's move into an examination; namely . . .

DR. BROWN'S
PRE-ENTREPRENEURIAL EXAMINATION

1. *True or False?*
Self-honesty is absolutely necessary for an entrepreneur to be successful.

2. *True or False?*
You can only learn through your own experience.

3. *Multiple Choice (choose one):*
Successful entrepreneurs must work
(a) only occasionally.
(b) less than their employees.
(c) very hard.
(d) (None of the above.)

4. *Fill in the blanks:*
There are three abilities which all successful entrepreneurs exhibit:

• **P** _____.

• **P** _____.

• **P** _____.

5. *Fill in the blanks:*
Successful entrepreneurs are _____ -
oriented, rather than task-oriented.

6. *Fill in the blanks:*
**There are three characteristics which all successful entre-
preneurs exhibit that cannot be taught:**

- _____

- _____

- _____

Just in case you get nervous on tests, let's go over the answers.
Yes, you need **self-honesty** to be a successful entrepreneur.
Self-honesty is made possible by the ability to be introspective,
which just about anyone can do. If you have taken the time to consider your motivations, you have been introspective. How honest
you are with yourself about your motivations, however, is another
matter. *Self-honesty is simply an accurate self-appraisal.* If you
suspect your solitary self-appraisal might not be accurate, do not
hesitate to get an outside opinion. A close friend, a trusted advisor, one's spouse or other confidant can be invaluable in helping
you pinpoint your strengths and weaknesses. A spiritual advisor
such as a rabbi or pastor might be beneficial or, depending on
your bent, perhaps a professional psychologist. Better to do it
alone, though, than not to do it at all.

Most people are not going to take the time to think about these
things but you had better if you plan to start your own business.
You need not become a part-time philosopher or amateur psychiatrist, but you do need to look inside and try to get an honest perspective on yourself. That is how you discover your primary motivations and your individual traits, as well as your strengths and
weaknesses as a business person.

Your self-appraisal will not remain static, by the way. You will
change, for better or worse. Your primary motivation will probably
not be as strong ten or twenty years from now, or may shift entirely. You may have learned how to overcome some of your more glaring weaknesses much more quickly than that, while others may
crop up that you were not aware of before. Just do not fool yourself now, whenever *now* happens to be, especially if *now* is the
time that you plan to start up your business.

Not everyone who wants to go into business and start up a
company is possessed of enough motivation or the right kind of

motivation and personal characteristics to be successful or even survive in the business jungle. Various personal characteristics and business skills are needed for success, too, such as financial insight, marketing ability, organizational capacities, people skills and negotiating prowess, to name a few of the more general ones. Some of them cannot be taught and the others would take too long to learn during a business start up. Survival may depend on more specific skills, like market knowledge, sales and distribution contacts and manufacturing know-how (again, naming but a few). So, if your self-appraisal shows you do not have these prerequisites, then you better not go into business without some help.

Unless you can be honest with yourself, chances are that you will try to go it alone and wind up losing your business and working for somebody else instead ... not necessarily by your own choice. That is covered by Chapter 11 of the Bankruptcy Code. Gratefully, this book only has ten chapters, so don't go looking for it here! Self-honesty will allow you to admit you need some help, and the accuracy of your self-appraisal will tell you what kind of help you need to go out and ask for. If you know what your strengths and weaknesses are, you might look to hire people that complement your strengths and compensate for your weaknesses. (We will cover how to handle all that in *Chapter 5*.)

You might think of taking on a partner, but be forewarned: Partnership is a way fraught with unseen dangers and potentially disastrous consequences. An awareness of the perils of partnership came to me at age seven in my very first business, one of those proverbial lemonade stands. I went to my mother and told her excitedly of my intention and she said okay, then told me what I would need. So I got an old crate and a stool from the garage, pitchers and glasses from the kitchen cabinet, made a sign with my crayons and a big piece of "cahd-board" (as we say in Boston) and found a jar to keep my money. Therein I deposited the working capital my mother loaned me in case I had to change a dollar bill. Meanwhile, she pulled together all the ingredients and made the lemonade.

I went outside and opened for business. As I sat there, I became a little concerned about what would happen if I had to go to the bathroom. Along came Sherman, my closest friend, and I said, "Sherman, would you like to go in business with me on this lemonade stand?"

And Sherman, being my best friend, said, "Sure."

So he became my partner and I promised to give him half of the profits at the end of the day.

When that time came, we counted up the money. We made thirty-six cents, so I took half and gave Sherman the rest. Then I ran inside to show my mother how well I had done.

She saw me coming.

"So, how did you do?"

"Great," I told her. "I made eighteen cents."

"You were out there all day and that's all you've earned?"

"Well," I said a little sheepishly, "I gave half to Sherman."

"What do you mean, 'you gave half to Sherman?' What for?"

"Well, I gave half to Sherman just in case I had to leave or anything. I made him my partner!"

My mother just shook her head. "Paul, it was our lemons, our sugar, our water, our pitcher, our glasses—everything that went into that lemonade stand was from our house. Sherman didn't put anything into it at all. Do you think it was right for you to give him half the money just for sitting there with you?" I do not remember my answer, but I do recall the lesson: **Do not give away equal shares of a business to someone who does not contribute equally**—and your partners rarely will! Unfortunately, I had forgotten that lesson by the time I became an adult and entered into my first real business, MetPath, which finally gave me pause to think (see *Chapter 2*). The point here is that sometimes one experience is not enough for some of us to learn a lesson.

Experience, that's the ticket! And the nice thing about experience is that you can learn from your own, or you can learn from somebody else. Not by their just *telling* you, but by their *showing* you. That is why I am trying to illustrate as many of the things I say about entrepreneuring with as many of my own and others' experiences as I can. But you have got to accept them before they mean anything to you. You have to believe that they are trustworthy accounts, delivered in good faith.

"That's obvious," you say? Not always.

The learning process, whether it involves personal or vicarious experience, always starts with *trust*. The phrase in literature is the *willing suspension of disbelief*, which is what allows us to gain insight from a play or a novel. If you cannot trust other people—like your business partners, employees, consultants, board members or suppliers—how will you make it through the business jungle? If you cannot trust your own experience, you will never learn from it, will you? Nor will you learn anything by observing someone else if you cannot accept the evidence of your senses. And if you cannot trust me, you will not get a thing out of this book.

Why should you trust me? Well, I have nothing more to gain from you—you have already bought this book. True, I might want you to buy my next book or even call me as a consultant, but you will only do that if you get something out of reading this book. And if you do read this book—you might as well, you have already paid for it—here is what could happen. You might try some of the things I have suggested. You may find that they work. If they work, you will then have had the experience yourself. Hopefully, you will trust your own experience. Then you will have learned something. Maybe you will buy my next book! Remember, though, I did not teach you anything. You get all the credit for learning it and perhaps you will gain a lot more, besides.

The attempt at self-understanding is certainly one well worth the effort. I have found that periodic check-ups of my motivations, traits, skills, desires, abilities, strengths and weaknesses is a valuable practice. These inward journeys are best taken whenever starting a new business and at several points thereafter. Starting an enterprise may be the first time you are forced to ask yourself some serious questions: Who am I? Can I do this? How am I going to do this? The survival and success of your business venture depend on your honest answers to these questions, more so than you can imagine.

I imagined all kinds of great things in 1967 when I started up Metropolitan Pathology Laboratory. And I was not shy to tell potential investors that it was going to grow to be one of the largest labs of its kind in the world, which it eventually did. I even began the company name with the word "Metropolitan," not because it was in New York City, but because I planned it to be in every major urban center in the U.S. and even abroad.

But back then, I knew very little about laboratory testing and even less about running a business. I was still in training to become a practicing pathologist. I thought I knew enough about business that I could not be hoodwinked, but that was about all. I was barely out of the box as a businessman. The only thing that saved me and the company from ruin was whatever self-honesty I could muster at the time. It was particularly important because as MetPath grew, I was able to hire people who knew more than I did about certain things where I was not very strong, like running the business. That way, the strengths and interests I perceived in myself at that time—in marketing, negotiating deals and raising money—would be complemented, for example, by others' prowess in administration, operations and purchasing.

In the meantime and ever since, it has been necessary to work hard to even stand still. Which brings us to the answer to the third question on our test: Successful entrepreneurs have to work **(c) very hard**. Had I been the type that demanded instant gratification, I probably would not have worked very hard at all once I started hitting the hurdles. Or I might have worked hard for a short period of time, then given up and gone off to take risks more apropos to a quick-hit nature, such as playing slot machines or scratching the silver off of lottery tickets. Entrepreneurs who want to be successful over the years or even to survive in the beginning, must have the ability to wait for things. That ability is better known as **patience**—which begins to fill in the blanks of question number three in the pre-entrepreneurial examination.

I call patience by another name: *the ability to delay gratification*. Delayed gratifiers do not need pacifiers. They want the real thing. They have the attitude that if there are some things worth pursuing, then there are some things worth waiting for, no matter how long it takes for either of those things to happen. They are confident people, secure in themselves, who are sure of their motivations and their abilities, able to postpone reward. There are plenty of people who cannot postpone anything. Instant gratifiers are not willing to wait through the years that things could take to work out.

Gratification comes in two flavors, business and personal. The rewards from business *per se* are satisfying only to business people. Most rewards within the business itself are moments of victory that burst colorfully and briefly across the long expanse of time's canvas: receiving that first investment, landing that first big contract, getting the price you want when you sell the company. They are things that would appeal to an instant-gratification type, things that call for champagne and celebration all around; the problem is, those things usually only happen once per business and do not happen right away. You may have to wait around for some time before they do. The instant gratifier, usually rash and impetuous, by that time will long since have moved on.

Delayed gratifiers are the ones who get to enjoy those moments because they know that to be in business at all is to be in it for the long haul. They know that things in business usually take twice as long as they should and usually work out only about half as well as they could. They know that the things that will bring personal gratification take even more time. That is what the delay is really all about, anyway. Delayed gratifiers know that the house in Palm Beach, the Lear Jet, the big bank account—or whatever personal rewards they want to realize out of their businesses—all will come later, usually much later. And they are willing to wait for it.

But while they are waiting, they are going to need a couple of other personal characteristics, as well; namely, the other two characteristics always present in successful entrepreneurs: **persistence**, the ability to keep trying to make things happen, and **perseverance**, the ability to go through whatever you have to go through to get to the end.

And what is the end? Well, the end is whatever your goals are. It just so happens that you need to combine patience, persistence and perseverance (each with a capital *P*) in order to realize your goals. Which brings us to the answer to question number 5: The successful entrepreneur is **goal-oriented**, rather than task-oriented. That does not mean the entrepreneur should not perform tasks. Rather, it presumes that an entrepreneur will have to perform many, many, many tasks, many of them tasks that you will not want to do. Being goal-oriented requires you to have patience, persistence, and perseverance, which allow you to *want* to do what you *need* to do. Goals make you *willing* to do the work.

I am sure you have heard about the necessity to set short-term and long-term goals before you start up your business. The reason you need to do that is because you need to have those goals to keep your eye on during the rough-and-tough times ahead of you. Entrepreneurs need reasons to do the numerous and sometimes seemingly pointless but necessary tasks required to start up and keep up a business operation. The entrepreneur is goal-oriented, not task-oriented. He is always looking for results, for the end point. If the entrepreneur realizes he does not have all the skills he needs to realize his goal, he can hire someone who is task-oriented to do the work for him. But because the goal is identified, the entrepreneur is willing to do anything that must be done to make it happen, even the most stultifying task. It does not matter if the goal first set is unrealistic. Even an unreachable goal may prove at the end to be a most valuable asset in terms of its motivational power.

The entrepreneur's ability to be goal-oriented is critical to his success in any and all areas of the business, even short-term projects. Let's say a computer programmer is hired to develop a system which will help the business run better and make a real impact on the bottom line. The project, as often happens, winds up taking twice as long as expected to complete. The entrepreneur will use every ounce of his perseverance to keep the business running in the meantime. He must also have the patience to wait until the job is finished and the persistence to keep moving the programmer and the staff along each day toward the goal of getting that programming task done.

Persistence could also be defined as a **bulldog mentality**, which fills in the first blank of question number six. Have you ever given a dog the end of a towel to pull on? I have never seen one that will let go before you do. I have never met one that said, "That's enough, I don't want to play anymore." (If I do, that talking dog and I are going on the road!) People usually throw in the towel but the dog never does. In many breeds, a dog that fetches a stick will not drop it at your feet either. You have to try to snatch the stick out of its mouth. If you can get it away, all that dog seems to think about is when you will throw that stick so he can go fetch it—again and again and again! You, the entrepreneur, have to be like that dog.

If you are planning to start up a company, the degree of your own stick-to-itiveness is often the only thing that will get you through the tough times. And there will be many of those. Starting up a business can be nothing but trouble, both personally and professionally. It is not for the faint-hearted. Time and money will constantly seem to be working against you; investors will be hollering for their returns; partners will not work out; employees will quit or complain; your family will wonder if you left town—I could go on but not right now, since I do not want to spoil the rest of the book! But I will reiterate here that the trouble these tough times bring can be handled if you are equipped with the proper motivation and the character traits mentioned above or are willing to ally yourself with someone who has the ones you do not possess. Otherwise, there is really no sense in going any further, because the chances are you will not get much farther.

And there is not much further to go in our examination, although I guess by now we should be calling it a self-examination. To review the answers so far:

1. **True**. Most successful entrepreneurs are self-honest and patient.
2. **False**. You can learn from anyone's experience.
3. Successful entrepreneurs must work **(c) very hard**.
4. **Patience**, **persistence** and **perseverance** are three abilities that all successful entrepreneurs exhibit.
5. Successful entrepreneurs are **goal-oriented** rather than task-oriented.

And, just in case you missed it, a **bulldog mentality** is the first of the three personal characteristics that all successful entrepreneurs exhibit that cannot be taught. Patience and perseverance must be learned. Introspection, self-honesty and humility (*especially* humility) must be taught. None of them are things with which we are born. But a bulldog mentality (a.k.a. *persistence*) is built into the successful entrepreneur, much as the money motivation is genetically predetermined. Persistence could be identified and explained; the lack of it could be pointed out to an erstwhile entrepreneur; but unless it is there at the start, not even the approximation of that quality quickly could be attained. To get it would take years and years of practice requiring precisely what is lacking: persistence!

A bulldog mentality, common sense, and interpersonal

skills cannot be taught because they are characteristics that come from inside, not outside an individual. Social and psychological engineers may still hold differently. So did the Bolsheviks, but their seventy-odd-year experiment at building the perfect Communist man has ended in utter failure, generating little except for political upheaval, social chaos and economic disaster. No Nietzschean "supermen" have yet appeared, nor do I expect they ever will. Neither do I think that trying to engineer any desired qualities in a person is possible, be they capitalist, communist, or entrepreneur—nor that such an attempt is a good idea!

Any attempt to engineer **common sense**, for example, is doomed from the start. I am not sure we could even define what the elements of common sense are, but when someone does not have any, that fact is sure hard to miss. I will never forget a classmate from medical school who fell into that category. One snowy Boston afternoon, we were crossing Harrison Avenue in the middle of the block when, all of a sudden, there was a howl close behind us, followed by a thud. We turned around and there was our friend, his books strewn all over the place, sitting in the street between two parked cars. The space he occupied was big enough for a snowplow, but he was not able to navigate it without crashing into the rear end of a big, late '50s sedan parked there. Rubbing his elbow, our classmate looked up at us and weakly proclaimed, "I haven't gotten used to the fenders on this model yet."

We just stared at him, the car and one another, knowing that here, indeed, was someone who would complain about being wet but would not have the sense to come in out of the rain. On the other hand, he did not seem to mind being wet, either, when the situation called for it.

As underclassmen, none of us could graduate unless we swam two laps of the university pool. The bunch of us jumped in and started off one day, along with our hapless friend. Though he managed to convincingly thrash around a bit, he rather quickly sank to the bottom of the pool. After fishing him out, we asked what happened.

"Oh, I can't swim," he admitted between gasps.

"You can't swim? Then why did you jump in?"

"It looked easy."

Hence, the famous adage: "You can lead some people to water but they might drown."

Common sense: It cannot be taught. Either you have it or you don't. Entrepreneurs need a lot of it, however, not to mention a great deal of uncommon sense. If you do not have either, maybe you should consider another career and not jump into the treacherous waters found in the business jungle.

But if you are in the entrepreneurial swim, another character-istic that is standard issue to a successful entrepreneur is a facil-ity with **interpersonal skills**. Now, you can teach someone to act as if they like people in some areas of business such as customer service work but even there the application of such instruction is limited. Write a telemarketing script for someone without genuine interpersonal skills and they will still come off as wooden, insin-cere, or so obviously "practiced" that most people would not buy a cold drink from them on a hot day. Tell a customer service employee with no interpersonal skills how to treat customers, and they will still ruffle feathers. Those feathers will have to be smoothed by you, the entrepreneur, if you want to keep the cus-tomers coming back. The professional audiologists I employ to test people's hearing in my current venture, HEARx, work much of the time with the two most difficult-to-deal-with groups of people: the elderly and the very young. If any of these audiologists do not care about people, their dislike will probably not improve after a few sessions with a squalling child. If that is the case, then they do not belong as audiologists.

Anyone without so-called "people" skills is not going to be a very good entrepreneur, either. People skills are absolutely critical to a business and not just in customer relations. There are many places besides the sales counter or the customer service desk where these skills come into play. There are relationships the entrepreneur must enter into with all sorts of people: financial sources, suppliers, employees, governmental regulators, bureau-crats, the media, consultants and many, many more besides. But they are *people*, first of all, and anyone who cannot deal with peo-ple has no place as an entrepreneur. You must be able to get peo-ple on your side if you want to succeed.

Having interpersonal skills means caring *about* people, not car-ing *for* them. If you want to hold peoples' hands all day, think about becoming a manicurist but forget about being a business person. The kind of caring I mean is something that makes you interested in what other individuals are doing and saying as it relates to your business dealings with those people. The only rea-son you know most of them at all is because you are in business, which more or less defines the entire extent of those relationships.

You may or may not be sympathetic with their ideas or situa-tions. Perhaps you cannot relate to their problems and maybe you do not even like them as individuals. But as far as your business dealings with them are concerned, you must sincerely care about what they want or need, be actively interested in what they are doing, and be perfectly willing to listen to what they have to say. You will have to deal with people at every turn and twist of your business, so you have got to want to get to know every cranny and nook of the people with whom you will be dealing. If that desire is not inside, no amount of wishing, teaching or practice is going to get it there.

Okay, that's it!

Time's up!

The self-examination is over.

How did you score?

Do you think you have what it takes to be an entrepreneur?

Are you willing to somehow acquire what you do not know?

And, most importantly ...

Do you still want to be an entrepreneur?

*   *   *   *   *

Auks range in size from seven to thirty inches long, their coloration varying from gray to black with white undersides. Their bills can be long and slender, or short, stout and triangular, depending on the species. Although they vary somewhat in appearance, all auks bear more than a passing resemblance to the penguin. Colored the same, they also have compact bodies and stand erect, supported by webbed feet on short little legs. They are sea-divers, too, dependent on the ocean for their food. The major difference is that, unlike their funny and flightless cousins the penguins and their unfortunate and quite extinct ancestors the great auks, these are sea birds that know how to fly....

*   *   *   *   *

3. Why?

The former Soviet Union is learning the hard way that people cannot be taught how to be entrepreneurs. Russia and the Eastern Bloc countries are beginning to understand, desperate as they are for businesses to start up, that not all of them will make it. Some will survive, but only because of the people they put in them. At least the governments there know enough to ask for help. I wonder, though, even given the proper motivation and all the personal characteristics necessary, if a totalitarian system can change enough to accommodate all these new entrepreneurs.

The difficulty is that at least some of them will want to build their businesses for reasons that do not exist in those places. Everything—all production and economic effort of any kind—had until recently been for the State and the State alone. But **the three reasons why entrepreneurs start up businesses** are quite different. One reason is **to build a small business**, primarily for themselves or their families. A second is **to build a business in order to sell it** for a good profit. The third is **to build a big business** for the sake of building a big business.

Those are the *only* reasons for an entrepreneur, any entrepreneur, to build a business, any business. Now, personal circumstances may force them in one or another of these directions to begin with, like being born into a family-owned concern. Given a choice, an entrepreneur might later chose to build up the family fortune another way and sell off the business, then go build a big business. So these reasons or goals for entrepreneurs may be blended in different ways at different times, much as motivations are. The bigger the business, the more complex the blend.

Just being in business, by the way, does not automatically make someone an entrepreneur. That kind of thinking merely invites mistakes and poor performance. Being in business does not define your motivations or your goals. You do. The fact that you happen to be in a business may actually only decide what you will do and where you will be for a certain period of time, if you do not make the choice. Born into a family where my father was a physician did not make me a physician, although I first started down that career path. Someone born into a tradition of restaurateurs may take over the family business, but that would not make that person an entrepreneur either. Even if the eatery was successful, it would be the result of the efforts and insight of some other family member or employee. If it were me, I would be dying to get out of the kitchen!

The idea of just putting people in business and expecting them to act like entrepreneurs is where the Russians and the Chinese are going to have trouble. A few generations now have been told what they will do, based on the State's assessment of their capabilities, balanced against the State's needs. If the State has too many gymnasts at any given point, woe to the gymnasts who wind up being farmers or bureaucrats and, as things have turned out, woe to the system! All of a sudden, the State is telling everybody to go into business, even though most everybody has never considered entrepreneurial motivations or goals, or even found it necessary to look at themselves, for themselves.

But the respective governments unconsciously started off in the right place as they began to grapple with their new economic mandates. They have been promoting the creation of small family-owned businesses. I jokingly say that entrepreneurs who start family- owned businesses do it in order to steal from the government and most of the people in those countries have already been doing that for years! But it will take more than that for them to be successful, as the bankruptcy rates in capitalist countries attest.

The majority of start-up businesses anywhere are *small businesses* and many are family-owned. Grocery stores, boutiques of all descriptions, copy centers, coffee shops, restaurants, card stores, antique dealers, machine shops, gas stations, furniture stores—there are just thousands upon thousands of them. Take your pick. And there is more than a little truth to my joke about stealing from the government. There is usually cash in small businesses that does not get reported—employees who get paid off the books, an extra car at home that is assigned to the business, and on and on and on.

The ability to make such financial maneuvers is a large incentive for entrepreneurs who start up small businesses. Another is that they can be their own boss. Nobody gets to tell them what to do. They do not have to answer to anybody about how they spend money and they get to control pricing, purchasing and salaries. They can sell whatever, whenever, and however they choose. Such freedom is something that most entrepreneurs would agree is desirable, but more difficult to sustain as a business gets larger.

The second reason for starting up a business is *to sell the business*. Obviously, such entrepreneurs are highly money-motivated and stay that way. They want to become rich in as short a space of time as possible and will therefore put together as profitable an enterprise as they possibly can in order to sell it. Their drives toward achievement and power will be sublimated to the money motivation, probably for their entire lives. But they will never become competent in running a business of any size because they have already gone on to their next business venture by the time growth starts occurring. They can be classified best as classic entrepreneurial opportunists.

I quickly could have fallen into that category, had I been so motivated, early in my business career. I was offered a deal to sell MetPath about a year after its start up. Revlon Corp. showed up on our doorstep to buy the company two weeks after we had arranged our first major financing. (*See Chapter 9 for details.*) We did not make a deal, because I was not in business to sell the company. Had I done that deal, or others like it early on, I would have been a millionaire.

But I was in business to build a big business, or door number three. I wanted to build MetPath into a Fortune 500 company and was not about to sell until I had accomplished that. I was money-motivated, sure, but I had set a goal and wanted to achieve it, period. I did not set up MetPath just to sell it and I did not set up HEARx to sell it either—which should be obvious to anyone who realizes that I have spent ten years trying to achieve the creation of a major health-care company devoted to hearing.

I hope readers, after recognizing that my own experience most closely parallels the third reason for building a business, have not drawn the erroneous conclusion that this book is designed only for those who wish to build big businesses. The size and scope of a business is transparent to the principles presented here. But there is one thing that must be big about entrepreneurs, no matter why they start up their businesses. It is a personal characteristic that I have not discussed until now. It is the key to any business, regardless of how much money an entrepreneur wants to make or how big a business.

We could have named it earlier. The characteristic first appeared in my son Mark's grand thoughts about the parking meters. It surfaced again in my goal for great things when I started Metropolitan Pathology Laboratory and yet again in the comments on goal-orientation. This characteristic plays such a major part in every aspect of a successful entrepreneur's make-up that I had to save it until now. It is, in fact, *the one absolutely essential, most necessary and preeminently valuable personal characteristic of every successful entrepreneur and business, large or small, that I have ever known or been associated with:*

Entrepreneurs must have **delusions of grandeur**.

It does not matter if an entrepreneur runs a multinational corporation or a local photography studio; the ability to be able to think big, to dream—these are successful entrepreneurs' most important possessions. Visions of great possibilities will keep them going when nothing else will, and the bigger, the more impossible, the more grandiose, the better!

If penguins dream, I just know that they dream they can fly! Sad to say, the only way a penguin will ever get to fly is if someone puts it on a plane.

But entrepreneurs can take off, powered largely by their own vision of things to come.

Will you get off the ground? That depends...

What do you see that no one else can?

$ECRET$ OF THE PENGUIN

Entrepreneurs are not made, they are born.

You cannot teach someone persistence, common sense, interpersonal skills, or how to be an entrepreneur.

Money must be the entrepreneur's primary motivation.

A Visionary Advantage

Chapter Two
The Owl: A Visionary Advantage

▲ ▲ ▲ ▲ ▲

Owls (order Stringiformes) are primarily nocturnal birds of prey found worldwide in every type of habitat. The owl's large eyes gather more light in dim illumination than those of other predators, allowing nighttime hunting. Its large orbs are directed forward, giving the owl a second advantage over other avian predators: binocular vision. This allows owls to perceive their prey in a three-dimensional manner. Other predators lack this perspective because their eyes are located on the sides of their heads. But owls' eyes also mark their greatest disadvantage, in that most are quite uncomfortable in broad daylight. Their eyes are so absorptive that they can be dazzled by bright light.

*   *   *   *   *

So, tell me...

What do you *think* you see?

There is no doubt you think you have this great idea, which is going to be a better and/or a bigger company than anyone can imagine. And of course, you already believe that you have got all the right qualities to be a great entrepreneur, including the willingness to ask for help when you need it.

But has it occurred to you that your wonderful idea might only be a flight of fancy? Do you think your delusions of grandeur could be just a plain old delusion, with no hope of ever becoming grand? Do you think that your vision is in focus, or is some trick of perspective making you see things all out of proportion? Is it possible, do you think, that your idea is not good enough to build a business around? And just how probable do you think it is that such a business can be built?

Face it, you are still in the dark. So, what do you think you are going to do next? I'll tell you....

Chapter Two: The Owl
▲ ▲ ▲ ▲ ▲

You think!

And not just any old kind of thinking, but some very serious thinking about your idea and how you plan to build it into a business. What you see at first glance may very well not be what you get. An idea is just a single thought, much like a glance is just a look. Even if you have an inspired thought, you really had nothing to do with it, no more than with that beautiful sunset you saw and now hold in your memory. Thoughts simply occur to us and we really have no control over what thoughts come into our heads, just like we have no control over the sights that offer themselves to our eyes. However, we do control which thoughts we keep in our minds and which sights we choose to focus on for more than a few seconds. Those are the ones we think about, the ones we want to see clearly.

Building a business from an idea is just as complex and imaginative a task as viewing a sunset and then composing a symphony or painting a picture. Before pen scores music or brush strokes canvas—or a business opens its doors—careful planning must be undertaken by the creative talent who conceived the idea. The idea will expand and contract many times before the right formula of notes or colors will be hit upon, or before your idea for a business will come into sharp focus.

Please do not confuse this creative thinking process described here with the writing of a business plan. That is an entirely separate matter. You will need a business plan, certainly. You already know that one of the first things you will need is money and a written business plan is usually needed for raising that money—which we now will begin calling **The Money**, or start-up business capital. Most investors who have **The Money** you need will want to see a document called a business plan, complete with financial projections. They will want to see it even if they do not understand what it says or do not care (*see Chapter 3*).

But **a business plan is merely an outline of your visions, only the tip of the iceberg of your business planning process**. And whatever you write in it is going to change—probably the day after you open for business and many more times after that, no matter how much money you get. But if you have really planned your business and thought things out beforehand, if you have played Devil's advocate from all the angles that you can think of and asked as many questions as you can, you will be much more capable of meeting the unexpected when it happens—and, believe me,. it will happen again and again! Entrepreneurs learn early to expect the unexpected.

So you will not be told here how to write a business plan. What we are about here is business planning, which demands more than word processing software and a spreadsheet package. It requires that you think about, in detail, exactly what it is you see when you think about building your business. Here is where you will begin a reality check on your delusions of grandeur to make sure they are not merely shadows with no substance. **Entrepreneurs do not need to learn how to write business plans, they need to know how to plan businesses.** I have written a few business plans and seen hundreds and hundreds more during my career. Over the last twenty years I have probably reviewed two or three a week, on average. The businesses they described were all different, but most of them shared one thing: They were all great-looking business plans! They all used high-quality paper, had title pages, tables of contents, introductions, Roman numerals, indented sub-headings, one and one-half spaces between lines for easy reading and were laser-printed.

People seem to get hung up on the mechanics of writing a business plan—how it should look, what should be included in what order, how to phrase certain things, the number of pages, the print typeface and even the size of the margins—instead of thinking about actually planning their businesses. They act as if investors really give more than two hoots about how the thing is wrapped! Capital sources are not going to give you any money on the looks achieved by your IBM or Apple presentation-design software packages. The business plan hardly even gets you in the door and it sure will not keep you there. What is going to keep you and your business interesting to investors is **the clarity of your vision**, not the clarity of the plastic covers that you use on your business plan.

But the unfortunate attitude persists that by getting the presentation format right, entrepreneurs somehow invoke the power of a magic formula which bedazzles investors into parting with **The Money**. Well, you will find no magic formulas here. If you want directions on preparing business plans, look elsewhere. There are lots of other books you can read to get tips on writing business plans and how to organize your thoughts. There are also many professional and not-so-professional lawyers, accountants and consultants to go to for help with actually writing a business plan, as well as some software packages. But they will not be much help for your creativity, I'm afraid. Most will just agree or disagree with your thinking, for a price.

Right now, it is just you and your idea, *mano a mano*, facing each other in a locked, windowless room with no furniture, and this book. Your object is to try to beat your idea to death with this book. If your idea survives your no-holds-barred attack of analysis and critical thought, then your chances of surviving in the business jungle and becoming a successful entrepreneur are vast-ly improved. And do not worry about hurting yourself or your idea. You both will survive the attack if your idea is a good one. If it turns out bad, do not try to hold onto it. Let it go! You have had one idea, you can have another, so be ruthless. Avoid the ego trap of spending what could turn out to be the rest of your life in the wrong business, just because you could not bring yourself to admit to having a bad idea.

Also count it a big mistake to fall in love with your idea before you really know what it looks like. A lot of people come up with ideas that they are absolutely enamored with and get so stuck on their concept that they think they are going to turn the world on its ear. But they never stop long enough to even ask, "Is this a good idea?" or "Will people want to buy this?" Take a spoon. Now, with careful design, you can make a spoon with a hole in the mid-dle. You can also figure out how to make lots of spoons with holes in their middles. But are people going to want a spoon with a hole in it? Who would buy it? People on diets? Dry cleaners? Food-haters? There would be more profit in selling the middles you cut out of the spoons as slugs to slot-machine vendors for testing their machines.

Statisticians tell us that the main reason new businesses fail is a lack of sufficient capital. They could not get **The Money**, in other words. The reason they could not get **The Money**, I propose, is that those businesses first were victims of poor (or no) planning and therefore could not attract the right investors. They might have thought they had great ideas and probably had great-looking business plans, but they could not see well enough or far enough to carry their ideas across the street, much less across a confer-ence table.

We are after clearing up your vision as much as possible before you start storming around the business jungle.

Now, just what is it you think you see that is so great, anyhow?

*   *   *   *   *

The seemingly neckless owl has the advantage of being able to describe a near 360 degree arc with his sharp-beaked head. This helps him to maintain visual con-tact of his prey without major alteration of his posi-tion, either in flight or when stationary. But the owl's amazing visual acuity is a greater asset. On each side of the base of the beak are several rows of small, curved feathers which form a ruff to support the long feathers that make up the large disk surrounding the eyes. The disk perhaps may aid in reflecting available light into the owl's eyes, further enhancing the night-hunter's ability to see in the dark. Combined with three-dimensional vision and its elegant, noiseless flight, these traits make the owl a truly remarkable bird of prey.

* * * * *

1. Your Idea . . .

Consider the owl, soaring across a moon-lit sky, a few hundred feet above the treetops. It is a fine night for hunting and he is very hungry. Something draws his attention down below in the forest. It seems to be moving, although that might just be a trick of the shadows.

Too high up to tell for certain what he sees below, the owl circles, lowers his altitude about a hundred feet and comes in from another direction. Now his sharp eyes pick up the movement again and there is no doubt that there is something alive down below him. But he still cannot make out how big it is, whether it is something he can eat or something that could eat him. He decides on an even closer look. He begins his descent.

Entrepreneurs pursuing a clear vision of their idea likewise must get a closer look at exactly what it is they have in their sights. The initial step in qualifying an idea involves a precise identification of what you think you see, which is, at base, one of two things:

1. **An idea for a product, which may or may not become a business**

OR

2. **An idea for a service, which has to be a business.**

Be well-advised that these are two very separate and distinct things.

In the first place, **just because you have an idea for a product does not mean that you are going to be able to build a business out of it**. And while it probably would be better if a product is **proprietary** (*i.e., patentable*), even one that is not proprietary still may be worth building a business around, if certain criteria are met. If you have invented something, first try to legally protect it by filing a patent application. (A *patent pending* attached to your product, by the way, often offers more protection than an issued patent, since it allows you greater flexibility in competitive situations.) If your vision is to build a business around that single idea, however, be very, very careful.

Hardly any companies are built around a single-product idea. Those that try usually fail. When you have a concept for a single product, the best thing to do is to get rid of it. That does not mean that you should immediately discard the *idea*. Just dispose of any idea you might have about building a business around it. Entrepreneurs with proprietary product ideas do not have to build their own businesses in order to make money from their inventions. They have the advantage over non-proprietary product or service ideas in that they can sell the idea to someone else, and let *them* build the business and deliver the product to the marketplace.

The major difference between developing an idea for a service and an idea for a product is that a product can be developed independently of the means of production, distribution or delivery. But there is no way of developing an idea for a service business without thinking about who will perform the service and how it will be delivered to the marketplace. **An idea for a service is always non-proprietary and *requires* that you build a business around it**. A component of the operation that delivers a service may be innovative or even proprietary, but that does not make the business proprietary. MetPath, for example, was one of the first with the concept of centralized, national testing facilities and we had testing machines made for us that no one else had. Those factors did create a much-needed competitive advantage for the business, important because non-proprietary ideas automatically place the entrepreneur in a more highly competitive and risky situation. But they did not make the business proprietary.

Anyone can start a laboratory like MetPath or a hearing-care service like HEARx, for example, just as anyone can start a car wash or a fast-food restaurant chain. If it is an old idea, there will be many competitors already. If it is a new idea and its time has come, then there will soon be many competitors. Unlike a proprietary idea that can be patented, there is no way to legally stop someone from copying an idea for a service, nor can someone be stopped from delivering a service.

An idea for a service is always an idea for a business. You cannot sell the idea, because no one is going to buy something that they can have for free. An idea for a service automatically carries with it the necessity of providing that service to someone, of delivering it somehow, because the people who will use the service are the only ones who will buy it. The ability to deliver a service is built in to a service idea; without it, there could be no idea at all.

The determination about what to do with your *idea, product* or *service*, is made by passing ...

DR. BROWN'S BUSINESS VISION TEST

- *Feasibility: Can it work, in theory?*
- *Producibility: Can a prototype be built?*
- *Replicability: Can it be made in quantity?*
- *Marketability: Can it be sold in volume?*
- *Profitability: Can it be sold at a profit?*

If you have a potentially successful business idea you will be able, once you get your vision properly focused, to perceive the answers to all of these questions. But to get your vision focused, you have got to really think about what you want to do and how you are going to do it. Remember before you start that there are some basic differences between how to look at a product idea and how to look at a service idea in terms of building a business, as we pointed out at the very beginning of this chapter. So it is a good idea to circle around and take a look at your idea from a slightly different angle, just to make sure that you can accurately describe what you are looking at.

When you first look at a product idea, for example, you really only have to go through the first three levels of the test—*feasibility, producibility* and *replicability*—before you have to decide whether or not you or someone else can turn the product idea into a business. One would really be flying blind if they tried to build a business around a product that could not be prototyped or determined to work as envisioned. Even non-proprietary products must be built and tested before an entrepreneur can try to build a business around them. Likewise with replicability: If you cannot reproduce your product faithfully, you cannot build a business out of it.

It is also important to understand that replicability has nothing to do with how many of a particular product have to be made. It does not matter if your product idea is for a ninety-nine cent novelty item that will have to be made in the millions for the masses or for a $999,000 piece of industrial equipment that will be sold one by one into a very narrow market. Two or two million, it is critical to know that each one you make will look, smell, feel, taste, and act just as well as the first one. Do not be fooled and make sure you do not fool yourself! Fail this part of the test, and your capital and your company will wind up being consumed, no matter how wonderful you think your product is or how much you want to be successful.

When it comes to considering an idea for a service business. (Need we say it again?): *An idea for a service is integrated with the idea of building a business.* Unlike product ideas, service ideas must involve thinking about building a business immediately, right from the inception of the idea.

Any consideration of *feasibility* automatically includes whether or not it can be brought to market at all. Thinking about *producibility* means planning the delivery mode—the type and size of a facility, the number and type of staff, the requisite equipment, etc.—for the service. Considerations about *replicability* involve, first of all, deciding whether you want to build only one or a number of outlets for your service. Then you have to think about many other elements, including whether or not the physical design you envision will be applicable across all situations that might be encountered in all locations. *Marketability* and *profitability* considerations are directly tied to the delivery methods the service requires. A product idea, as we have already pointed out, can be determined to be theoretically sound without knowing how it will be delivered.

Either way, what you see during planning will suggest what to do next with your product or service idea.

IF ... THEN

- If any idea looks like it will fall short in any one of these areas ... then you must think about how to deal with the problem before you think about going to investors.

- If the idea is for a service business and you cannot resolve the problems in your mind ... then you probably will not be able to solve them in the real world either. Abandon it and find another business to think about. (If you cannot fix it at this stage ... then no one else will want to either.)

- Likewise, if your idea for a business is based on a non-proprietary product and you cannot see it working in any one of the above areas ... then neither you nor anyone else will be able to build a business around it.

- If the idea is for a proprietary product and it falls short ... then you may not be able to build a business around it, but someone else may be able to. How you get rid of it will depend on which of the criteria are satisfied.

On that last point, do not just abandon your idea outright! If you think your proprietary product can be proven technologically feasible and a prototype can be produced that looks like it can be replicated, then you might be able to sell it to someone else. Just because you cannot prove that a proprietary product idea can be reproduced or profitably delivered to market does not mean that no one else can do it. Most entrepreneurs just do not have the wherewithal to carry it all the way through. So, once you verify a proprietary product's feasibility and produce a prototype, consider selling the concept to someone else and gain your reward. If you take this route, however, be careful. When you show your product to people who are interested, do not forget to have them sign confidentiality agreements first, even it you have a patent. Ideas are easy to steal. If no one bites, then you can discard your idea or at least put it on the shelf to tinker with later if it shows promise.

If no one else seems interested in making much out of your idea, then you can be relatively certain that you cannot either. It may be a great idea, but you may have to accept the fact that you just cannot build a business out of it. And if it is a single-product idea and no one is interested, then you can be almost absolutely certain. Ninety-nine times out of a hundred, there is no single-product idea that will bring a reward sufficient to build a business.

That does not mean there is not a lot of money to be made in a single product, or that a lot of entrepreneurs will not try. Look at Pet Rocks or Cabbage Patch Dolls. They were wildly successful products. There is only one problem: Can you tell me where to buy a Pet Rock or a Cabbage Patch Doll today? Nowhere, except maybe at garage sales, and that is exactly where you most likely will wind up if you try to build a business around a single product. Even if you decide to try building a business with a single-product idea, you probably will not even be able to begin anyway because you will probably never get **The Money** from investors to start it up. But if you want to use your own money, don't say you were not warned. Most investors will not go for a single-product idea because they are going to be asking the same questions as you are, particularly this one: *How much money can possibly be made on this deal?*

That is why it is much better to save yourself all that trouble and sell your single-product proprietary concept to a company that can afford to buy it. Let them do all the additional product tests, initial production runs and in-depth marketing studies. Let them take the product and market it through their existing distribution channels. You sell the idea outright for a lump sum or sign a royalty agreement and take a nickel every time they sell one of your whiz-bangs. They make a lot of money, although it is more likely they will make a *little* money. You might make a little money (and maybe a *lot* of money), but at least you will be debt-free and ready to move onto your next whiz-bang idea with maybe a little bit of money to fund its development.

Let's go back now to a single-product idea that you are getting ready to abandon because nobody wants it. Here is where it pays to think things through. Maybe your proprietary single-product idea can be turned into a product that has multiple applications or one that can be sold into more than one market, with just some minor technical alterations or repackaging. It would be better if your idea starts out as a multiple-application product. But no matter how it arrives, an idea for a proprietary product with more than one marketing dimension is an idea that an entrepreneur may be able to build a business around.

Just do not forget to put that idea through the vision test again, starting right at the beginning, no matter how many things your whiz-bang can do. Even though it may seem like the second time around, you are really dealing with a new product, a new concept, something different from your first idea. Without revisiting your vision again and again, you could easily trick yourself into seeing what you want to see rather than what is really there. The questions must each be thought all the way through, over and over—unless, of course, you care to learn the hard way, as I did.

Casting around for a business venture to get involved with after I sold MetPath, I got involved with starting up three product-based companies during the mid-1980s. Each appeared to offer a great opportunity to build a business, but only one is still in operation and it has become moderately successful. The other two were "learning experiences" (an excellent euphemism for "failures"). One of them was also an excellent object lesson of the failure to think things through and properly evaluate an idea.

What attracted me to the company Medex was a patented product developed for people with broken wrists. Called the Web-Guard, it was a small plastic device that snapped onto a cast at the space between the forefinger and thumb, allowing relatively normal use of the hand without interfering with the healing process. The inventor already had been making the product in small quantities in his garage, so we sent it up to Tufts University's Department of Orthopedics. They thought the Web-Guard was super and were of the opinion that everyone who had a cast put on their wrist could use one! So three of the criteria were satisfied: The feedback from Tufts said it was feasible; the prototype already had been produced; and it seemed easily replicable in large quantities.

Profitable? The product cost only a few cents to make in volume, and the selling price would give us a big margin. Marketable? Didn't our technical advisors at Tufts turn handsprings over this product? Every hospital, doctor's office, medical supply house and clinic would buy large quantities of these things. Was anything missing? My partner was sure we were going to make a big pile of money. I liked the product, I liked the person who wanted to be my partner, and I put $150,000 in the venture for about 45 percent of the stock with the intention of managing the business. I was not going to make the mistake of being a passive investor.

Dumb, maybe, but not passive! Let's just say that today I have become very concerned whenever anybody tells me they are "sure" about anything, especially about making a lot of money. The people at Tufts were flipping over the product, all right, but we forgot that researchers are not business people, they are "cloud" people. Academics tend to have their heads up in their clouds and their feet not touching the soil of the business jungle. They are quite happy that way and can only give an unbiased, honest opinion if they *are* that way. Our mistake was to assume their approval meant that it was going to be marketable at a profit. Not that we forgot to apply critical thought to these things; we just did not apply *enough* critical thought. Too little, anyway, to do the kind of in-depth study that would easily have shown exactly what we were missing, to wit: *How does anyone sell tiny little pieces of plastic in a sophisticated marketplace?*

The researchers' enthusiasm may have been partly due to the fact that they did not have to pay for their test products. There was no way we could sell the products and build a business. How much would somebody pay for a small piece of plastic that looked like it cost three cents to make, anyway? Not enough, certainly, to make any kind of a profit. The marketing and distribution expenses simply buried the financial return. The Web-Guard actually turned out to be an excellent example of the kind of product idea that should have been sold to a big company that could have supported the extensive marketing and distribution that such a product requires.

I hooked onto another simple principle concerning product-based ideas while fishing around for a business during those post-MetPath attempts:

THE FIVE-YEAR
BUSINESS SINKER

The opportunity for success in a business built around
proprietary product technology is greatly enhanced
if the product can be sufficiently developed and
brought to market within five years' time.
If it takes any longer than five years
to develop and bring the product
to market, the opportunity for
success is reduced
almost to
zero.

The likelihood of building a successful business with proprietary product technology that takes more than five years to develop is very unlikely. The main reasons are that the time window
beyond five years is too long and the financial drain too large for
investors to wait for a return on investments that are usually big
and could be massive. A gentleman called me not to long ago to
say he developed a concept for a new artificial heart product, for
example. All he said he needed was $600,000 the first year, $10
million the next year and $20 million in the third. With that he
thought he could make a product and have a dynamite company.
Well, I estimated that his chances are similar to those of an owl
intent on capturing, carrying off and eating an entire cow. First of
all, he would not be able to corral that kind of money for a concept for a single-product company. And I guarantee it would take
him a lot longer than three years to get the product perfected and
the business off the ground. It is safer to say that he might starve
before he got his first taste of profit, if experience is any teacher.

Attempts to build businesses around concepts in genetic engineering or new pharmaceutical products offer some further
insight into the financial difficulties that can be encountered.
Some have been funnels for terrific amounts of money, counted
not in millions of dollars but in the hundreds of millions. The
entrepreneurs who started some of them up have had to sell off
more and more of their own interest in those businesses in order
to continually raise **The Money** that kept them going. The
founders had the ideas and started the companies, but by the
time the first products got to market, big companies had swallowed them. Some of the entrepreneurs may have wound up owning a minuscule percentage of the companies they conceived, and
maybe even still had a job. Genetic engineering to solve the problem of muscular dystrophy or building an artificial heart are not

businesses that entrepreneurs should consider starting up alone. Taking on a corporate partner before losing control would be a much better idea (see *Chapter 7*).

There are other potential complications that can drastically diminish the opportunity of an idea for a business, no matter how good. A unique birth control technique was developed which used a silicon-based material to block a woman's fallopian tube. The product had been tested on thousands of patients who experienced no pregnancies and no complications, and the process was also shown to be reversible—a number of women became pregnant after the material was removed. After testing, they went to the FDA to get approval to market the product.

"You have not done any mouse studies," said the FDA.

"But we have done tests with thousands of patients, and we've had no problems!"

"We are sorry," the FDA replied. "But under our guidelines, you must do mouse studies."

Do you have any idea how small the fallopian tube of a mouse is? Suffice it to say that it has been at least ten years since the idea was hatched, and there is no telling how much longer it might take for the product to reach the marketplace. It is not unusual for such regulated products to take that much time to be born. The average amount of time for a new drug to reach the market is ten years, for example. Even if it only took five, chances are that a lone entrepreneur literally has no business having an idea like that. Still, everybody underestimates the time it will take, thinking things will happen overnight. They do not.

The opportunity to build a business is much better if a proprietary product can be built and brought to market in less than five years, provided, of course, that the whiz-bang lends itself to multiple applications or markets. The building of Permark involved just such a product situation. As we related in *Chapter 1*, the inventor developed a hand-held instrument for doing microsurgical pigmentation. It started out as a machine for ophthalmologists to apply permanent eyeliner for cosmetic purposes. By analyzing the opportunity the product idea presented, however, many other uses were envisioned. Dermatologists could color in anything from a hair transplant to damaged skin, for example. Then the opportunities grew to include a wide variety of applications among other medical specialists, from surgeons, who could use the instrument for reconstructive breast surgery, to radiologists who treated cancer patients.

The business started up in 1986 on the strength of those considerations, but we continued to pursue other types of possibilities that our earlier analysis had uncovered. Before long a new power supply was invented and developed, greatly increasing the machine's available power. That allowed the unit to be redesigned so that it could do more than just micro-surgical pigmentation. The product soon was expanded to include another device on the same hand-held unit, which performed dermabrasion, a process which "erases" skin irregularities of various types. All of these things were accomplished within three years of the company's inception, at which point the company had grown to just under $1 million in sales.

The time window was short enough, sales levels were high enough, and the future prospects of the business seemed bright enough—particularly considering the continuing product and market developments—to keep investors interested in supporting the company, even though it had not begun to make money yet. At present, the company is still growing and beginning to be profitable, and the product is still evolving: Permark, in 1990, began developing a small surgical saw and a drill that will work off the same power supply. The lesson here is that the opportunity to build a successful business around a product idea was realized within five years of the inception of the idea.

There is no time limit on how long it will take for a service business to become successful, however. It took seven years for MetPath, a service business, to become profitable, but once it started making money, sales and profits advanced almost exponentially each year until it was sold. The reason it was successful, I believe, was because MetPath was able to differentiate itself sufficiently from its competitors. *(How that difference evolved is a line of thought that properly belongs in the next section of this chapter, so we will hold off on that.)*

Take a moment to review the business vision test and see if you can identify what it is that you have been trying to see. Your thinking primarily has been directed toward identifying exactly what your idea looks like; whether or not it looks like a good idea; and whether or not it looks like it has a chance to be turned into a business. Your thinking, then, has been filtered through a **qualitative analysis** of your idea, an attempt to assess its possible potential as an idea, *per se*. This effort may convince you that your idea is a good one that can be turned into a business. Great! Congratulate yourself heartily, and then ask yourself the next question: "So what?" You have not gone far enough with your thinking yet! Your idea must be looked at from every angle, turned over and over in your mind until every dimension has been exposed to view.

"I've done that already," I think I just heard you think.

Well, if you have done that already, then you have to look at your idea again and again and again—in a different light, from another angle, under a variety of conditions—to make sure that what you saw the first time was not an illusion.

"Yeah, I've done that already, too," you think.

Well, think again! **You, the entrepreneur, must modify and correct your ideas *mercilessly* before you can *think* about showing it to anybody else.** It is much too early to even start looking for someone to help you write a business plan, especially because you really do not have the full picture yet. So, if you have not done so already, pick up some paper and a very sharp pencil. Use it to try to poke as many holes in your concept as you can, inflating and deflating your trial balloons and estimates at least three more times than you think is necessary.

If you think this is an overly cautious approach or just too burdensome a task, understand that you have more than likely missed several key points about each aspect of your business idea, just because you are a human being. No one gets it right the first time, the second time, or even the third. Some might argue that no one *ever* gets it *all* right. But if you take the time and do some really exhaustive planning, your chances of success will be greatly enhanced. Then, too, you just may avoid the *really* heavy burden that a failed business can put on your shoulders.

There is just an awful lot to think about if you want to turn your product or service idea into a business, and you are at least a chapter and a half away from attempting to turn your business planning into a business anyway.

So don't start flying around believing you are ready to go and get anything just because you *think* you can see what you are after.

Whatever you think you see, there is much more to it than first meets the eye.

* * * * *

Its nocturnal habits and ominous hooting sounds have associated the owl with the supernatural and the otherworldly in the mind of man. The owl was used in the Middle Ages to characterize the idea that man was in "darkness" before the coming of Christianity. The barn owl of Europe was long looked upon as a bird of ill omen and eventually as a symbol of disgrace. But the symbolism most widely associated with the owl is that of intelligence, although popular characterizations seem to confuse intelligence with wisdom. A food manufacturer even uses an owl—wearing glasses!—to symbolize its brand of potato chips. Owls first became symbols of intelligence, however, because it was thought that their large, eerie eyes could peer into the future and presage events.

*   *   *   *   *

2. Your Business . . .

Consider that owl again while *it* continues to consider whatever is moving around on the ground below.

Now just at treetop level, the owl floats on the air currents, his wings twitching to adjust to minute changes in wind speed and air pressure to maintain altitude. His eyes never leave the target, his head shifting continually in an uneven staccato of movements as he relentlessly follows his prey. He sees it clearly enough to know that whatever is down there is something alive that is not too big for him to handle.

But now he has a new set of questions to think about. How is he going to get at that mouse or squirrel or rabbit or bird or whatever it is down there? What speed should he attack at? Can he get through those trees? Will it stay in the open or will it head for cover? Is there more than one down there that cannot be seen yet? Are there any other predators in the area?

As these questions run through its mind, he circles, keeping the prey in view while he thinks things over...

You, the entrepreneur, need to expand your thinking if you hope to build a successful business. How far and how well your idea will travel as a business depends on more than just the quality of your idea. Once you enter in, the success of your business will depend on how well you perceive the often unstable environment of the business jungle. **Qualitative analysis, or possibility thinking, has gotten you this far.** Not exclusively, of course, since there are no hard and fast borders in the mind when it comes to creative thinking. Any attempt to define the inherently subjective qualities of any idea also will involve some estimates about how big, how much, how many, how long, how often, and other quantifiable criteria.

These objective elements, once the view broadens from the idea itself to the larger consideration of building a business, eventually come to dominate the entrepreneur's thinking process. Your thought, your idea for a business built around a product or service, must be tested against some hard realities external to the idea itself. I digested that fact when my son Mark moved into junior high school, taking his entrepreneurial tendencies with him. One Friday night at the dinner table, my wife Cynthia asked him how things were going at school.

"I had a great week," he said, between copious mouthfuls of food. "I made thirty-seven dollars."

Cynthia and I looked at one another, wondering what he meant. "You mean," I ventured, "you got a job after school?"

"No, no," Mark said, gulping down his milk. "I made the money during school."

We looked at each other again, now a little concerned about his announcement. How does a seventh grader earn thirty-seven dollars during school hours? As much as we trusted Mark, the first thing that came to our mind in those days—and the first that comes to parents these days, too, sad to say—is that controlled substances were somehow involved with his windfall profits. The next question was delivered with great trepidation.

"Ah, Mark," Cynthia ventured. "Could you tell us how you earned thirty-seven dollars while you were in school?" Then we both swallowed hard and held our respective breaths.

"Oh, easy! I just noticed," Mark said, with a bit of relish clinging to his chin, "that all the kids were hungry in last period." Looking at Mark, Cynthia and I certainly did not find that hard to believe! "So I thought: Why not run downtown during lunch hour and buy candy bars and sell them to the kids at school? The candy only costs me a quarter apiece, and I can sell them for seventy-five cents each before and after the last period."

Our mutual sighs of relief greeted that explanation. A couple of months later, I asked Mark one day after school how his food service business was doing.

"Oh, no good," he admitted, between bites of a Chunky candy bar. "I got out of that business yesterday."

"Why was that? I thought it was a great idea."

"Well, it was," Mark agreed, as he polished off the Chunky, "until other people caught on and started selling candy bars for sixty cents. That was okay for awhile," he said, reaching in his pocket and pulling out a Fifth Avenue. "But then the competition got so bad that prices went down to fifty cents and then to forty cents, and they look like they'll go down even further. It just isn't worth going downtown anymore."

And he was obviously, but by no means unhappily, forced to gulp down his leftover inventory.

Unless, like Mark, you plan to eat your own idea for a business, your thinking has got to become an exercise in **quantitative analysis, or probability thinking**. You have already decided that your product or service idea presents a good possibility for building a business. But how big do you think that business will be? Who is going to be your customer, and how do you think you can reach that customer? Who is your competition? What do you think you will need to build that business in terms of money and people? If your business ever gets to be in business, what do you think the chances are that it will make a profit and survive the complex environment of the business jungle?

The answers to those questions are gained by looking at your business from...

DiFF*ERENT* PERꜱᴘᴇᴄTIᴠᴇꜱ

The Marketplace

The Strategies

The People

These must be thoughtfully considered to evolve a credible business in order to prepare a business plan that investors will want to hear about before they give you **The Money**. An idea for a service is immediately dependent on these objective considerations. Remember, a service business starts out as a non-proprietary venture. But that does not mean that a service business does not involve innovation! Exactly the opposite is true. But when it comes to innovation, the difference between a proprietary, technological business opportunity and a service business opportunity has to do with the **timing and frequency** of innovation.

A product-based business requires an entrepreneur to come up with one idea for a product that does not exist yet, and then probably to develop and improve that single product over time. A patentable invention, from the standpoint of building a business, automatically sets a business apart in a market. But no such instant uniqueness is conferred on a service business. Look at take-out-only Chinese food establishments, one-hour photo labs, quick-lube garages for automobiles—they have no automatic proprietary edge with their businesses. An entrepreneur with an idea for a service business who wants to be successful has to innovate and keep innovating. He must essentially take something which already exists and try to do it faster, cheaper or somehow better than anyone else—and then keep doing it over and over again to stay ahead of the competition.

The largest clinical testing laboratory in the U.S. when MetPath raised its first major infusion of outside capital in 1967 had revenues of between $1 million and $2 million. By the time I sold MetPath, its sales were over $100 million. We were processing 32,000 patient samples a day, every day. What we had to invent was just about everything, including the design of the room to handle the specimens, the size of the table on which to put the specimens, and a refrigerator that would hold 32,000 specimens times ten days, or 320,000 specimens a day. We had to design the width of our corridors to handle the cart traffic that level of processing required, and design our own data processing system because no one else had anything close to what we needed.

We did a lot of this as we went along, of course, but we had to think most of these things up from scratch. It was done because, **if an entrepreneur can develop or acquire something proprietary within the business framework, that enhances the value of the business.** An executive from one of MetPath's competitors, Bristol-Myers, once approached me and questioned my decision to push one-day turnaround of test results to our customers.

"You're giving everyone their reports back the next morning by working all night long," the executive stated, a little smugly. "Medically, there is no reason for you to do that. Nobody sees the patient the next day, so why do that?"

"Simple," I answered. "The difference is that I'm now receiving 2,400 samples a day, and you guys are still processing only 420 samples a day." Until he viewed it from my perspective, that business innovation did not seem worthwhile. But it was very worthwhile, not because it was absolutely necessary to operate a lab, but because it increased the size of the business—in this case because it was something that the customer perceived was necessary or (more likely) because the customer was convinced by MetPath's sales representatives that it was necessary. Over time, such service has in fact become necessary, leading us to surmise that the only reason it was not necessary before is that no one had ever done it before. Well-conceived, innovative concepts in any business can often set trends that did not exist before.

There is an interesting misconception that has resulted from the general necessity for innovation in business, coupled with the popular belief that innovation means creating a high-technology product. Most people probably would define entrepreneurs as innovators who are engaged in chasing down technological opportunities and trying to build big businesses around them. The reality is far different. Our society hinges to a large extent on entrepreneurs running small service businesses within a variety of markets, such as consumer, professional, business, industrial, government, or some subset of a market. You name it, someone is doing someone else a service—nursing home, machine shop, grocery store, messenger service, car repair, research, dry cleaner, travel agency, clothes boutique, print shop, beauty parlor—in literally thousands of ways. Visits to business and industrial parks, malls and downtown areas—or a stroll through the Yellow Pages—will prove the overwhelming diversity and numbers of non-proprietary service-based entrepreneurial pursuits. The bulk of entrepreneurs, then, are engaged in trying to build businesses that are intrinsically no different from perhaps hundreds of businesses already out there.

Some of these businesses are small by choice or circumstance, but most are only small because they have not gotten big yet. How big the entrepreneurs who start them up would like them to become depends, first of all, on their individual delusions of grandeur. They simply may not want to build a big business. But if they do, there are some advantages in starting up a service business over a product business.

A proprietary-product business opportunity tends not to be developed into a big company by the entrepreneur, first of all, because it tends to be acquired before that can happen. The computer industry is full of examples of small, quick-growth technology companies being bought out left and right. If that is your game plan, then head for Silicon Valley in California, or maybe Austin, Texas, where there are a lot of high-tech companies or a lot of research going on. Just do not forget to take along a lot of money, or at least this book, because start-up costs of technological business opportunities are usually very high.

A non-proprietary business opportunity usually takes a smaller initial investment to start up, takes longer to develop, tends not to be acquired early and can in many cases be built into a large company by the entrepreneur—without losing financial control of the business. That is why I predict there will be more and more people employed in service businesses, simply because you tend to stay employed longer with a service business than with one based on a technological product innovation—as soon as your whiz-bang gets out-tekked, there goes your business. The longer an entrepreneur manages to survive the business jungle, notwithstanding profitability, the more likely it is that people will continue to reinvest. If that thought is more to your liking, then stay where you are and finish reading this book.

No matter the size of your ego or your business, the same objective criteria apply to ideas for small, medium or large businesses—at least for those hoping to be successful. First on the list is **identifying the marketplace**. A wide-angle market analysis or market research begins with a demographic view of the population that you will be trying to reach, otherwise known as the customer.

The primary factor that will decide the size of your company is the size of your customer base now and in the foreseeable future. This view will determine the size of the market for whatever it is you are selling, and whether or not it is a growing market. The larger the customer base, the larger your margin of error if things do not go according to plan—and, trust me, they will not. A large market at least allows the entrepreneur the simultaneous advantage of being able to maintain adequate revenue from a relatively small share of the marketplace, while at the same time making it easier to keep investors interested in supporting the business.

When MetPath started up, the existing market presented a very big opportunity: Over $3 billion dollars was being spent annually on laboratory testing. Fourteen years after I sold the company, MetPath in 1996 (twice renamed, first as Corning Laboratory Services and then as Quest Diagnostics) was approaching $2 billion in a market that had grown to over $25 billion. When I started up HEARx, I again saw a big opportunity. The annual market for hearing aids in 1987 was already $2 billion, projected to grow to more than $10 billion over the next twenty years. That is a pretty good-sized market to get a small piece of... all I want to do is build a $500 million company.

But don't think that I, or you, have to rush! Remember, if you want to build a business, your whole focus is to **stay in business as long as you can**. So keep those delusions of grandeur healthy and flexible, and do not go weighing down your thoughts by setting them in stone. They are going to change anyway, which is one of the few things in business about which you can be relatively certain. Another pretty sure bet is that, whatever the marketplace you are thinking about entering, you are bound to have **competition**. The entrepreneur needs to think about how many competitors there are, how big they are, how deep their pockets are, and how they run their businesses. This phase of market analysis is very simple and straightforward, but it can create problems for the fledgling entrepreneur. The trouble comes from overconcern with the competition, especially when the other players in the marketplace are larger, when there are a large number of them, and when their individual resources are much larger than yours. This can be an overwhelming vision for a new business person.

Worry about them all you want, but your worry will not help one bit in building your business. Look at it this way: Your competitors do not even know you exist yet, but you know about them, so you have the advantage for the moment. Learn everything you can about them and see where you might be able to improve on what they are doing. What is the product? Ice cream? Go buy some of theirs and taste it, see how much it sells for. Clothes? Go buy your competitors' pants and try them on. What is the service? A gym? Visit them, even join one, and see how you are treated by the staff, what programs they offer, and how they are priced. How big, how many, and how rich the competition is should not negatively affect your business planning. It should assist you.

Looking at the forces arrayed against you is intended to help you, not hurt you. The fact of the matter is there will always be competition and, most often, the more the better, unless the market is truly overcrowded. The heavier the competition, the more likely the potential reward for those who succeed. It would be highly unusual—a dream of dreams!—to come up with a worthwhile idea for a business that involved a marketplace where no one had ever before been. Competition is just something you will have to contend with, so you better learn as much as you can about it.

An understanding of the competition also brings a deeper understanding of the marketplace, since the competition is always looking at what is in store for them. They are constantly doing market analysis, too, and some of that comes out in annual reports and in the financial media. There are also a lot of market research firms who make it their business to supply other businesses with information regarding the future growth, composition, customer, technologies, labor supply, and other elements of the marketplace. They look beyond the competition, and so should you.

There are many other influences that can have an impact on what will become your marketplace and therefore on your business. The best time to think about them is before your idea becomes one of many businesses doing business in the business jungle. The other influences that are external to the marketplace generally include:

- government regulation and legislation that could affect the rules of the marketplace;
- economic, political, and social trends that may affect the customer's buying habits;
- financial and economic trends that could affect the availability of money; and
- technological developments outside of your particular industry.

The development of the personal computer, for example, has had a terrific impact on all aspects of business, from finance to administration to design to production to marketing, and innovations there will continue to affect the entrepreneur. The stock market plunge in 1987, the savings and loan debacle, the realignment of the financial services industry, the problems that commercial banks have with bad loans, and economic phenomena like inflation and recession—all of these have and will affect the money available to businesses.

Chances are that an entrepreneur will not be dissuaded from starting up a business because of such external conditions, good or bad. Any entrepreneur deserving the name will possess sufficient drive and desire to outweigh the negatives and take advantage of the positives. But these things must be considered now because these are things of which investors are very aware. They will want to know if and how the entrepreneur intends to deal with them. Entrepreneurs will have to think things through very carefully to be able to respond to investors' fears and concerns regarding the business environment that their new company will face. They are going to want answers and you are going to need more than a few yourself.

After starting up businesses in the face of all of the above and building successful businesses while such things were going on (and they are always going on, one way or the other), I can report that sometimes external forces do help. MetPath, for example, was to some degree legislated into success. The first development was when the Clinical Laboratory Improvement Act, a federal law, was passed. It regulated laboratory personnel, inspected facilities, and set up quality control procedures; things sorely needed in the industry at that time. The next was a patient billing law passed in New York State, which mandated that labs bill patients directly, rather than billing the physicians. All of a sudden, the medical profession began choosing labs on the basis of quality and service, rather than on the basis of how much money could be made off of the laboratory tests. The final assist was offered by something called the Padavan Act, again in New York, which made any kind of kickbacks illegal between the doctors and the labs. All of these were critical to MetPath's survival as a business and helped the company grow.

Ethical considerations may require you to take a stand for what you believe in, which just might help your business. When I testified before Congress in favor of change in the clinical laboratory industry, I was not very popular among the thousands of small, poorly operated labs that dominated the market. But the law was formulated and passed, which dramatically changed the number and type of laboratories in the market over the next twenty years (which, by the way, was one of the business objectives of MetPath). So my opportunism, if you will, was also guided by ethical considerations. It turned out to my advantage but could have gone the other way just as easily. That would not necessarily mean that I could not have built MetPath. It just might have taken longer, which would have been fine with me as long as we had the money to survive. The point is that being in business means to be able to take advantage of opportunities, and an entrepreneur's ethical concerns expand rather than limit those opportunities. Legislation is expected in the hearing-care field that will undoubtedly change that marketplace and help HEARx in the long run, as well.

Legislation, however, is a two-edged sword that can destroy a business as easily as it can help it. I have watched several businesses flounder and go down the tubes because they were not properly prepared to make their product or service meet legal requirements, such as was the case we recounted earlier concerning the company confronted with a mouse's fallopian tube. Another group in Florida years ago developed a medicine that stopped herpes. They went ahead and did all of their clinical trials and tests for that product in Mexico. And then they tried to bring it back into this country, but the FDA would not approve it. They had run out of money by then, so the product never got off the ground and neither did the company.

The key for the entrepreneur is trying to know what to expect, and attempting to understand what might have to be done before it has to be done. Now, you cannot cover every probable future event, but you can do the best you possibly can. What you envision will happen in your business or marketplace will seldom happen the way you think it will, anyway (a reality exposed in all its gory detail in *Chapters 5 and 6*). The point is that, by thinking about as many probable scenarios as possible, the entrepreneur is prepared for just about anything and therefore can move more quickly and effectively to meet changes as the circumstances warrant.

Odds are that as you consider the various strategies you may employ in building your business you are probably worrying about holding onto your present job long enough to put together a business plan. Your idea for a business will by now also have become quite an enterprise in your mind, having evolved several segments with multiple elements, each poised to enter a multiplicity of markets. Whatever you do, try to keep most of it under your hat for right now. Meanwhile, as you continue to strategize, **start making distinctions between public strategies and private strategies**.

When MetPath started up as Metropolitan Pathology Laboratory, the public strategy for the business was to set up a large clinical laboratory that would service the metropolitan New York area. But the rest of my strategy—the majority of my delusions of grandeur—was something else, to say the least. My private scheme was for the company to become International Medical Services, which would have had three separate areas of business: a laboratory services division; a medical products division; and a financial services division. The problem with the concept was that, even though it was truly a grand delusion, a twenty-nine-year-old clinical pathologist with no track record in business whatsoever was the one having the idea. If I went out to raise money and told anybody about IMS at that point, they never would have given me any money and probably would have had me locked up. It was all written down, but all that could be revealed was the clinical laboratory piece of the puzzle—the public strategy. The private strategy that contained all my delusions was unveiled slowly. As MetPath grew, so did my name and image and reputation, and more and more of my delusions of grandeur could be told because I had become more believable.

An entrepreneur's public strategies have got to be realistic and reasonable. Too many people come up with plans that include all their delusions of grandeur, and the result is that they simply appear self-deluded. If you are successful the first time, more can be told the next time. Steven Jobs was able to start up Next Computers with the stated intention of building the next generation of personnel computers because Steven Jobs can say whatever he wants after having built Apple Computers and people will listen to him. But if an entrepreneur with little or no experience in building a high-tech business tried, he would only be laughed into the next generation. Save yourself the embarrassment and frustration. Keep your best thinking to yourself until the time is right for you to let other people know about it.

There are, however, some **other people** an entrepreneur will need to tell things to who can help realize a strategy, public or private. These include consultants, certain employees and maybe even a partner. Now is the time to consider these people very carefully and decide how much of your delusions you should share with them. Entrepreneurs can be guided in that decision only by their own sensibilities, but common sense says that caution should be exercised when sharing your plans with anyone else.

Caution must also be the watchword concerning what others are telling you. A lot of entrepreneurs rush out and hire consultants without paying much attention to their credentials. Very few consultants have ever had their feet on the ground for very long in the business jungle. They are most often theorists, not entrepreneurial tacticians with years of experience. Even if they have some experience as businessmen, few have ever run a business as an entrepreneur. They are primarily good for saying no, for telling you what you cannot do, not what you *can* do.

Accountants and academicians are particularly suspect in this category. Accountants are great for telling you what not to do, and they always have good reasons: "There isn't enough money," "You'll lose your shirt," and so on. They are great for the downside, but do not rely on them for the upside potential of an idea.

Academicians are a little different, but are still only good for saying no—even when they say yes. When you talk to the professor of chemistry at Imaginary University and he tells you that your new compound does not make any sense scientifically, do not waste your time pursuing that idea because the professor is probably right. But if he says the product is good, and tells you to go ahead and build a business around it, be very, very careful—as we should have been with the Web-Guard mentioned earlier.

Whatever kind of advisors you use, think first about who they are and where they are coming from. Listen to their opinions, then go and figure out the business side of things yourself. Do not bend their facts and figures to fit your version of reality, but take them at face value. Use them to help keep you from going off the deep end or heading off in the wrong direction. Trust your own instincts if you do not agree with their conclusions, but try not to distrust their facts. If you need a second opinion, get one, then make your own decision on how to proceed. You will make many seat-of-the-pants decisions, but that is something entrepreneurs do best. The entrepreneur often steps where others fear to tread.

Those employees who will be stepping along with you require consideration as well. We will be talking a lot more about the people you hire in *Chapter 4*. But before you start hiring them, think about where they are going to come from. If you need skilled labor or specialized professionals, make sure they are available where you will need them. As far as management personnel are concerned, mull over your own strengths and weaknesses and try to figure out what traits others should have that will be complimentary to your own. If you are a technical or scientific expert, who is going to raise the money? If you are a good negotiator, that does not mean you will be able to market your product or service.

Think about the possibility that you will probably never be able to do everything required of an entrepreneur by yourself. Then think about whether you want to hire the talent to help you, or whether you want to take on a partner. As already indicated, a partnership is a difficult proposition—and that is not sour lemons from my childhood, either! Equal partnerships simply do not work. Unequal partnerships may work; at least they have a better chance of working than partnerships where the shares are split 50-50. The inequality that might make a partnership work can be either financial—one partner owns more of the business than the other—or territorial. If you structure a partnership where the financial split is 50-50, but one partner is an inside person and the other is an outside person, that might theoretically be feasible. But still not likely.

A 50-50 business partnership is very hard to maintain, just because people do not see things the same way, no matter how similar they seem otherwise. Just after I opened the doors of Metropolitan Pathology Laboratory in that two-room apartment across the street from Columbia Presbyterian Hospital in New York where I was still a resident pathologist, I took on a partner. The act should have carried a strong sense of *deja vu* for me, because I had done almost the same thing twenty years earlier with my lemonade stand. But I had forgotten, and took on a partner because I was worried about what would happen if business started coming in and I could not be there. I asked my best friend, Paul, if he would pay half the three month's rent I had paid on the apartment in return for being my 50-50 partner in the business. He agreed and we began the struggle to get the business started.

We began having problems about a year and a half later, in the fall of 1968. We by then had a real lab, and we were doing about $3,000 a month in test revenues. The equipment was there, the customers were coming, everything was beginning to work, but we were not making any money. We were starting to fight more and more often. I wanted to buy wastebaskets, and he said that cardboard boxes were fine. I wanted to go get stationery printed, and he said a rubber stamp was fine. I wanted to get curtains to make the lab look better, and he said that since no one ever came there anyway, why bother? The problem was that we both thought we had the same skills, the same ability, the same everything, including shares in the business, but we did not understand that was the problem. We just knew that our partnership was deteriorating.

Finally, Paul came to me and suggested that we end it.

"Paul, this is not working," he said. "We should split. Why don't you buy me out?"

"Fine, Paul. What do you want for your half of the business?"

"Well, Paul," he answered, not hesitating an instant, "I figure it's worth about $35,000."

"That's ridiculous, Paul. We are not going to have that much in sales for this entire year, and God only knows if we are ever going to make any money at this, and you want me to give you $35,000? That's absurd."

I did not know what to do, so I went to our mutual accountant who suggested that I tell my partner that I agreed with him, that the business was worth $70,000, that half of the business was worth $35,000, and that my wife Cynthia and I would sell him our half. And the next time I saw him, that is exactly what I said.

"No, no," he immediately shot back, adding a few more "no-nos" for emphasis. "I don't want it, Paul. I'm selling my half, I'm not buying your half. If I buy your half the business will collapse. But if you buy my half, you'll probably make this into a big company."

Probably without realizing it, Paul had neatly encapsulated the heart of our differences. We were suffering from double vision! Paul did not or could not or would not see what I saw. Paul did not believe that there could be a big business called International Medical Services, or MetPath, or even a smaller, successful one called Metropolitan Pathology Laboratory. Paul lacked that vision, and therefore lost faith. He just wanted out. Paul had no delusions that would help him hang on through the hard parts of building a business, large or little.

"Paul," I said patiently, "if you cut an apple in half, you have two equal halves. You cannot have two halves of an apple where one half is bigger than the other. So whatever you are willing to pay me for my half is what I should pay for your half." And after a long drawn-out argument, I agreed to buy his half of the business for $7,500.

Now, there was something else I wanted to look at. What was it? Let's see... First was the marketplace, then the systems, the people...

Oh, of course!

The Money!

Now, how could I miss something that important?

What could I have been thinking about?

What do you think?

*   *   *   *   *

Ranging in length from the pygmy owl's mere five inches to the great horned owl's two-foot-plus height, there are 134 owl species in two families: **Strigidae** *(123) and* **Tytonidae** *(11). Although roof eaves will do for a barn owl and the burrowing owl will share a prairie dog's digs underground, most owls live in trees. The ubiquitous bird was once classed with hawks and eagles [order* **Falconiformes***] but they are not closely related. Surviving mostly on small mammals and birds (although a few relatives are fish eaters), an owl kills as a hawk does. But the owl soars alone as the premier hunter of the avian world, stalking its prey in virtually noiseless flight, with unmatched vision.*

*   *   *   *   *

3. ... and You!

Have you ever been with someone who is just sitting, staring off into space, and ask them what they are thinking about?

"I don't know," is a common enough reply, often followed by, "Nothing, really."

Then they usually change the subject. What they are really saying is that they do not want to bother putting their thoughts into words. Unless they are brain damaged, it is certain that they are thinking about something and they know what it is, even if they are lying. Some practitioners of transcendental meditation, I believe, claim that the most advanced state of consciousness that a person can attain is to be able to think about nothing. Perhaps such enlightenment has something to do with brain damage; in any case, the experience most likely would be the only one that would be truly indescribable.

The entrepreneur must describe his thoughts, however, if he ever plans to build an idea into a business. Yet the process by which one arrives at such a description often seems like walking on a path that is not there, taking steps that seem to lead nowhere. It is only after you take the step that the path somehow appears under your foot, at least for that moment. Building a business is an open-ended, creative process; as much an art as it is a science. It is affected by individual experiences, intuitions, a sense of timing, emotions, and a host of other human influences.

Here there are no borders between fantasy and reality. At best those lines become indistinct, blurred by the confluence of plans and schemes, hopes and dreams that the entrepreneur entertains. And that, as you may have heard before, is just the way it is, and you might as well throw in another "So what?" This is only the beginning! Wait until you actually start up your business. You may very well look back on this time with pleasant nostalgia. If you get **The Money** . . .

Oh, right! **The Money**! I promised we would address that. Let's begin with a question which should bring the outlines of your vision into sharp relief:

How do you think you will look to an investor?

That is the ultimate aim and test of everything you have been thinking about to this point, because you are the one who has to go and get **The Money** to start your business. Your idea, your business, the opportunity they represent and the strategy you have evolved may look great to you, but you are the one who has to make them look good to investors. The printed business plan which you distribute to investors will not do it because it does not contain all the information that they will want to know, only you

do. The writer of the plan, your accountant, your lawyer, your consultants, your spouse, your business partner—none of them will
do it either.

**You, the entrepreneur, are the idea, the business and every-
thing else, as far as investors are concerned.** By the time you
get around to talking to investors, they will want to see and hear
a lot more than just a prepared presentation. They will want face-
to-face answers to their questions from you about your plans for
your business, and only you can do it. If you cannot give them
detailed answers without referring to a no-matter-how-neatly-
bound sheaf of papers, they will be giving you the gate instead of
The Money. No one will wait around if you say, "Uh, just a
minute, okay? I'll go and get my business plan and that will
answer all your questions." (If you come across any investors who
believe that business plans will answer all their questions, send
them over to my office, will you? They have a few million things I
would like to talk to them about.)

But to get investors to believe that your idea, your business,
and you look as good as you think you are is going to require the
best story that you can tell. Investors love a good story and, even
if you have already built a successful business, investors do not
want to see a business plan that reads like *War and Peace*. They
definitely do not want to hear a tall story and would prefer a short
story, a fact that serves to emphasize just how important it is to
qualify and quantify your thinking as much as possible before you
start talking to investors. Entrepreneurs who have already built a
business may have more to say and investors may be predisposed
to listen to them a little longer than they will listen to your story.
But yesterday's successes likewise will not produce one single dollar for any new venture unless the thoughts are first well-devel-
oped and then well-delivered.

So your ability to tell a good story is really what it is all about.
Your idea and your business will amount to nothing unless you
can get *The Money*, and you will not get *The Money* unless you
learn how to talk to investors, those very necessary and often very
cunning inhabitants of the Business Jungle. It all comes down,
finally, to you.

Now that you think you understand yourself, your idea, and
your business, there are only a few things left to consider. First of
all, decide who is going to help you write a business plan that will
make your idea, your business, and you look as good as possible
on paper. Next, contemplate how you are going to turn all the
planning you have done into a story that will make you sound as
good as you think the business plan looks. Finally, figure out how
you will find a bunch of investors who will look at your business

plan, listen to what you have to say and maybe give you what you have been thinking about most of all anyway right from the start, namely, **The Money**.

And that is all there is to it. Except, of course, that before you can do any of that, you have to think about a few other things, like: how much you think your business is worth; how much money you think you will need; and just where you think you will find those people who might give you **The Money**—and all of that is in the next chapter.

This is precisely the point where *your idea, your business, and you* all come together. Coherence will be the result of the chaotic process of creative thinking that at times appears to defy logic. As you twist things one way and then the other, you may be hard pressed to put what you see in any kind of order. You may despair of ever making sense of it all, particularly when things look backwards, sideways, and upside down, all at the same time—and they will. Your thoughts will seem oddly circular, and you may also notice some repetition in your thinking.

Well, don't give any of it a second thought! That is just the way it is when you begin to try bringing order out of chaos. Who told you this was going to be easy? Just keep trying to find your path and try not to get confused by apparent contradictions and redundancies.

So, tell me . . .

What do you think you see?

$ECRET$ OF THE OWL

**A great idea cannot always be made
into a successful business.**

———

**Developing your business strategy requires
being able to see
both the forest and the trees.**

———

**The size of the potential market for your idea
will often make the difference
between business success and failure.**

Polly Wants the Money

Chapter Three
The Parrot: Polly Wants the Money

▲ ▲ ▲ ▲ ▲

PARROT *(family* Psittacidae, *order* Psittaciformes*) is the name given to a large group of birds, generally with richly colored plumage and possessing at least some degree of mimetic ability. The unusually long-lived birds share several other traits, including large heads, strong jaws, razor-sharp beaks (even the smallest can inflict a painful bite), and claws with the first and fourth toes pointing backward which give them a strong, hand-like grip. These intelligent and capable creatures need relatively longer nest care than other birds, however, to give them adequate time to develop and coordinate their complex motor responses.*

*   *   *   *   *

You probably think your new business looks pretty good, don't you?

Well, you should! You have made a few things happen. Perhaps you have scratched up a little cash and made a prototype of your product, and it seems to work very well, every time. Or maybe you have done some preliminary market studies that indicate there is more demand for your service than you imagined. You have tons of confidence, burgeoning energy, a positive outlook and the emotional support of those you hold near and dear. Even if you have to risk everything and seed your idea with your own hard-earned cash, you are certain that the time to leave the nest has finally arrived. Only one thing is lacking: **The Money**, enough capital to bring your vision to reality.

Before heading off in search of that capital, however, consider for a moment that an entrepreneur at this early stage of business development is similar to a baby parrot in some tropical rain forest. The young bird will not be fed by his parents anymore and must fly off to find a meal or perish in the attempt.

A fledgling entrepreneur is likewise at a point of no return. Either he finds some capital or the business will die young. The entrepreneur is just as hungry for **The Money** as any parrot is for food, but the parrot has an advantage: natural instinct will lead him to his first meal. Entrepreneurs are hardly as well-equipped. Most brand new business people have little experience when it comes to getting financing, their efforts more than likely limited to personal loans and home mortgages from banks. Business financing, they find out quickly enough, is a tougher nut to crack entirely; in fact, it is doubtful they know the three ...

BASIC QUESTIONS OF BUSINESS SURVIVAL

1. *Where do you get The Money?*
2. *How do you get The Money?*
3. *How much of The Money do you need?*

... much less the answers.

Happily, there are answers. So don't worry—a very important bit of advice, since entrepreneurs just starting out tend to worry altogether too much about everything, especially about getting **The Money**. Driven by fear and possessing scant knowledge of things financial, they may often waste valuable time concocting poorly conceived and overcomplicated business plans that leave them with great dreams and zero cash. After one or two misdirected efforts, some may become so fearful or demoralized that they never get off the ground. Many others, perhaps driven by circumstance or personality or pride or their spouses or whatever, press on blindly and wind up crashing soon after takeoff. Usually, such disasters happen when an entrepreneur does something stupid—like someone I know *very* well who nearly gave away his company before it got started. But more about that a little later.

Be advised for now that if you hope to avoid such unhappy scenarios, the financial area of the business jungle first must be explored thoroughly. And beware! Budding entrepreneurs must have all their wits about them at all times. If you wish to hold onto your idea, your company and your skin when hunting financial sources, you must understand fully the tricks and traits of your quarry. Here is where the reality of doing business first meets the dream of having one. This is definitely *not* the time to be traveling the ozone in flights of fancy. There are too many concrete concerns to confront on the jungle floor if you are ever going to get **The Money** and really take off.

All of those concerns are connected by a single thread: **the risk**

factor. Investors, for their part, take an entirely pragmatic view about risk. As far as they are concerned, the only ones risking anything are themselves, by putting up **The Money**. And each one thinks he will be the only loser if the business does not get off the ground. So before investors will seriously consider putting up hard cash for a new venture, they want some assurances that the entrepreneur in question is going to give it his best shot. What it comes down to is that every investor has the same question: Just how much of a risk is the entrepreneur willing to take?

Consider that baby parrot again, ready to fly. Once he jumps off the edge of the nest, he is committed! Everything he has, all his ability and his hope for the future, are tied up with that first step. He goes hungry unless he goes out on a limb. Likewise, **an entrepreneur's demonstrated degree of commitment is absolutely the initial deciding factor for investors** when they consider putting money into a new venture. Since investors are putting their money where their mouths are, they first want some kind of assurance that the entrepreneur is able to walk the walk of business success, not just talk the talk. Words, after all, are cheap. Investors will turn a deaf ear towards any new business person who does not tangibly demonstrate a willingness to undertake the risk of entrepreneurship, no matter how good a story sounds.

Your money or your time are the only things available that will demonstrate the degree of your commitment to an investor, and there are times it requires both. A case in point: When I began talking about starting up HEARx in 1986, I went first to all the professional investors who made a fortune from their investments in MetPath a few years earlier. Yet not a single one would give me any money for the new venture. I could not understand why but I soon found out: They all had short memories. Those investors simply were not ready to invest in my new venture, despite my proven track record—a "what have you done for me lately?" attitude.

They said, "Listen, Paul, why don't you just go sail around Palm Beach? You're not going to go through starting a business again, are you? Of course you're not! How can you go back to work and build another company? Just relax! Enjoy life!"

Nobody believed I was serious until my wife and I sold our house in Massachusetts, our apartment in New York, her antique store in New Jersey, and moved to Florida full-time. Then, when I put $1 million of my own money into the business, everybody said, "Well, why didn't you tell us you were serious? Of course we'll give you some money!" And they did, once I demonstrated my willingness to commit a large sum of my own money to my new enterprise. If you have some cash, invest it in your business. Money, as far as investors are concerned, is what commitment is all about anyway. It is certainly tangible, and money speaks volumes about commitment to investors.

Now, I know there is someone reading this who is saying, *"But that's easy! How about when you don't have any money, like me? How do you demonstrate your commitment then?"*

Patience! Patience! Didn't I just say a few paragraphs ago that there are two elements to commitment? Obviously, money is a good way for entrepreneurs to show potential investors their intention to walk the talk, but it is not the only way. The other way is time, and of that the new businessman possesses plenty. If the old adage that time is money is true, then the new businessman is loaded! Just like money, however, it's what you do with your time that counts. If the erstwhile entrepreneur has a job and does not give it up to work full-time on a new business, for example, that will not sit very well with investors. Not only does that portend a too long, too slow haul for the start-up of the business, but it also speaks volumes about the entrepreneur's lack of faith in the idea. There are few who would invest in a part-time proprietor of an untried business. So, if you do not have any money, be ready to walk away from your job and invest all of your time in your business. And that includes weekends!

Granted, such a decision can be uncomfortable to make, but entrepreneurship is not for the faint-hearted. The beginning stages of a business always create circumstances that require difficult choices, testing one's degree of personal commitment. Not long after I started Metropolitan Pathology Laboratory, MetPath's forerunner, I was drafted into the Navy. I was commuting back and forth to New Jersey three or four days a week from the base where I was stationed. There was no way I could quit my job, unless I wanted to start up my business from federal prison in Leavenworth. I sat down with my wife and told her that I really did not have much time for her, the marriage, the kids or much of anything else at that time. It was not easy, but I had to make my family aware that the business would have to come first in my life for awhile. I explained that if I made the company work, the marriage and the family and everything else would do well in the long run. It turned out that I was right, but—talk about risk!

Over the years, that kind of all-or-nothing attitude has helped develop a high level of trust between me and those who invest in my ideas. People understand that attitude reflects someone willing to put all the eggs in one basket. They also have come to believe, properly, that I will watch out for their money as if it were my own. They have learned that I am not going to take one egg out for myself when nobody is looking. I have never bought "company" airplanes or boats or apartments or anything like that for my personal use, or sold stock to anyone with the idea that it would make me rich at their expense. Not that I don't want to get rich! I do, but only from what I can accomplish.

And I never, never, *never* trusted my luck. Getting **The Money** will not be a result of luck, but a lot of hard work along with a lot of stress. I do not believe in luck, good or bad, and could never accept the idea that anyone's circumstances ultimately could be blamed or credited to chance. Next time you hear someone in business say, "I just ran into a streak of bad luck," check your initial response. You *know* that is an excuse, that it is a cop-out, and that somewhere, somehow, someone screwed up. The business opportunity came and went, and the entrepreneur was unprepared to take advantage of it. Luck had nothing to do with it.

If luck mattered, then I was certainly unlucky in the summer of 1969. I had been drafted only six months after MetPath had gotten its first investors. Stationed at the Portsmouth Naval Hospital in New Hampshire, I ran the company via Ma Bell and the Eastern Airlines shuttle for eighteen months. I was continually on the road, reassuring old investors and trying to interest new ones, while at the same time putting my two cents into the business. Daily telephone calls from Guy Seay, my Harvard co-alumnus whom I had hired as MetPath's vice president of finance, kept me up to date about what was going on when I was not there. The call I got one fine fall morning, however, almost made it unnecessary for me to ever have to show up again.

"What are we going to do?"

The voice on the phone was Guy's, and he was upset. "We've got a $37,000 payroll this afternoon and we have $18,000 in the bank. What," he repeated pointedly, "are we going to do?"

I had nothing brilliant ready to reply. Our immediate options seemed grossly unattractive: one, write everyone a check and wait for half of them to bounce; two, write everyone a partial paycheck and tell them we will make it up to them next week; or three, write no checks and tell everyone that we will try to pay them next week. At least that way we would have enough money to pay some of our other bills and stave off the end for a little while. Great choices, right? So we agreed to try and raise some money from our investors to make up the difference, and Guy would call me back by 2:00 that afternoon, before the banks closed.

Several frustrating hours later, we both had come up empty. Just as Guy was about to call with the bad news, his phone rang.

"Hello, Guy," the voice on the other end said. "John from the Bank of New York here. How are you?"

Not at all sure whether perfect health or dire straits was the correct reply, Guy let out a noncommittal, "Well enough, I guess.

How are you, John?"

"Fine, just fine. Listen, Guy, you're not going to believe this," John went on, "but do you remember that $50,000 loan you and Paul applied for about four months ago? Well, it was finally approved by our loan committee just this afternoon. So, if you're going to be in New York next week, why don't you come in and sign the papers?"

"You're right, I don't believe it."

"What was that, Guy?"

"Oh, nothing, John, nothing. Ha-ha!" Hardly stopping for breath, Guy pressed on quickly before this obvious hallucination ended. "Well, gee, John, that's great! Listen, I was on my way into New York anyway this afternoon. Maybe I could sign the papers and we could finalize the loan today."

"Oh, I wouldn't want you to make a special trip, Guy."

"No, no, it's okay, really! I had to go and pick up a few things for Paul anyway," Guy nearly shouted. Regaining control, he added a little more calmly, "I'll just come over to the bank and then you can deposit the money in our account. Is that okay?" The ensuing two-second silence saw Guy nearly crush the telephone in nervous anticipation.

"Welll... sure," John decided. "I guess we'll see you in an hour or so."

"I'm on my way," Guy said, and so, once again, was MetPath. The impossible had happened, but it had nothing to do with luck. The money did not come out of the blue. If we had not filled in the loan application early enough; if Guy had not made all the speeches, cultivated a relationship, and made a friend who supported our application before the bank's loan committee, then we would not have gotten **The Money**. We were not lucky. We simply were given opportunities and were prepared to take advantage of them. Why the call came then, at precisely the right moment, is not something I can easily explain. I just call it a miracle (one of nine at MetPath) and let it go at that.

But don't go expecting miracles, either, when you are trying to raise **The Money**.

It is much better to be counting dollars when you are trying to start up a business.

So let's explore the first of those three basic questions of business survival and see on whom you might count for . . .

The Money.

*   *   *   *   *

Parrots are brightly colored, raucous birds found throughout the equatorial belt in the Americas, Africa, Asia, and the Australian regions. There are over three hundred species of these garrulous birds, including noisy little lovebirds, parakeets, and budgies; the larger and no less voluble crested cockatoos, keas, and lories; talkative Amazons and African Greys; the shrieking Goliaths of the rain forests, the giant black cockatoos of New Guinea; and the three-foot-high macaws from Central and South America, whose powerful jaws crush nuts that take man a hammer to crack. They are highly prized for their colorful and unique appearance.

*   *   *   *   *

1. Where Do You Get The Money?

There are really only four sources of capital that you, the new entrepreneur, can approach when beginning to search for **The Money**. Before you start out to get that start-up capital, however, you need to know that . . .

SOME OF THE FOLLOWING CAPITAL SOURCES ARE BETTER THAN OTHERS

- *Banks*
- *Wall Street*
- *Professional Investors (venture capitalists)*
- *Private Investors*

Banks really are the last place to expect to find **The Money**, although they are often the first places that entrepreneurs look. That was true in the '60s, when I started MetPath, and likewise in the '80s, when I started HEARx, and it will no doubt continue into the next century and beyond, unless bankers' attitudes change drastically. Not long after we opened HEARx in 1987, a large Florida bank was willing—if we bought a certificate of deposit (CD)—to loan us 95 percent of the amount of that CD. We would get the loan for only one point above prime rate. What a fantastic deal, right? They take our money and then give some of it back to us, and charge us interest to boot! That is like a retailer renting you an umbrella on a sunny day with the provision that you return the umbrella if it even looks like it might rain. Banks are exactly the same: They do not even want to risk the chance of getting wet.

Still, developing a strong banking relationship is necessary for any new business—even crucial, as has been the case for me often enough—since they are convenient and steady sources of operating funds once your business is on its feet. Plus, their connections in the financial world may help later on with contacts and introductions. But banks are businesses that make money by loaning money. They want their money back and they want a profit, too, which they call interest. But unlike investors, banks will not wait until they can get it out of your profits, so they take it out of your cash flow, a little at a time.

And before they will even consider giving you some money, you have to come up with collateral, usually in the form of receivables or hard assets. A bank might loan fifty to seventy-five cents for each dollar's worth of your receivables at a couple of points over the prime interest rate. They might even add the value of your inventory onto that, but don't count on it. If there are furniture, fixtures, and equipment, perhaps they will consider a loan amounting to 50 percent of their value at three to five points over prime. That office building or factory you have with all those special design elements is worth no more to a bank than the going market price for the least-desirable property in the area.

So, let's add it up:

Banks want collateral.
+ Start-ups don't have any
Scratch banks as a start-up capital source.

And while you're at it, scratch **Wall Street**. Few small or first-time businessmen possess the contacts, experience, or financial wherewithal to head straight for Wall Street and a public stock offering. (If you think you do, turn to *Chapter 7*.) There, investors only believe in a great story accompanied by a great track record, and you do not have either one. Most start-ups do not need the kind of money that Wall Street can afford anyway, where it is easier to raise a whole lot of money but tough to raise only a little. So if you are raising money for a small to medium-sized start-up, forget Wall Street.

The only way that most new businesses can find investment capital is through a **private placement**, which means raising money outside of the stock market. Private placements are the domain of two distinct capital sources: **private investors** and **professional investors**. Is one better than the other when it comes to a brand new entrepreneur trying to raise money for a brand new business? I certainly think so.

Let's look first at *professional investors*, also known as **venture**

capitalists. They share several traits that an entrepreneur needs to know how to recognize:

- Venture capitalists **make a living at investing**. They want to make as much money as possible out of each investment. As a rule, they are decidedly better at negotiation, market analysis, and other investment arts than even experienced entrepreneurs.

- Venture capitalists **try to minimize their own risk as much as possible**. They hunt in packs, tending to invest with the same group in each different deal. Their pooled resources give them more to invest, allow investments in more than one enterprise, and automatically provide a source for subsequent rounds of financing in each separate deal. Most venture capitalists will probably demand 50 to 75 percent of an investment target in order to maximize their potential profit and further minimize their risk.

- Venture capital groups **vary in size**. They may have at their disposal anywhere from somewhere around a million dollars to hundreds of millions of dollars. The amount that a group will invest in a venture relates directly to the amount of dollars it has available. For example, a $750,000 investment is probably not of interest to a $5 million venture capital group because that is too much money for it to put in one place. A group that size is more interested in making $100,000 to $250,000 investments. On the other hand, $750,000 is too small for a group with $500 million because at that level it would soon have more investments than it could effectively manage. The ante for such a group probably needs to be at least $2 million.

- Venture capitalists **tend to invest in success**. Unless a company has already made money or the entrepreneur has some other kind of historical plus—a track record of building other businesses, recognition as an expert in a particular field, a management team composed of defectors from a big company—it is unlikely that very many venture capitalists will even get past the executive summary of a business plan for a brand new company.

- Venture capitalists **like to specialize**. They pick certain industry categories, such as retail or high tech, and seek to invest exclusively in those areas. They develop expertise in those investment areas and usually will not invest outside of what they know. An entrepreneur looking for capital to produce God's answer to biotechnology will only waste time and effort trying to raise money from a venture capital group specializing in oil and gas exploration.

- Very large venture capital groups **manage other peoples' money**. An entrepreneur talking to a mega-million venture capital fund seldom, if ever, will be dealing directly with the original investors. Instead, the contact point will be individuals empowered to manage all of those investors' funds. Managers usually receive a fee based on a portfolio's total value.

- Venture capitalists **believe in projections**, period. Even if venture capitalists like you and your product or service, the only thing that will make a potential investment look good to them is if the numbers appear to work out. And they want to know everything relative to you and your business since before it began to back up those numbers, as well. If you bring them a sample of soap you want to produce, they will want to know if you have statistics proving beyond a shadow of a doubt that people bathe every day!

- Venture capitalists **tend to be both greedy and cowardly** when it comes to money. They are greedy in the sense that they want to make as much money as possible, even at someone else's expense. They are cowardly because they very rarely are investing their own money.

Perhaps the most important thing to remember about these sophisticated money sources is that they are all at least as hungry or bright or greedy as anyone else, sharing among themselves one primary concern: *Money*—unless it is *More Money* or, better yet, *Big Money*. They do not have to worry about things like setting up a business, employee relations and production runs. Their only business is making money and all they really care about is how well their investments perform. Venture capitalists may sign on to share the financial risks of the venture that shows some potential, but at the first hint of trouble, they begin hearing the drumbeat of doom. They get very nervous and start demanding things, because all are terrified of losing their *Money*. Few treat losses lightly and most will not hesitate to eat entrepreneurs alive, stripping the carcasses bare for whatever gain they can feed on when there are too many mistakes or if things do not happen as anticipated.

The more perceptive among you probably have figured out that venture capitalists are not my choice of investor for the new business person. But also understand that the dreadful possibilities just stated are not meant to deter anyone from seeking them out. My purpose is only to alert entrepreneurs to the deadly dangers that await the rash and untutored who head off in that direction. I know, because I was one who did. My first effort at raising capital, in fact, turned out to be the closest I ever came to losing my company to venture capitalists.

Metropolitan Pathology Laboratory was little more than a year old when I was introduced by the friend of a friend to a group of venture capitalists interested in backing the company. I was more than anxious to meet with them, considering:

That while still a resident pathologist, I was running the lab with an increasingly contentious partner from a much less than luxurious two-room apartment across the street from Columbia Presbyterian Medical Center in uptown New York;

That both of our wives were the drivers for the company, picking up and delivering the test samples and reports;

That the business I started with $500 borrowed from my father-in-law only had a volume of $3,000 a month, with zero profit;

That I had to supplement the family income by working nights.

I was indeed considering all of that and more when I met with the venture capitalists in their very comfortable offices. It was a heady moment for me and I was feeling like I had finally arrived. The room we were sitting in was bigger than our two-room apartment and my sense of self-importance grew steadily as they outlined the deal.

Yes, of course they would give me $1.5 million! All they wanted was 49 percent and I would still control the company with 51 percent. How could I refuse?

We shook hands. We went off to draw up the papers and I started looking for a bigger office. The next time I met with them, my hopes were high. But as we sat down to review the contract, one of the assembled venture capitalists put those hopes on hold.

"Paul, we've been thinking," he began, smiling but serious. "You're only twenty-nine years old and you've never run a company before. You have never even been in business. And we're about to give you a million and a half dollars. Now, I'm sure you can understand that we are a little nervous about giving you that much money."

"Sure," I agreed. "I can understand that." What else could I say? After all, no one had ever offered to put $1.5 million in my checking account.

"What we would like to do," he continued, "is have a purchasing committee that will review all purchases over $5,000. Now, you'll be on the committee, but at least we'll feel protected about how the money is spent."

My lawyer started to say something but I cut him short and hastily agreed to their demand. I was not about to lose the chance at all that money over what I thought the small matter of a purchasing committee. So once again it was smiles and handshakes all around as we went off to rework the agreement. I began thinking about how nice it would be to have only one job. The chances of that happening looked as good as the contracts we were ready to sign a week or so later at what was supposed to be the final meeting. But it was not to be.

"Paul, we've been doing some more thinking," said the same smiling but serious face across the conference table. "Now that you've got some money, you'll be hiring employees. But you've never had anybody work for you before. How are you going to determine how much to pay them? Do you know what the going rate is for a secretary or a lab technician?"

I admitted I did not know, but added that it should not be too hard to find out. "Well," he went on, "we can save you some time by forming a compensation committee. And that way we'll be assured that nobody will get a crazy salary compared to somebody else in the industry."

After he reminded me that I still would own 51 percent of the company and "would be on the committee, of course," I agreed to the compensation committee, again hushing my lawyer. Another round of handshakes and off we went, only I was not smiling anymore, but getting impatient for the chance to move the lab out of the apartment house.

Another "final" meeting was set up. We were again ready to sign, when once more I heard...

"Paul."

It was Mr. Smiles again. *Now what?!*

"We've done a little more thinking..."

Thinking? Really!

"...and we're nervous."

You guys? No kidding!

"We've gone over your proposed price list," my no longer smiling but now very serious friend intoned, holding the list in front of him like a piece of junk mail. "We need to know how you arrived at the prices you charge for the tests you perform."

"I just choose them," I said honestly.

"That's what we thought. Look at this," he said, sliding the offending piece of paper across the table to me. "Isn't it true that Columbia Presbyterian charges eight dollars for a pap smear and you charge only three dollars?"

I could only nod in agreement, uncomfortable now with what I thought had been a smart move, i.e., charging a low, fair price that would help build my customer list.

"Paul," he went on, "we need to have a pricing committee. Now, you'll sit on the committee and, of course, it's still your company. But we feel we should have some control over pricing."

At that my lawyer, who had been brooding darkly throughout the one-sided exchange, rose abruptly. He called me out into the hall and started in:

"Paul, do you realize what's going on?" The beads of cold sweat dotting my brow and my glassy-eyed expression must have told him I probably did not, so he pressed on.

"Listen," he said earnestly, his face a few inches from mine. "Two weeks ago they cut off your left arm. Last week they cut off your right arm. Now they're starting on your legs. If you sign this, it's not your company anymore." That woke me up a little, and he paused to let it sink in.

Then he shouted in a hoarse whisper, "THINK! What decisions do you get to make when they have control of purchasing, salaries and pricing?" Not many, I admitted. "And it won't end there. Maybe they'll let you decorate your office any way you want," he spat out. Irony dripping from his lips, he mercifully delivered the *coup de grace*.

"Paul, I've been thinking ... tell them to take a walk!"

His language was a bit more colorful than this edited version and I could hardly miss the point. So we went back in, tore up the documents, and walked out on $1.5 million.

My lawyer, bless his retainer, awakened me to my peril just in time for me to avoid potential disaster. I had been naive enough to believe those venture capitalists were impressed with my potential to manage the company and make the deal work. The truth was that they would have been equally happy with just the reverse! That experience and a few others—MetPath required capital infusions every eighteen months, on average, for the thirteen years I ran it, from the time it started up early in 1969 to the time I sold it in 1982—served to convince me that venture capitalists invariably follow a set pattern. They try to get as big a piece as they can of a company with their initial investment, anticipating they can pick up the rest later when the business has run out of money.

This is particularly true when negotiating with a group which may be putting very little of their own money into deals, but are making a living by representing other people's money. They want to make money for their clients, and if they make too many mistakes they will be out of the picture before too long. So they are going to try to protect against future losses any way they can when they negotiate the initial deal. One favorite way is to put themselves in a position to take over the company if things do not work out as projected, as that group tried to do with me.

They may have honestly liked me and my idea, but what they believed in were the projections for a new business in a multi-billion dollar clinical laboratory marketplace that was fragmented and ripe for consolidation. They were ready to invest all that money because of the large market MetPath was entering, which made my financial projections all the more believable. What they were betting on was not my success, but their ability to work a deal that would eventually give them control of my company and a foothold in that market.

It would have been easy enough after an experience like that to pack up my tissue slides and go get myself a real job. My track record was not, after all, very promising. I had been through a year of running a meager lab, gaining a profitless income by servicing a small customer list out of a two-room apartment. I had accomplished this only while moonlighting from my $6,000-a-year position at the hospital. I did not have any money, I sure was not making any and I had just walked away from the first real money that came my way. But after taking a hard look at my position, I found myself not at all ready to give up. Common sense, a bulldog mentality and my delusions of grandeur (remember them?) refused to let me view my recent failure at raising capital as anything but a temporary setback. I believed in what I was doing, I was excited about the future, and I was determined to succeed.

True, I was right back where I started. But I also was free to move in a new direction. At least I knew who not to go to for **The Money** and soon I found out where I should have gone in the first place: **private investors**. Relatives, friends, business acquaintances, professional connections such as lawyers and accountants—these are all individuals who do not make their living at investing. They come in two flavors: wealthy and non-wealthy, or, as the Securities and Exchange Commission likes to put it, **accredited and non-accredited**. The SEC, which governs private as well as public stock offerings, defines a non-accredited investor as anyone who cannot demonstrate a net worth of $1 million or income of at least $250,000 annually for each of the preceding three years. An accredited investor can.

Accredited or non-accredited, private investors believe in the entrepreneur—you! Wealthy or not, they are willing to go in there and take risks, often simply because they like you. It is also true, however, that they do not want to lose their money. They get particularly shaky because they are playing with their own funds and not somebody else's. Just how nervous they become is in proportion to the size of their investment, relative to their net worth.

Accredited (read *wealthy*) private investors are concerned about things like track records, market share, return on investment and how soon they can get their cash out. This type of investor is, after all, an individual who could easily handle a $100,000 or larger investment all by his or her self. These investors did not get wealthy by making mistakes and they are cautious about making investments, since just about everyone they meet is asking them for some! But if accredited investors believe in an entrepreneur, and if they like him, they most likely will invest. However, they will usually want to know a bit more about that soap you want to make than just how well it performs in the shower. Accredited investors will probably ask to see something on product development, preliminary market research, estimated sales, and profit potential (which, if you read *Chapter 2*, you probably *think* you know all about).

Most entrepreneurs just starting out usually do not get a chance to answer those queries since they do not know any accredited investors. They are not easy to find either, since they keep a low profile to avoid spending their lives fielding requests for capital. A personal introduction by someone whom the accredited investor knows and trusts is just about the only way to get in to see one.

Non-accredited investors are a lot more accessible. They may be a bit short in the wealth department compared to their accredited cousins but they are often comfortably well off, with a little money put aside to invest in the hope of making a little more. They are not usually greedy or out to make a killing—which is fortunate for them, since they often have little financial or investment expertise. Their investment activities generally are limited to simple pursuits, such as finding the highest interest-bearing checking accounts and the lowest credit card interest rates, searching out high-yield CDs and mutual funds, and perhaps playing the market a little on their own or through a local broker.

Unsophisticated they may be and perhaps even a little foolhardy, but these retired professionals or business people, neighbors, friends of friends—just about anyone—can be the best thing that happens to an entrepreneur just starting out because where they are short on money, they are long on belief. They might put $5,000 or even a few thousand above that into your company easily enough, just because they like your family, have known you for years, or think you are a good person who deserves a break. They often make emotional rather than intellectual decisions about their investments. Ask them for $10,000 or more, however, and you will frighten them away. You cannot expect to get very much capital from a single non-accredited investor—but then they do not expect too much from you either.

The least demanding of all investors, non-accredited investors are not out to make a fortune. They just do not want to lose any of the limited funds they possess. They do not care and might not even know about the SEC's 144 rule, even though they should for their own protection. It says investors who are buying stock in a non-public company are locked in for one year from the date of their investment and cannot take their money out, if the company goes public. Neither do they rely on the fancy financial formulas and extensive market research so common among professional investors. If you ask a private investor to back that soap manufacturing company of yours, he will probably ask for a sample, then decide how much to invest after taking a shower and seeing how it lathers up.

My own early efforts to raise start-up capital, after my first failure with venture capitalists, was soon aimed at just such private investors. At least they seemed much less threatening than that group of professional investors who nearly had me for lunch. Even if it meant a lot more effort and some handholding with friends and relatives on my part, it was better than the handwringing I would probably still be doing if I had given away 49 percent of my company before I had opened its doors. So, after a few recomputations, I lowered my sights, if not my expectations. I knew that I would need to get only about $250,000 from some number of private investors to get the lab out of the apartment. But there were some obstacles. The first one I faced was how to decide how much investors should pay for stock in the company, which had to be based on how much the company was really worth. My problem looked something like this:

DR. BROWN'S BUSINESS VALUE TEST
(Choose a value for your company)

(A) $100,000
(B) $200,000   (C) $300,000
(D) $350,000   (E) $500,000   (F) $1,000,000
(G) $3,000,000 (H) More (I) Really Don't Have A Clue

My answer, like most entrepreneurs just starting out, was that I really did not have a clue. So I let the government do it for me. SEC regulations currently state that a private placement can involve any number of accredited investors, but only a maximum of thirty-five non-accredited investors. I did not know any wealthy people (which turned out to be incorrect and will be explained in a moment), so I set my target at thirty non-accredited investors. I felt it would be fair to give each of them a one percent share of the company for an $8,000 investment. That would give me the $240,000 I needed. And a little simple math gave me the value of my company: If one percent was worth $8,000, then 100 percent must be worth $800,000.

Yes, it was entirely arbitrary and, yes, it was also very easy. So? Everything does not have to be hard! Regardless, it served to accurately establish a value for the business.

After I figured that out and was about to begin chasing non-accredited investors in the fall of 1968, one of the members of the venture capital group I recently had walked away from called me up and said he was sorry that things did not work out, but that he liked my idea. "I told them you wouldn't go for the deal," he chuckled over and over. "I told them so. I knew you'd walk out." As he spoke, it dawned on me that he was still interested in making an investment, this time on his own. He went on to say as much, that he and his father, both accredited investors, were willing to make a private investment.

His call first of all brought salve to a badly bruised ego. So all of my time spent preparing for those meetings was not wasted after all! Someone was listening, someone who perhaps saw what I saw. Just as importantly—make that *more* importantly—he brought a good portion of **The Money** to the table, investing $80,000 for a 10 percent equity stake in the company. With that much assured, all I had to do then was raise the remaining $160,000 of the $240,000 I needed from non-accredited investors.

Still smarting from my recent run-in with venture capitalists, I wanted to make sure that nothing would go wrong in raising the rest of **The Money**. So I got a little carried away and included a promise that any investor who did not like the deal after a year could get his money back. Since I believed in my idea, I did not expect to fail. Sounded reasonable to me! Had I told my wife about that move, she most likely would have thought it anything but reasonable. So I didn't tell her. Things worked out, anyway. Good thing, too. If we would have had to return nearly a quarter of a million dollars out of my $6,000-a-year annual salary, there is no telling what would have happened.

But it worked, and by December 1968, the offering was closed.

Chapter Three: The Parrot
▲ ▲ ▲ ▲ ▲

I had raised **The Money** and MetPath was born. Granted, $240,000 was a lot less than the $1.5 million I had walked out on a few months earlier but at least it helped assure me that I was not crazy for turning down all that money. I probably would have been certifiable had I agreed to the terms of the deal that the venture capitalists had offered. I wanted to build a big company and they would have taken it away from me before I even got a chance to try. But the real problem was not them or my state of mental health. I simply did not know the nature of the opposition. Come to think of it, I was not even aware that they *were* the opposition until the battle was nearly over.

What I found out in the end was that I needed a much better strategy before I went up against venture capitalists again. All too willing to give away so much for very little, I nearly sold out my dream the first time someone waved cash under my beak. As far as strategies go, it was closer to business suicide than anything else. Operating as I was, it did not much matter if I was out to win or out to lunch; the simple fact was that I did not know with whom I was dealing. But they certainly had me pegged: One green businessman, sure to get what was coming to him. I thought they were my passport to fortune and success, while they were busy punching me a one-way ticket out the door.

My vision did not extend past my considerable delusions of grandeur on the one hand, and my obviously pressing but hardly hopeless live-in, work-in situation on the other. Nor had I stopped to think that I might need more money soon, or that by holding only 51 percent of the company, I was but a hair's breadth away from losing it. I did not know then that I probably would have had no choice but to return to those same professional investors in short order for additional funds, with no margin left to give away any more of the company without losing control. The rest would be history and I would get only a footnote—and so much for my delusions of grandeur.

The great thing about private investors as capital sources, on the other hand, is that it is a lot easier for an entrepreneur to maintain control of the business. Most private investors are not interested in running your company. The entrepreneur gets to decide just how involved they will be. Besides being the least avaricious among investors and requiring little in terms of justification and explanations, private investors allow an entrepreneur to finance a new venture by taking small amounts of money from a number of sources, rather than a lot from a few.

There are several reasons why that is desirable. First of all, you stand a much better chance of getting **The Money** if you only ask for a little bit rather than a whole lot. Plus, if you take only a little bit of money from each investor, none of them are likely to get distraught if they lose it. And by selling small chunks, you will not wind up with one big investor who is effectively a partner in the business. Take a big chunk of **The Money** from one investor or an investment group and you will have someone on the phone all the time with suggestions, second-guessing your decisions. Investors with a lot to lose are apt to panic at the first hint of trouble, showering you with questions all day long: "Are we going to sell more units? How much more money do you need? Why are expenses so high?" and so on!

The key for the entrepreneur is to be selective when dealing with any investor willing to part with some of his money. Avoid the "whiners," the ones ready and willing to complain when things do not work out as you planned—which they won't. If not everyone is cut out to be an entrepreneur (as you learned in *Chapter 1*), then not everyone can handle being an investor either. Look instead for the "winners," private investors who seem to have more than a modicum of belief and enthusiasm for you or your dream and are willing to commit to the long haul, not those looking merely for a quick return on their investments. Both you and your investor will be much happier. Most importantly, once you find these angels, hang onto them! They will be ready to invest in future deals—perhaps with a little coaxing—if you make money for them in your first venture. More importantly to the new entrepreneur, they will undoubtedly prove to be key sources for additional funding during the start up to help make that first venture a success.

It should be obvious by now that just finding the right investors in the financial jungle can mean following a path full of pitfalls. And this in only the beginning! Locating and attracting the right investors is a question of looking good enough so that they will want to talk to you.

Once you find them, however, just looking pretty will not get you **The Money**.

Then it becomes a question of whether you can talk as good as you look.

*　　*　　*　　*　　*

Parrots can develop huge vocabularies and learn complex tricks in captivity. Only a few sub-species, however, excel in copying the human voice; smaller parrots, for example, have voices too tiny to carry human tones at all. The talking parrots that come readily to mind are the multi-hued, scratchy-voiced Amazons, usually caricatured as possessing vocabularies learned at the shoulder of patch-eyed, peg-legged sea captains. But the best talkers are the African Grays, very attractive ash gray birds with bright red tails. Found throughout Africa and Madagascar, these birds surpass all others in tonal quality and mimetic ability, making them perennial favorites throughout history . . . .

*　　*　　*　　*　　*

2. *How Do You Get The Money?*

I suspect you think things really look good now.

You think you know where you can get **The Money**. You have done your homework and come up with what seem to be a pretty neat business plan. You have completely committed yourself to your new venture, quitting your job in order to devote all your time to building a business around that great soap you developed. It really impressed the first investor you gave it to (your father) because it also cleaned the bathroom tile when he took a shower. The only hitch is that one investor will not be enough.

Now comes the hard part: Preparing yourself to go out and sell other potential investors on your deal. That means becoming a salesman. No matter how good you and your business look on paper, if you cannot talk, you will wind up taking a bath and getting stuck with a lot of soap. Putting together the necessary documents for a private placement is one thing, but being successful depends on whether you can sell investors to go for the deal. Just because they like what they see or read does not mean that they will make the investment. Your small private investor might be getting a lot of flack from his wife because he has lost money on other deals. The professional investor is probably looking at a half dozen deals besides yours at any one time. Your business plan will be just one more sitting in the pile on his desk, and they all look at least as good as yours or they would already have found the circular file.

Getting **The Money** requires both show *and* tell. An offering circular is merely a door-opener. Its purpose is to make your proposed venture look good to investors and get you invited to make face-to-face presentations. You have to talk well enough, once you get in the door, to turn their considerations into cash. If you want to hear investors say, "This deal sure sounds like a chance for me to make some money, so here's my check," then you have to be able to talk as good as you look.

Now comes the so-called "Dog and Pony Show," when the entrepreneur gets to take his act on the road, traveling wherever investors are. They are not going to come to you, even if they like you a whole bunch. Plan on doing some serious talking: If you need thirty-five private investors to put up $10,000 apiece, for example, then you are going to talk to a lot of non-accredited investors and maybe a few accredited investors before you will get your $350,000. However many private investors you think you need to reach your capital goal, expect to present your case to twice as many as you hope to wind up with. Consider taking a public-speaking course, hiring a consultant to find the inconsistencies and errors in your presentation style, even getting a voice coach if you think you need it. Personal style is important in all fund-raising situations and a sense of humor is invaluable, both with individual investors and in more formal presentations.

Individually, private investors usually will not take up a lot of time, particularly if you are not asking for a lot of money. But remember that they become increasingly skittish as the size of the potential investment increases. Ten thousand dollars is a lot of money to someone who does not have a lot of money. Even if you get past their spouses, small investors will want the blessing of their lawyers and accountants, so expect to spend some time there as well. Eventually, it may come down to a potential investor simply asking, "O.K., now, level with me. Am I going to lose this money?" If your answer is a candid, "Not if I can help it, because I'm going to be working my tail off to make us all rich," they are a good bet to make the investment on such small reassurance. More sophisticated private investors, on the other hand, will be asking more questions about the business, your projections and the marketplace, so you better have the answers on the tip of your tongue.

All of your investors will eventually want to see your offering memorandum, a document that is basically a compilation of facts and figures about you and your company. It includes things like historical information, management biographies, current financial information and a few other things, like risk factors the business faces (potential and ongoing lawsuits, competition, government activity relative to the marketplace, etc.). Its purpose is actually to protect the entrepreneur and the company from any possible claims of misrepresentation. But there is nothing in it that will make the slightest bit of difference to a private investor who already has been "sold."

If you have talked well enough and he has decided in favor of an investment in your company, one of two things will happen when he gets the offering memorandum:

1. What you told him will be corroborated by the document and he will look for the piece of paper that he has to sign to commit to the investment; or

2. He will not even read the document but just look for the piece of paper to sign to commit to the investment.

Remember, this is a private investor, accredited or non-accredited. He probably knew and liked you before you asked him to invest or knows and trusts someone who has already invested. He likes the idea, too. He has realized that you are committed to the project. After that, it is all a matter of style, a question of how well you have made your case in personal, face-to-face presentations. If you have already talked as well as he already knew you looked, then, before he gets the offering material, you should have been able to infect him with your excitement, enthusiasm and desire.

The infection may take on a life of its own after that, without any further prompting from you, if it gets into the right group. When I went out in the original private placement to raise the $3 million necessary to fund HEARx in 1986, things were proceeding with difficulty until I made a presentation to an acquaintance of mine who belonged to a country club. He got interested and before long he was talking to his friends about the deal, and they talked to their friends, and in ten days I raised $1.8 million from nine or ten people by word of mouth.

But all that is just a walk in the park compared to all the talking you will have to do once you start negotiating with professional investors. First of all, the minimum ratio of presentations to successful deals becomes 10-to-1 rather than 2-to-1. It may seem to take forever and sometimes does. Venture capitalists will want market statistics, financial projections, cash flow analyses and more. It is always more, more, more and the entrepreneur must talk, talk, talk each time they demand something else. A new vocabulary will be required; unusual terms will start popping up, like "performing due diligence," "protecting our investors," "board representation" and "right of first refusal." The general meaning is that the entrepreneur must begin to jump through hoops that venture capitalists will expect him to jump through regularly once the investment is made.

Most investors in start-up companies expect a return on their investment that is greater than the money they make on savings account interest, bonds, or even the stock market. Professional investors expect a bit more: **they want to make at least five times their money in five years**. If a set of financial projections will not allow that kind of profit, most will reject the deal no matter what other factors are involved. Knowing that, the entrepreneur just has to match his projections with the return demanded by the investors.

Too simple? Well, let's see if we can't complicate it a little. Let's say you want $2 million and are willing to give up 40 percent of the company for that amount. That means the company would have a post-deal or initial value of $5 million, and a 40 percent share would be worth $2 million. Now, the brighter among you are probably saying, "Ah-Ha! I get it. Just increase the projected $5 million value in the fifth year to $25 million. Then, since 40 percent of $25 million is $10 million, and $10 million is five times the $2 million investment, *voila! J'ai le fait accompli, non?*

Well . . . *Non! Il n'est pas fini.*

You still have to prove your company will be worth $25 million in its fifth year. The answer is to understand how investors will verify your projections. Keep in mind that a sophisticated investor will not believe your projections until he applies a couple of formulas to them. Right off the bat, he will probably cut them by at least half since he knows that everything in business costs twice as much and takes twice as long to accomplish. Then he will use what is called a **P/E (Price/Earnings) multiple**. This imaginary number, usually between ten and twenty, is used to determine the projected value of a company. That value is then figured against the amount of the original investment, and must yield the investor at least five times that amount over five years.

This is how it works: When an entrepreneur projects after-tax earnings of $2 million in the fifth year, the investor cuts that in half to $1 million. He then multiplies the $1 million by a P/E of 10, fixing the company's fifth-year projected value at $10 million. If the deal gives him 40 percent of the company, his return after five years would be only $4 million, merely two times the original investment. Even if the investor does not cut the projected earnings in half and uses the same P/E multiple of 10, the result would be only $8 million in the fifth year, four times the initial investment. Either way, the deal is in trouble.

Now, let's raise projected earnings in the fifth year to $5 million. The venture capitalist will halve that to $2.5 million and multiply it by a P/E of 10. That means the company's projected value in the fifth year would be $25 million. This makes the venture capitalist's 40 percent share worth $10 million, or five times his original $2 million investment. Now the deal has a good chance of getting **The Money**—if it passes one final test. Before an investor will hand over $2 million, he will want assurance that the numbers being presented are not just a figment of someone's imagination.

First of all, the investor will want to see that the business plan provides for a marketing plan and sufficient personnel to realistically meet the financial projections. But the key is in market share. **The bigger the market, the more believable the projections.** If the market an entrepreneur is going after is big enough, then all the things that matter to a potential investor—the amount of the investment, the financial projections, the value estimates of the business, the possible return on investment—appear relatively believable.

Let's look at an example. If I start up a business attacking a $100 billion market, with projections that show a 0.1 percent increase each year, at the end of five years it will have one-half of one percent share-of-market. That is a $50 million business. And if I am only asking for a $2 million investment in exchange for 40 percent of the company, the probable earnings after taxes in five years will be more than sufficient to provide a return to an investor that is five times his original investment. The market size makes those assumptions very reasonable. But don't go overboard. Start up a business in a $100 million market with projections that say you will have all the business at the end of five years, and everybody you show it to will laugh. Enter a $1 billion market and project that you will have a company worth $800 million in five years, and the laughter will be just as loud.

The really funny thing is that, since the advent of the personal computer, everybody's numbers come from the ceiling. It is laughable how much easier it is to do projections now. Years ago, when someone said to you, "Go back and redo the numbers," it was a major undertaking. You had just spent two months working on those numbers by hand. Going back over them and recalculating them could take just as long, prolonging the fundraising period. Now, it takes a few seconds! You load your Lotus into the PC, decrease G&A by two percent, and your profits are automatically recalculated to show an increase of two percent. You can print out a completely new document in about fifteen minutes and be ready to go back to the investor with completely revised projections.

Potential investors know that what they see is not necessarily what they will get and that projections are merely a gauge of what a business might be able to do. They know that everyone can churn figures out, twisted and turned almost instantaneously just by tweaking a couple of parameters. Investors also know that projections will not give investors any firm handle on the entrepreneur's ability to perform whatever that tweak indicates. Even the entrepreneur who created the projections does not really have a true picture of just how it is that he will accomplish such fantasies. Still, many sophisticated investors persist in asking for projections covering as much as five years.

As far as entrepreneurs are concerned, such long-term projections are worthless, other than for targets. Quarterly, monthly and tomorrow's projections are the only ones really meaningful to the new business person, but those are useless to venture capitalists.

Professional investors want long-term financial projections on which to base their investment decisions. Small matter that the projections are tailored to suit each different situation and may have been created only a few moments before they were delivered. The belief is still that numbers do not lie, so investors place great stock in them. The fact is that, yes, numbers do not lie, but what they tell you depends on what you believe is the truth.

When I was raising capital for Permark, a call came in from a venture capitalist who had reviewed our projections.

"Paul," he said, "I think you can make more money in the fifth year. As it is now, you only show that you'll be earning 18 percent pre-tax. Are you sure you cannot earn more money as the company develops?"

"Perhaps," I replied. "Let me go work on the numbers and see what I can do. I'll get back to you." I hung up with him and talked to our controller.

"They said we're too pessimistic," I told him. "Increase profits from 18 percent to 22 percent for the fifth year." I could have called the investor back an hour later, but I waited until the next day to break the good news to him:

"You know what? You were right! We can get up to 22 percent in the fifth year."

"Oh my God, that's wonderful!" He was excited. "There's no problem *now* in valuing your business at $5 million."

All I did was have a few numbers changed on a spreadsheet. The investor knew me, knew my track record, and had already sold himself on the investment. He also had been around long enough to know that reality is seldom a match for the many projections he had seen over the years. But he still wanted that last little bit of assurance. Once I knew what he wanted, I could give it to him. As long as the projections are grounded in the reality perceived by the investor, one number is as good as another, no matter what happens later on. It is that simple, and can be even simpler.

While I was starting up another venture a couple of years later, I went up to Chicago with an offering memorandum under my arm to see a venture capitalist. He lost no time in explaining to me that he had a system for evaluating potential investments.

I said, "Oh?"

"Yes," he went on. "If I like the concept, I assume everything will do half of what you project and never be worth more than ten times after-tax earnings in the fifth year. After I do those two calculations, I want to get at least five times on my money in five years."

"Oh," I said.

He quickly did a few computations.

"Oh! This works out," he concluded. "I should get seven times my money in five years. You've got it. We'll invest $100,000."

That was the end of the conversation. The projections looked so good that I was there hardly more than seven minutes and I said, oh, maybe two dozen words in all. Sometimes you hardly have to say anything at all; just stand there and look pretty.

No matter who you are making presentations to, the point is to be creative, to play to your audience, to make the best out of every situation where there is a chance you might be able to raise **The Money**. There is an old sales motto that says, "Sell the sizzle and not the steak!" That is just about perfect advice for an entrepreneur trying to raise start-up capital. He does not have much else except concept to sell anyway, and that is his biggest advantage.

That's right, I said, *advantage*.

The potential of the company and its concept are what makes it valuable in the beginning, and that is what you should be selling to investors. But if you have begun to earn money, your business will be valued accordingly. Your concept and its exciting potential by then has become hostage to the profit and loss statement. Once the steak is cooked, it is much harder to sell the sizzle. As soon as you start to make money, the numbers determine the value of your company and how much capital you can raise. The numbers had not yet taken over when I rushed into the second and third private placements for MetPath in 1969. Twice we had run out of money—and that is not the best time to raise capital—and twice I was able to get **The Money** to keep the company going without having to give it away. That experience proved to me that, when it comes to fundraising, what you say is often the difference between survival and extinction.

It doesn't have to get to that point, though.

Not if you can figure out how much money you will need in the first place.

*   *   *   *   *

So amusing did ancient Romans find African Grays that they brought them to the Eternal City in great numbers. But not all of those parrots wound up spouting Latin phrases from some patrician's perch. So many were imported that the excess—probably those who could not cut it in the speech department—were skewered, cooked, and served at some of the best Roman tables as Epicurean delights.

*   *   *   *   *

3. *How Much Of The Money Do You Need?*

Things don't look so good at the moment, do they?

You seem to have done everything right, but your start-up is sputtering. You went out and got **The Money**, and still managed to hold onto the lion's share of equity in your company. There are no profits yet, but sales have been growing steadily. Yet your accountant has just told you that, unless you get some more money, you will be heading for bankruptcy court.

What happened?

Easy!

You knew what to say in order to get **The Money**, but you did not know how much to ask for. I know, because that is exactly what happened to me with MetPath.

Almost immediately after completing that first private offering for $240,000, I was back asking for more from many of the same private investors. It happened a lot quicker than I expected; in fact, we had just moved the business out of the apartment in New York. We were able to buy equipment, hire some people, and build a real lab in Teaneck, New Jersey, but thirty days after we opened, it took another $250,000 investment or we would have gone right out of business.

Seems I had underestimated my expenses, but on the positive side we had built up sales to $15,000 a month. That sales increase allowed me to raise the value of the company so that when we returned to the investors for more money, we only had to give up 10 percent of the company at a higher price per share. We completed a $2.50-a-share offering in April, 1969, and felt we finally had enough capital to get us through the start up.

Wrong again! Once more I had managed to underestimate expenses and overestimate sales growth, which meant there were no profits on the horizon. As a result, we needed yet another capital infusion of approximately $250,000 in November 1969 so we could stay in business. Back I went to private investors, including many of the original ones, but sales had still increased enough that we only had to give up 5 percent of the company, now at $5 a share. All of this happened just seven months after the lab opened in Teaneck, and it was a wonder that we survived, considering that I was commuting from the Navy and spending as much time fund raising as I was running the business. But we came through it with the business intact, and a couple of very valuable lessons.

During those second and third fundraising efforts, I realized that there are going to be money problems in every company's start-up period, no matter how well you plan against it. The cardinal mistake is to say, "Oh, **The Money** I raised is enough, because my projections show that it's going to work out." There is never enough! Those few months taught me a simple truth: **Entrepreneurs should get at least twice as much money to start out with as they think they are going to need.** Otherwise, **The Money** invariably will run out before you know it. Getting more money from private investors is hard enough, but it is much easier to do before you run out than after.

How much money you need to raise is directly linked, by the way, to how much of the company the entrepreneur wants to give up in order to get it. If you do not mind building a company for someone else to take over, then it does not matter. But if you want to hold onto your company, you cannot give up financial control.

Today my rule of thumb is that an entrepreneur should never give any investor more than 40 percent share in a start-up situation. Back then, I just presumed I would have to give up whatever the investors wanted because I did not have any money and they did. After it was over, it dawned on me that no one was going to give a business tyro $1.5 million unless they controlled what then was the merest chance of building a nationwide $100 million chain of clinical testing labs out of one tiny operation barely making ends meet. I had absolutely no business in negotiating with professional investors under those circumstances. I would have wound up with absolutely no business at all had the negotiations turned out differently, simply because even $1.5 million would never have been enough to support the ambitious business plan I had developed.

The company was worth about $5 million on paper by 1970, and by then I had given up 45 percent of the company for a total investment of approximately $750,000. True, I would have gotten twice that much and given up only 49 percent of the company to those venture capitalists back in 1968, and the company might have been worth even more. But it is likewise true that I would not have had control of the company in 1970, and also probable that I would not even have been there. Back then, I did not know how to talk to venture capitalists, so I kept my mouth shut. If it had not been for my lawyer, that would have ended me.

I kept my mouth shut on one other occasion that I can remember, but this time it saved me. Sometimes not talking can close a deal, too. At least I was around to see MetPath heading for deep trouble in the summer of 1971. This time, it was not a question of not making the payroll; it was a matter of going out of business. *C'est fini! Kaput!* The company was out of money, period. Yes, one more time! A group of venture capitalists, recommended by a few doctors who were impressed with MetPath, expressed an interest. After they reviewed our projections, we structured a deal that would give them 10 percent of the company for $1 million at $6.25 a share. I knew that I was at a disadvantage now, and I knew that they knew that I knew. When my lawyer and I met with them in June, 1971 to iron out the terms of the agreement, we all knew I was in for a bad time.

Now, perhaps the most time-honored caveat of deal-making is to **always negotiate from a position of strength**. Yet there I was, weak from my desperate need for capital. The demands began almost as soon as we sat down, and I quickly found out just how bad it was going to be. At every turn, there always seemed to be a phrase added to each point under discussion, something like, "... and if this or that happens, we get paid thus and so."

"What do you mean, thus and so for this or that? That's ridiculous," my attorney stormed at their first demand.

One of the investment firm's principals turned to me and said, "Paul, tell your [expletive deleted] attorney to shut his [expletive deleted] mouth, or we leave!"

I turned to my attorney and said, "I don't see any reason why we can't pay thus and so for this or that. Let's go on. What else?"

"Well, in case such and such occurs, we want even more thus and so."

Again, my lawyer howled, and again, a warning was delivered. The entire negotiation went like that; every point was contested. Finally, I took the lawyer aside. "Look, take it easy! There's no problem. I don't care about any of those issues they've raised."

"But they're going to take over the board, and gain control over the whole company!"

"They're not going to take over the board," I assured him, "and they're sure not going to take over the company. It's going to work!" So I acceded to their demands, got the money and went back to work.

The conditions (known as **affirmative** and **negative covenants**) that were being placed on the deal really were minor points, as far as I was concerned, compared to getting that check so that MetPath would survive. The investors' demands were predicated on the fear (or hope) that my projections were wrong and the deal was not going to work out. They were simply trying to protect (or position) themselves. But that was their game plan, not mine. As it worked out, my attorney was half right. They did attempt a takeover, but it failed with help from a friendly bank.

I was sure the deal would work out because I was certain that

MetPath would be successful. My delusions of grandeur told me that it did not matter if there were penalties for being wrong because I did not expect any of them would ever be enforced. I was not losing anything. I still had control of the company — something I managed to do for all of the fifteen years I headed MetPath, by the way, even though at the end I owned less than 12 percent — and the concessions I was making were getting my company what it needed. I saw the deal from the standpoint that it rewarded me if my projections were right. So I did, after all, negotiate from a position of strength: I had enough self-confidence (the investors might have thought it was arrogance) to know when to keep my mouth shut.

Today, entrepreneurs starting up a business are finding it even more difficult to raise start-up capital, since many venture capitalist firms avoid start-ups and seek to reduce their risk by waiting until the second or third round of financing before making an investment. Ever since the stock market collapsed in 1987, most investors have also become increasingly worried about how they are going to get their money out of a deal. There are not many ways to begin with. The company can go public or be sold to another company, giving the investors an opportunity to sell their stock, get their investment back, and make a profit. But no investor can get very excited these days about taking a 10 percent share of a company that may never be able to be converted back into real money.

First-time entrepreneurs anxious about raising **The Money** likewise must choose their capital sources cautiously. Remember, some investors are practiced predators who know how to make themselves sound better than they are, hoping to trap the unwary.

The more attractive you look to them, the more they will want to have you for dinner—and not as a guest.

The only way to avoid being the main course is to know what you need and how to ask for it.

Just be careful who you talk to!

$ECRET$ OF THE PARROT

*"Potential" is more exciting than "reality"
to prospective investors.*

---

*Too little—or too much—money
can ruin a start-up business.*

---

*"Your business" means
not giving up control to investors.*

Leader of the Pack

Chapter Four
The Wild Horse: Leader of the Pack

▲ ▲ ▲ ▲ ▲

The wild horse [family Equidae] first appeared more than 50 million years ago as the small hyracotherium or eohippus of the early Eocene epoch. Sporting four toes on its front feet, this "dawn horse" may have had a five-toed ancestor. But the modern three-toed equid family includes only horses, asses, onagers and zebras, all of which man has tremendously reduced in their wild state. So-called wild horses, such as those that range the open spaces of the western U.S., are really feral, i.e., once-domestic animals released or escaped from captivity. There were, at one time, large herds of native North American wild horses, but today's breeds descend from European breeds introduced in Colonial times, particularly by the Spanish. Mysteriously, some ten thousand years ago, wild horses became abruptly extinct in the New World for as-yet-unknown reasons.

*   *   *   *   *

Many years after my fumbling foray into the lemonade business, my mother came to visit her now-grown and hopefully wiser son and family. Richard was eleven and Mark was eight at the time, and she was very concerned, as most grandmothers are, in the progress of her grandchildren. The eldest was doing very well in junior high school, particularly in math, and had become very interested in the stock market and other things financial. And that was all that Grandma needed to hear.

"So, what do you want to do when you grow up," she asked Richard the achiever, about two sentences after she hugged him hello.

"I guess I'll go work for MetPath, Nana," he said. As his grandmother's smile broadened, Richard beamed and quickly added,

"I'll work in their finance department."

"That's wonderful, Richard," she beamed back, as only grand-mothers can. "Keep up the good work!"

Encouraged by that report, my mother later sought out Mark, the soon-to-be entrepreneur (it was a year yet before he would start shoveling snow at parking meters) and asked him what he thought he might do when he grew up.

"I don't know, Nana," Mark said, uncomfortably scuffing the ground with his eight-year-old feet. That answer did not satisfy her, being a grandmother.

"Well, you'll probably do what Richard is going to do," she said, smiling her grandmother's smile.

Mark perked up, now very interested and undoubtedly not wanting to be outdone by his older brother, and asked, "Why? What's Richard say he's going to do when he grows up?"

"Why, he's going to go to work for MetPath," she said, glad that this news seemed to interest him. "Didn't you know?"

"No."

"Well, that's what he said!" she said, with mock gravity. She realized that she might have come on too heavily; after all, Mark was only a little boy. How could he know what he wanted to do at that age? So she tried a different tack, determined to encourage her younger grandson too.

"Wouldn't you like to work at MetPath with your father?"

Mark stopped and thought about that for a second or two.

"Well, maybe. And I know what I'm gonna do first," Mark vowed unhesitatingly with all the sober certainty an eight-year-old could muster.

"Why, Mark, that's wonderful," my mother gushed, taken aback by his sudden surety. Then she added with great grand-motherly interest, "What are you going to do?"

"I'm going to fire Richard!"

Obviously, Mark had come to two conclusions: one, that he was going to be in a position to fire Richard and, two, that Richard was not an employee he would want to hire in the first place! No doubt that sibling rivalry was clouding his entrepreneurial vision a bit at the time. The point of the story, however, is to illustrate that you, the entrepreneur, must have a very clear idea of the type of employees you want to be part of your new company and how you intend to deal with them.

An entrepreneur must lead his company the way a stallion leads a pack of wild horses. The pack members choose to follow an unflinching and sure-footed leader without question, as long as they believe he knows where he is going and what he is doing. They trust that he will not lead them to dry gulches and bitter grass when they seek food and water. When danger threatens, the herd relies on his protection and guidance, certain he will not head into a blind arroyo when they must escape. Those horses have made a decision that the leader is fit to lead, that he knows what he's neighing about.

Mother Nature, of course, uses instinct to prepare the wild horse to be the leader of the pack. Similarly, it is plain old horse sense that prepares the entrepreneur to lead a company's employees through the Badlands of the Business Jungle. Common sense provides the entrepreneurial animal the basic understanding to **form a philosophy for employee relations**. That other basic entrepreneurial quality—interpersonal skills—allows the leader of the pack to effectively communicate that philosophy to the employees. In other words you, the entrepreneur, must know what to say, as well as how and when to say it, when it comes to successfully understanding and fulfilling your company's personnel needs—which to a greater or lesser extent depends on meeting the needs of your company's personnel.

It is not what *they* think they need, most often, but what *you* think they need. You must be the arbiter of your employee relations policies. Your employees should not be the ones to dictate how you will be dealing with them but they *will* be, by default, if policies are not established from the outset. You are the leader. You must set the tone and direction of your relationships with your employees, not the other way around. Remember what we said back in *Chapter 1*, that caring *about* people is different than caring *for* them? Here is where it becomes most important to remember that distinction, because there is no other place in the business jungle where the idea of "family" is more apt. Your employees can become one big happy family and that can be wonderful for them and for your business. But unless you, the entrepreneur, sincerely and properly identify as the head of the family, it could be more like a large family feud.

Fairness, understanding, kindness, support, and all the other human urgings that families bring out in people are also right and proper in a business setting, as long as they are rightly and properly set on a business footing. The business family is far different than the ones built by blood and marriage. If you want a *family*, go get married and have kids! If you want a business family too, go find some investors and hire some employees. But before you do either, you better have a good idea of exactly where you want your relationships to be heading.

Employer-employee relationships require the employer to form a philosophy for **interviewing, terminating and, most importantly, motivating employees**. I developed my own version of an employee relations philosophy when I started up MetPath, and it has proven out so well that I used it when I started up HEARx and in every venture in-between those two companies. I am famous for my interviews among employees, probably because I have told every single person I have ever interviewed the following:

"If you want to be successful here, let me tell you five things that you need to know as an employee." And then I tell them exactly what I expect of them.

The five little gems I drop on employees are a distillation of my philosophy, which is plain in language and simple in meaning.

But I think I will hold off a little before telling you what those five statements are.

After all, this is not a job interview.

Let's just see if you can figure out where I am heading.

*   *   *   *   *

When grasses became common on the plains of North America during the Miocene era about twenty million years ago, this had a terrific impact on the wild horse. Browsing species which remained in the forests gradually became extinct, while grazing animals survived with the more abundant food supply of the prairies. This phenomenon was due primarily to an adaptation of the teeth of the Equinae. Grass is a harsh substance, always contaminated with dust and sand. The low-crowned teeth typical of browsers could not survive the damage from the abrasion of grass and grit. Grazing animals like the modern horse, however, have long, prism-shaped teeth with folded enamel ridges surrounded by cement. As the teeth wear down, the folds constantly expose sharp new cutting surfaces, and the teeth are tall enough to provide the wild horse a lifetime of chewing. This is a very good thing, since horses eat about 90 percent of the time. As a comparison, cattle only eat about 50 percent of the time.

*   *   *   *   *

1. Interviewing Employees

Forget what I just said about telling you later.

I changed my mind.

I want to let you in on those five things I tell employees *now*, instead of waiting until the end of the chapter. So, the first thing

I say to an erstwhile employee in an interview is that I expect he or she ...

Sorry. I changed my mind again. I really *don't* want to get into this right now. In fact, I'm not sure I want to tell you what those five things are, anyway, because ...

Did you say something?

What do you mean, *"Jes' hol' on one dad gum minute there?"*

Now, I know the person who just said that has no idea what *dad gum* really means. I suspect they learned the phrase between jobs while sitting around watching *Bonanza* reruns on television. I am sure that you would like to know what *dad gum* means. I know I would! Maybe...

"Hey!"

Are you speaking to me?

"I don't care about the meaning of dad gum or gol' durn or even dad burn, for that matter. I care about what those five things are!"

Well, if that's the way you feel about it...

Had enough? Of course you have! But let me explain the reason for this little digression. It is meant to illustrate how very disconcerting and upsetting it is when you do not know what to expect, when someone decides to change direction on you without any warning.

The illustration, limited as it is by the printed page, hopefully serves two purposes. First, I want to remind you that, if you ever intend to get off that couch and become an entrepreneur, you had better learn how to handle sudden movements. They will be happening all the time when you start up your company. Second, I want to direct your attention to the idea that employees do not appreciate it when you tell them one thing about the conditions of their employment and then go and do another. And they are even worse off when you tell them nothing at all. Part of your job as employer is to project an image of certainty and create islands of calm in the sea of constant change that is business, while at the same time harnessing employees' energy and talent to meet those fast-changing conditions.

Projecting an image, by the way, is not a euphemism for "lying to them and making up stories." Here it means giving potential employees an accurate representation of what your company is all about, relative to their potential employment. Many employees thrive on problem solving, a lot enjoy a fast-paced work environment, and most will welcome changes in routine, at least from time to time. All will get plenty of that in a start-up business, but they will become very discomfited unless you tell them the rules under which they will be operating. Sure, an employee will know to do the obvious things: come to work on time, put in a good day's work, do not steal from the company, and never park in the chairman's assigned parking spot near the front door. But if that is all you expect out of your employees, do not expect very much out of your company because, by definition, employees are the major part of the company. A company, says the dictionary, is "an association of persons for carrying on an industrial or commercial enterprise." And you, the entrepreneur, are the leader of the pack.

Entrepreneurs must demonstrate their leadership to employees by letting them know up front what is expected from them, stated in no uncertain terms. Otherwise, you wind up with a bunch of confused and disgruntled employees who spend more time bellyaching than working, while you spend more time fielding complaints and answering demands than running your business. Of course, that was not your intention when you hired them. You would like your employees to be happy and productive in their jobs and careers so that everyone will prosper. But if you do not tell employees just what their role is in helping create that kind of successful business environment, or keep changing the rules, they will sooner or later do more or less what they please until corrected or shunted off in a different direction. And you, in time, will become nothing more to them than someone to be second-guessed, avoided or outsmarted as much as possible.

If your employees come to think of you as the scatterbrained boss who cannot make up his mind and keeps changing directions, the cruel overseer with the whip, or the bumbling idiot who does not know anything, it will be very difficult to change those perceptions. Such negative images get started much more easily than you can imagine. It just takes one employee to get the ball rolling in the wrong direction through rumor and innuendo; unless something halts the momentum, it can spoil the workplace and even bring down a company. The best way I know to stop it is not to let it get started.

Entrepreneurs must clearly view the tangible and intangible conditions of employment expected on both sides of the paycheck. These conditions must be communicated, for to be silent invites chaos and high rates of turnover.

What are the chances that you would consider or keep an employee who does not know how to do what he was hired for? By the same token, what types of employees will be attracted to or stay with a company where the boss does not bother to (or just plain cannot) communicate what is expected of them? The answer to both questions is, "Not good!" Most complaints about employees would not exist if employers would just ask themselves that last question, develop an employee relations policy, and then tell the employees what direction they will be heading before they are hired. The very act of communicating directions has a salutary effect. The interviewees get the idea that the interviewer is some-one who knows exactly what they want and where they are head-ing. The most immediate result is that the company will wind up with better employees. The ones who are hired will want to hold onto their jobs as much as you want to hold onto them. Plus, there will be fewer mistakes in hiring, and the problems that poor employees present to a business can be dealt quickly and effec-tively because everyone will know the rules.

The interviewing process is so crucial to the start-up business, in my estimation, that **the entrepreneur should interview every potential employee for as long as he possibly can**. I interviewed almost every job applicant who came to MetPath for the first seven years of the company's existence. Had I the time, I would have interviewed every single person because that policy allows insights from two directions, plus an advantage. The employer gets a look at those potential employees and what motivates them. The employees get a face-to-face look at their potential employer and the sense that they can become an important part of the compa-ny. The entrepreneur gets the advantage: A chance to describe all the things which employees might consider "bad" goings-on—the long hours, how hard everybody was working, how many were giv-ing up family time and vacations. The conditions I presented in those interviews often (exactly half the time, in fact!) would con-vince prospective job-seekers not to come on board, which was just fine with me.

My wife, Cynthia, once commented that I had no right to make people work as hard as I made them work. My reply was that I was not making them work at MetPath. They could work anywhere. They chose to work at MetPath. And if they were going to work at MetPath, then they were going to have to work hard. So a lot of the people I interviewed never got past that first condition. It would have been easy for me, as a marketing-oriented person, to soft-pedal it and talk them into coming. But the only people I wanted to come work for me were people who wanted to come work for me, so I let them know what I expected from them, right from the start. I let them decide whether or not they could hack it with me. Then I decided about them.

Of course, there were exceptions. I made up my mind to hire MetPath's first director of marketing before I delivered my little speech because he impressed me as exactly the type of employee I wanted. He was an advertising space salesman who came into my office trying to sell me a page in the magazine he worked for at the time. He made his pitch, which was not bad, but we had no money to spend so I started to get rid of him.

"Look, Dick. This is the first issue of this magazine and I am not about to spend all this money on an ad in an untested, brand new product. Why don't you come back after you've published a few more issues?" He hardly took a breath, but jumped up, leaned over my desk and launched back at me.

"Dr. Brown, that's exactly why you MUST take a page in this magazine!"

I looked at him like he was crazy! I was intrigued by his reasoning, though.

"What do you mean?"

"I mean there may never BE a second issue of this magazine! But EVERYBODY'S going to read this FIRST issue, even if they never read the magazine again. It's a PERFECT opportunity to advertise because EVERYONE in the country that you want to reach will see it."

He stopped for a breath, and in that moment I decided that whether or not I bought an ad, I wanted this bright, quick, and aggressive young man to come and work for me.

I changed the subject and asked, smiling, "Would you like a tour of the lab?"

"Sure. But what about the ad?"

He definitely did not lose sight of his objective very easily, which only added to my resolve to hire him. Finally, after our walk through the lab, I sat down again with him, making certain I delivered my litany of five employee musts. Before he left that day, I offered him the job as our director of marketing. It was his turn to look at me as if I were a little screwy when I asked if he wanted the job.

"What do you mean?"

"What kind of a salary do you want?"

And he said, "I don't know. How much do you want to pay?"

Now, I would try not to tell people how much I would pay, but get them to tell me what they wanted. That way, I would neither pay too much nor insult them by falling below what they thought they were worth. I had a salary range in mind and, as long as he stayed within it, I would make the offer.

"Well, I...," he began. "Er... ah... I'd want... well, les'see... I think I'd want... gee... *at least $25,000 a year!*" he finally blurted out.

"O.K. What else?"

And he said, "What else? Oh! Well, let's see... I'd like a car, because I'll be driving around a lot."

"Fine. What else?"

"Ah, more? Er... Well, I'd like some stock in the company... and benefits... and...." He went on a little longer, hemming and hawing all the way, until finally he finished.

"That's all fine," I said, enjoying the look of total bewilderment on his face which turned to panic with my next words. "Congratulations," I told him earnestly. "You are now the new director of marketing for MetPath!"

"What do you mean?"

"Just what I said."

"You mean I can have all those things?"

"Yes, that's what I mean," I replied, matter-of-factly.

"Well, I have to go think about it."

"What do you mean?" Now I acted bewildered. "What is there to think about? You just told me everything you wanted and I just agreed to give you everything you wanted. Why aren't you starting tomorrow? When am I going to know?"

"Tomorrow," he managed. "I'll let you know tomorrow."

Obviously, nothing like this had ever happened to him before and he was absolutely stupefied. He called the next day to say he would take the job. More than that, he stayed many years with the company.

Usually the choice of an upper-level manager is not so obvious, and a number of applicants are scheduled to be seen. Time must be taken to meet them and subsequent comparison and consideration of their relative merits means that at least a few days and, more likely, a few weeks will normally intervene between an interview and a job offer. It will take even longer if you start interviewing the spouses of executives, as I did following one particularly unsettling experience.

I interviewed a prominent Ph.D., a chemist from the state of Washington just before we were going to officially open the MetPath lab in New Jersey. He was flown in at our expense and he was finally offered the position of director of chemistry. It was a key spot and he accepted, agreeing to start on a Monday. When he did not show up at the morning meeting we had scheduled, we figured he had plane problems. But we did not hear from him that day or the next. Finally, on Wednesday, I called out to Seattle where he was working. I fully expected to hear that he was no longer working there, but the switchboard put me through to him. When he came on the phone, I was more than a little upset.

"I thought you were coming in Monday as our director of chemistry," I said, "and we haven't heard from you. Is anything wrong? Where were you?"

"Oh, it's you, Paul," he began uncomfortably. (Who else could it be, unless he was doing this to more than one person at a time!) "I've been meaning to call you." (My, how thoughtful!) My wife refused to get on the plane."

So he didn't get on either!

I was flabbergasted. After that, I began interviewing people with their spouses. Cynthia and I would take them out to a late dinner and in the course of the evening's discussion we would be able to tell if there was a chance that the prospect was not coming. We could also tell, if it looked like they would come on board, whether or not they would be happy. At least four times during the company's early development we discovered through these dinners that the spouse had already made the decision not to come and so we passed on making the final offer. These double interviews effectively reduced to zero the possibility that a spouse would ever short-circuit me again. I would make the speeches, telling them what I would expect of them, while Cynthia would say things like, "Gosh, it's just incredible how many hours the people work at MetPath." And the next day it would be "Thank you, but sorry" from one side or the other if we had scared them off or they did not feel right to us.

I have always considered that a major learning experience for me. However, I do not suppose that you would personally consider this chapter any kind of a learning experience at all unless I divulge just what my five directions to the new employee are without further delay. So, here they are, presented more or less the way I deliver them:

FIVE THINGS PAUL BROWN
TELLS ALL POTENTIAL EMPLOYEES
WHETHER THEY WANT TO HEAR THEM OR NOT

"If you are going to work for me, there are five things you need to understand:

"**One:** I expect you to **put the company first.** If you are not prepared to eat, sleep and drink the company, then maybe this is not the place for you to work.

"**Two:** I do not want to lie to you. You are entering a sink-or-swim situation. There is no time to train you to do what must be done. **If you have any doubts about your experience or ability to do the job, then maybe you better not start.**

"**Three:** I only want to hire people with **the initiative to make decisions** on their own. A bad decision can be corrected, but nothing can be done when no decision is made.

"**Four: I will fire you quickly if you screw up royally,**

because I have found that someone who makes one major mistake will probably make another.

"**Five:** I divide everyone up into two categories: the talkers and the producers. The **producers will be rewarded,** and they won't ever have to ask for it. So just go out there and help us succeed and I'll take care of you. I never mind making anyone rich who makes me richer."

These guidelines were never written down, just delivered more or less the same way to everyone I ever interviewed for employment at any company I have ever led, from maintenance people to senior managers, receptionists to researchers, secretaries to scientists. When we finally got a personnel director in our eighth year at MetPath, the company had simply grown too large for me to handle the interviewing anymore. At one stretch we were hiring over one thousand people a year for positions all over the country, so I had to finally delegate authority in that area to a personnel director, even though I still interviewed all the top managers—including the new personnel director.

Lou came out of a gigantic corporation to work at what, by any comparison, was a very little MetPath. The fact that there were no written personnel policies made him a little uneasy ... well, to be honest about it, he showed up and went into total culture shock. He arrived for work his first day with several boxes of personal effects but they sat unopened in his office. One day, two days, a week went by before I spoke with him. He admitted that he was uncomfortable and thinking about going back where he came from. We waited and things finally started coming out of the boxes, so I asked him if that meant he was going to stay. "I have a wall clock in my car," he said. "When I bring that in, I guess it means I'm going to stay." So we waited some more, until one day this big clock with a barometer showed up on the wall, and he was all smiles.

Along with the clock, however, came his advice that when I interviewed I was never again to use the "guillotine" guideline, as the fourth one was called. He felt that since MetPath was really not a little company anymore the chief executive officer should not say things like that. It might intimidate people, particularly the corporate types who would now begin applying for jobs at a company that was heading for the big time. Lou strongly urged me to refrain from using it. I am by no means convinced that he was right, but I also follow the rule that **entrepreneurs must trust the people they hire and try never to second guess them.** Otherwise, why spend all that time and money looking for good people in the first place?

It will soon become apparent that there is always room for minor screw-ups, anyway, which is what happened when we entered that peak period of hiring I mentioned earlier. We were very busy, so a system was devised in the personnel department in order to keep up with the volume of job applicants.

Everything was working fine until, one afternoon, a maintenance worker showed up in the executive offices. He was holding his employee badge, our information booklets and all the things that new hires received under the new system. The people in the personnel department assumed he had just finished being processed and was reporting for work. The man was all excited and wanted to thank the vice president of personnel for having hired him. Never before, he said, had he been hired for a job where they did not make a big fuss, and how nice it was to come to a company that just hired people without a lot of rigmarole.

We thought that we had plenty of rigmarole, so we investigated and found that we had hired a new employee who had never even been interviewed. Seems that his application for employment wound up in the "approved" pile by accident, and everyone was so busy that nobody noticed.

At least when I interviewed people myself that would never have happened! So I occasionally dusted off and brought out the guillotine, despite Lou's opinion. Like the time an "experienced" technician somehow started the lab's largest testing machine running backwards and blew out all the power in the building. The execution took place quickly; by the end of his shift he became an ex-employee because he had endangered the company and proven himself unreliable. **Reliability** cannot be over-emphasized as the most desirable personal characteristic an employee can possess. If you can rely on people to do their jobs right, if they show up where and when they say they will; if they get to work on time and do what they were hired to do on a regular basis, if they do not liberate items from the workplace or cheat on expense accounts—if they can be found reliable in all areas—there are few things more valuable to an employer.

Also, **entrepreneurs need people who can do things right the first time.** I always tried to hire people I thought could hit the ground running and do the job. When I began staffing the laboratory at MetPath, I hired fifteen lab "chiefs" for each of the various testing departments and nobody else. That way I was sure that the job would get done right. When regular lab technicians were hired later on, they moved into an environment that had been set up by people who not only had years of experience but who had been on the job themselves for months. We also sought to **hire employees**

who could take the initiative at any level and get things done, even if such aggressiveness meant they would occasionally make mistakes. Things are happening very fast in a start-up business, so you need people who are willing to put their heads on the block; too many are stunned into inactivity because they are worried about making the wrong decision.

When someone exercised initiative and screwed up as a result, there was never a guillotine. When MetPath was very young — the company had thirty-five employees at the time—we had to get out a mailing of three thousand-plus letters to doctors one evening. The mailing had to get out by a particular day but the insert from the printer was late. It was finally promised for the next morning, but we did not know if we could trust that. If it came in the late afternoon, we would miss our deadline because we would never be able to label, stamp, and stuff all the envelopes in time to make the mail. So we made the decision to put the labels on the envelopes before we left work that day, to put the stamps on, and box up the envelopes so that when the printer brought the insert over we could quickly stuff it, seal it, and get it into the mail. Just about everyone in the company sat on the floor all over the office and put everything together. It was dark by the time we went home.

Later that night, at about nine o'clock, one of the drivers came in who knew we were doing this mailing. "I don't believe it," he said to himself, looking at all the letters sitting neatly boxed in the mailroom. "The idiots worked all day on the mailing and they never took it to the post office. Lucky for them I have a friend there who will take it from me this late, and the thing will get mailed and I will be a big hero." So he took them, banged on the door of the P.O. at 10 P.M., and his friend took them and mailed them all— every one of them an empty envelope with a stamp on it.

The driver was not a hero but he did not get fired either. In fact, he worked there at least a dozen years, until I left the company. He had shown courage and initiative and I would never penalize anyone for trying hard. In fact, I would rather have somebody working for me who would take it upon themselves to make that kind of decision than to have an army of mistake-free employees who never show any initiative. People with initiative are critical to a business in the start-up mode. An entrepreneur is not looking for cattle, but for people with the spirit and stamina of wild horses. You don't need it at General Motors, where initiative may not get noticed and might even be considered bad form. But in a start-up taking the initiative often means the difference between survival and success. As I still tell every potential employee that I interview, a wrong decision can be corrected, but nothing gets done if no decision is made. (By the way, we made the mailing the next day, this time with the driver's help—I think we made him lick all the envelopes!)

Not far behind reliability and initiative on my list of preferred employee characteristics are **loyalty** and **dedication**.

When a company is small, there are no committees and task forces to study a situation. You have a few people who get together on a regular basis to decide what is going to be done and then you have a small group of people who carry out those decisions. So you really do not need to hire a pack of thickheaded mules who are unwilling to take direction, hesitant to get involved and unable to think on the fly. Employees who can see the flame in an entrepreneur's eyes and try to add some of their own fuel to the fire are part of the driving force needed in the race to reach a business destination.

The problem with things like reliability, initiative, loyalty, and dedication is that they are hard to gauge in the short time it takes to interview someone. It becomes all the more important that you take the initiative and try to get your delusions of grandeur into the heads of your employees as soon as possible so that those hidden qualities have a chance to come out. Given the five prerequisites listed above, it would be difficult for anyone without at least some of those qualities to accept a job. That is part of the creation of an *esprit de corps*. Even at the early stage of the job interview, put the excitement and fast-paced action of being part of a growing business on the table in front of them. Tell them that if they are hired they are going to like coming to work at your company because the people they will be working with and for will be a lot like they are.

Employees will leave a job that pays a lot of money if they hate the boss or the company and dislike the people with whom they work. Since entrepreneurs have precious little money to pay big salaries in the beginning, it is fortunate that the reverse is true, too: Employees will work longer at a job paying them a low salary if they enjoy being around the boss and the other employees. People liked coming to work at MetPath. We had employees who changed companies and later came back to work for us there because they missed the action and all the excitement we generated.

But it takes more than co-worker's enthusiasm and an entrepreneurial pep talk during job interviews to sustain those kinds of feelings and attitudes among employees.

What helps most in the long run is learning how to keep them together and keep them following the leader, once they become part of the pack.

Oh! And by the way ...

Anyone who actually *does* know the etymology of the phrases *dad gum, gol' durn* and/or *dad burn*, please contact the authors in care of the publisher!

*   *   *   *   *

The wild packs of horses that populated North America were christened with many colorful names. The mustangs, broncos and cayuses were primarily descendants of the Barb and Arabian breeds that first made their way to Florida with the Spanish conquistadors. Later, English colonists imported and bred horses, some of which likewise made their way to the wild. Interbreeding has made the wild horse's history here otherwise difficult to delineate. Even harder to ascertain with certainty is a psychological profile of any horse, wild or tame. They seem a mass of contradiction and paradox, at once courageous and timid, affectionate and unfriendly, ungovernable and docile, hotheaded and phlegmatic, teachable and obtuse. As among human beings, brothers and sisters may be poles apart in temperament.

*   *   *   *   *

2. Motivating Employees

An employee's individual goals and motivations for working are similar in type to an entrepreneur's motivations, but there the similarity ends. The general likeness makes it fairly easy for an entrepreneur to identify the things that move employees. The trick becomes finding ways of providing a work environment within which those urgings can be satisfied by the employee. So it behooves the entrepreneur building a business first to recognize that **employees are not motivated in the same way or to the same degree that entrepreneurs are**. Someone who starts up their own business is a horse of a different color, indeed.

When it comes to money, for example, most employees are simply interested in making a living. Although they may dream of becoming wealthy, the risk of organizing and leading a trek into the business jungle is not one that most will take to get there. Employees place achievement more on a task-oriented footing, such as doing a good job or finishing a difficult project. Landing a job with a Fortune 500 company is a more likely goal for them than building a Fortune 500 company. The more goal-oriented types seek a career, perhaps a stock-option and profit sharing plan capped by good retirement benefits. The desire for power is limited to creating a little supervisory fiefdom in the kingdom of the entrepreneur, so to speak, or maybe becoming a power behind the throne at an executive level, a trusted advisor and confidant of the entrepreneur.

The motivations of employees are simultaneously more basic and more complex than those of the entrepreneur. Many employees may not understand their motivations or know what their goals are. Again, this makes it important for entrepreneurs not only to have delusions of grandeur in the first place, but to use the ability to communicate their vision to employees as quickly and effectively as possible. That is why I have always been keen on trying to motivate people during the interview process. There is no earlier or better time to create a lasting impression.

As time goes on, keep letting your dreams out into the open where the employees can see them—even when some of those dreams are nightmares. The only nightmare I can remember having in my whole life as an adult was about MetPath. We had a procedure for handling blood samples that had to be tested. We would take them in all day long and then number them in the evening, rack them, and put the racks in one of those huge industrial-sized refrigerators. The next morning, we would take the samples out and start processing. We were processing about two thousand samples a day at the time we made a decision to begin using pre-numbered labels. I was in the lab late one night after the labels had been delivered, happily labeling away with the rest of the staff (note, entrepreneurs, that you indeed do everything in a start-up business) and by midnight we had all the labels on and the samples safely stored in the big, shiny refrigerator. We left and everyone went home and went to bed.

The next morning I woke up and went to the lab at 7 A.M., as usual, ready for work. I decided to stop by the room where we had been putting the labels on the night before. I pulled open the refrigerator door. The draft from that action sucked out all 2,000 labels in a flurry onto the floor, which left all 2,000 tubes of blood sitting in the refrigerator, and all 2,000 looking exactly alike.

What really happened was that I awoke from that nightmare at 4 A.M., literally in a cold sweat. My pulse rate had to be about 160. I awoke mumbling to myself that no one had ever tested to see if the glue on the labels would stick to the glass tubes in cold temperatures. So I got dressed in a panic and sped to the office, went to the refrigerator and—very carefully!—opened the brushed-steel door. And there, staring back at me, were two thousand samples, all neatly racked, with labels intact.

The next day I was telling some employees that my nightmare should prove to them that I was not kidding when I told them that they would have to literally eat, drink and sleep the company. I thought I was the only one so addicted to the company that I would have those kinds of dreams, but I found out that most of the employees at MetPath already had experienced such nightmares themselves. I told this same tale to Shareen, who works in our accounting department at HEARx, and she replied with a knowing smile, "Well, Dr. Brown, I must be a member of the team for sure. I've already had my nightmare. I dreamed I was putting all the bills into the computer system and Mr. Faichney (the president of HEARx) walked in and asked me how it was going.

"And I said, 'Oh, just fine, Mr. Faichney! See for yourself.'

"He looked over my shoulder at my computer screen and began to get very angry. When I turned around to look, I was horrified."

When she had turned around, the screen on her computer was flashing the message:

**PAC-MAN
GAME 2
READY TO PLAY**

Like me, she awoke with a start, shaking. I once estimated that 15 percent of the people who worked for MetPath were "company addicts" and I believe that holds true in most enterprises. These are people who cancel vacations, do not go to parties, and do things for the company at the expense of nearly everything else. The business will not work if the entrepreneur is the only company addict, although he is the only one who really has any reason to be. Still, addictions are not reasonable things. We had people at HEARx working in the office until late afternoon on New Year's Eve, December 31, 1990 because we were going to start providing hearing tests to patients of a major institution on January 2, 1991. One of the area managers wound up working late into the night before the holiday, getting everything set up.

Donna did not have to do that. She was a salaried employee. Why would she choose to work on New Year's Eve for no money? She had *dedication*, in a word. Of course, most employees are not *that* dedicated, and many may not be impressed at all with your vision. But they can be impressed by you, which is where *loyalty* happens to come in.

Loyalty within a company is very often motivated by the force of an entrepreneur's personality, not the business or the principles he espouses. One of MetPath's top executives once remarked that many of the people who worked hard "were not working hard for the company, but for Paul Brown." They had developed a relationship with the boss who interviewed them; the person who knew six hundred of them by name as well as their wives' names and their kids' names; the employer that seemed to care about who they were and what they wanted; and the man proved that he could deliver on the promises he made when they first met him. **Loyalty to the chief executive officer can ultimately be transferred as dedication to the company**.

An employee's loyalty to the CEO also can put the entrepreneur into situations that require responses that are above and beyond the call of duty, as Jill could tell you. Jill was a spectacularly beautiful young woman who wanted to be an elementary school teacher, but came to work for MetPath instead because there were no teaching jobs available. She became one of our customer service representatives who early on manned phones at desks that were lined up right outside my office. Come to think of it, all our customer service representatives were women—and pretty women at that. But I am sure that had nothing to do with stationing them where I would have to walk past every time I went in and out of my office! Anyway, that's how it was set up. One Saturday, I arrived and headed for my office and, as usual, I could scarcely get past them.

No, it was not because they were so beautiful. I was simply in very real physical pain, suffering from back spasms caused by a slipped disk! It was especially bothersome after I flew on the air shuttle between Boston and Newark, commuting between MetPath and the naval base in New England. I was the only person I knew who would sit for takeoffs and landings, but during the flight was allowed to lie down—on the floor, in the aisle! People had to step over me if they wanted to get to the bathroom, but the floor was my only choice. I was making the trip three times a week, trying very hard to start up my business while performing my military service. After each flight and the half-hour drive from the airport, I would show up at MetPath only to crawl in the door, drop my attaché case and overnight bag, and hobble into my office so I could lie down on the floor, hoping the spasms would go away.

On one such day I was on my office floor when Jill came to the door crying. She was having severe abdominal pain and said she had been waiting all morning for me to come in so I could examine her and tell her what was wrong.

"You've been waiting for me?" I replied. "What help can I possibly be to you in this condition? Why didn't you call your doctor?"

"Well, Doctor Brown, I knew you were coming in and the pain was terrible," she said in between heart-wrenching sobs. "So I decided not to take a chance on going out of the office. *Please* help me! *Please*, the pain is so bad!"

"Jill, *think* about what you're asking! I'm on the floor," I said, with as much professional dignity as one can manage in such a position. "I'm in a lot of pain myself. How can I possibly examine you? *Please* go and call someone else!" Now, mind you, I was looking up from the carpet at this very attractive young lady, whose beautiful eyes were full of tears.

"Oh, Doctor Brown, *please*! You're the *only* one who can help me." My resolve weakening quickly, I gave it one last try.

"Jill, think about this," I said, when her crying abated for a moment. "The only way I could do that is if you join me down here on the floor."

"That's all right, Dr. Brown," she said. "I don't care. You just *have* to tell me what's wrong. There's no *time* to go anywhere else. I'm afraid. The *pain* is getting *worse*. You've just *got* to help me."

"Jill, please listen to me," I said as patiently as I could, since she seemed to be missing the point somehow. "I want you to *really* think about what's probably going to happen here. If you lie on the floor, you will have to be on your back. Then I am going to have to crawl over you to examine you, because I can barely move. And then someone is going to walk in here, and we're both going to be startled. I'll be rolling onto my back, away from you. Whoever comes in is going to see us both on our backs on the floor of my office with startled expressions on our faces. How do you think that is going to look?"

Well, it probably would have looked mighty odd, but nothing like that happened. Jill prevailed and the exam was accomplished with one of the other customer service girls standing a somewhat perplexed guard at my closed office door. Jill was not having appendicitis or anything else more serious than a painful ovulation. That was over twenty years ago. Recently, I saw her quite by accident while I was standing with my attorney in the quiet and stately corridors of a courthouse. Still an attractive woman, she came over and stood next to me and got my attention.

"I'll bet you don't know who I am," she said.

"Sure I do, Jill. I just hope you don't need another examination right now!"

"No, Doctor Brown, I don't. Besides, you're standing up!"

We laughed, and my attorney had no idea what we were talking about. But she was amazed that I would remember her, while I did not see how I could forget her, considering that we had once been on the ground floor of MetPath together!

More to the point, that little drama clearly demonstrates how much stock employees can place in their employers as individuals.

It often takes more than just personal charisma and delusions of grandeur to secure the allegiance of employees. Sometimes it takes placing some stock in the hands of employees, since the **desire for wealth** is a sure-fire motivator among most employees, probably *numero uno*. The reason why so many employees work so hard in my companies, I believe, is not only because of my personal involvement with them or my attempts to get to know them. I think that my high level of interpersonal skills takes a back seat to the fact that I make every single employee an *owner* of the company. It does not make any difference if they are clerks or vice presidents, every person in HEARx is a shareholder, as they were in MetPath and in Permark.

Two methods were used to give employees ownership. All employees who start with HEARx, for example, are given a ten-year option to buy HEARx stock at its price-per-share on the day they are hired. Each employee is assigned a certain number of shares of stock that they can purchase. A supervisor would be assigned a larger block of stock than the janitor, relative to the contributions each makes, but the janitor still gets his stock. An audiologist, for example, will be able to buy between 7,000 and 10,000 shares at that price anytime over the next ten years. The plan vests at the rate of 25 percent a year over the first four years of employment. That means that if an employee bought 10,000 shares of stock on day one of his employment, 100 percent of the current value of that stock would be available to the employee after four years with the company.

If you do not believe that this can make someone wealthy, consider this: If those were 10,000 shares of MetPath stock held for ten years, that would have meant a value of almost $500,000 when MetPath was sold to Corning. When Corning's stock split later on, the value of those shares increased to over $1.5 million— not bad compensation on top of a regular paycheck! There is an additional ownership option that can be used to attract top-quality management personnel. High-level managers were offered either stock options or blocks of restricted stock that would have to be returned if an executive did not stay for a specified period, but it would be all theirs after that period of time, even if they left the company.

If employees as a group own between 10 percent and 20 percent of your company, each one will undoubtedly take more care about their jobs and everything else about your business because each one feels he or she is being taken care of. Everybody likes to have a piece of the action and this plan is not something unique. When you come to **other financial rewards**, however, such as bonuses and profit-sharing plans, my employee relations philosophy departs sharply from the rest of the business world.

The first time we could afford to pay bonuses at MetPath, they were awarded to the lowest-paid employees first, not to management. And each year thereafter, when we made more money, the level moved up another notch on the pay scale. We did not reach the management level until the third year of profitability. The rationale is simple: The workers are the ones who make the business work on a day-to-day basis, and I want to keep those people happy. Starting out, it was only a week's pay, but it gradually increased to two-weeks' pay and up, until bonuses of at least a month's salary were being paid to everyone in the company. That meant they were literally being paid for thirteen months and only having to work twelve, not counting vacation time.

There are other things besides money that entrepreneurs should think about to motivate employees. When someone comes in on the ground floor of a new and developing company, for instance, he or she has no idea what the potential is for the job. So **career mobility** has become one of the promises I make to potential employees during the job interviews. Along with the "be prepareds," I tell them that the sky really is the limit, given the size and scope of the company and that they can advance as far as their capabilities allow. I started doing that at the beginning of my entrepreneurial adventures, and my promises had to be more than hot air. If I was going to be successful, my employees had to be successful as well. As time went on, I have been able to prove that I meant what I said because there are many success stories to tell.

Donna Taylor is one. She came to HEARx as an audiologist in one of our hearing centers when the company opened in 1987. She was rapidly recognized and promoted, first to area manager and then to regional manager. She became our vice president of operations within eight years, making over $100,000 a year—all as a result of being in the right place at the right time and doing her jobs well.

Career mobility can get someone excited about joining a new company and so can **geographic mobility**. Metpath was in sixty-five cities when I sold the company, but we started out in one. HEARx was operating in three cities within three years, with multiple locations in each, and after nine years has hearing centers in seven states. The breadth of the vision for the company allows the entrepreneur to offer a potential employee some flexibility about where he works and lives, from cross-town to cross-country. If the employees work hard, the company grows and the visions are realized, which allows even greater flexibility. If the spouse of a valued MetPath employee was transferred to another city, chances were we could move that employee to work in that same city.

It is not a good idea to give up on a good employee just because of a change in their personal situation. If we had people in HEARx who wanted to live in a certain city and we were going to open a hearing center there, we would offer them the chance to work there if they were good performers, someone we wanted to keep. Such policies tend to create a positive attitude that can pervade an entire company. Employees believe that management cares, management believes that their contributions are appreciated and everyone from top to bottom believes that the company offers solid opportunities and is a good place to work.

But there is more to employee relations than that. Entrepreneurs have to concern themselves with **little things**, too. A few small examples:

- There were few signs of "executive privilege" at MetPath. There were never any assigned parking spaces, for example. You want to park near the front door? Great! Come to work earlier than I did. I was usually at work early, so I got to park there.

- We used a Rusco time-card system and there were two clocks: an entry clock, which everyone punched, including myself and all the executives; and a ready-to-start-work clock that hourly employees punched in addition to the entry clock. If the chairman of the board carried a Rusco card and punched in and out every day, no one could complain about punching the clock!

- At no time was there a separate dining room for executives, only a massive cafeteria that fed two thousand people a day at its height. When I worked there and ran the company, I got in line like everybody else did. I did not have my secretary call down and say, "Dr. Brown is coming down now, make him a special lunch the way he likes it." A cafeteria offers an excellent opportunity to meet and socialize with your employees. The mistake is to remove yourself because you think it is beneath your dignity.

My philosophy is best expressed by these little things that say, "We're all in the same boat and everybody rows. There are no privileged characters." Sure, some vacation times were longer than others, benefits differed, salaries varied, but **entrepreneurs must take care not to de-motivate anyone by the way they conduct themselves**. A few Metpath executives visited a company in

Boston that we were looking to acquire and received an important object lesson on this point. The CEO took us through the entire company. Not one person in the whole building said to him, "Good morning, Dr. Whatsyername." He did not say anything to anybody either. He walked into a room, announced that it was such-and-such a department, and then he led us out of the room. No introductions, nothing; and no one in any department said a word or even looked up from what they were doing. Finally, he made a big demonstration of the fact that he had no offices for his managers, that he wanted them in the open and to all feel equal. Then we saw his office: a 20-by-40-foot palace of executive privilege if ever there was one.

I think that motivation by example is the most powerful tool an entrepreneur has in his tool kit. The boss owns a block of stock, everyone knows he is aiming to get rich, and why not? They know it is his company, that he started it up. But if everyone else can have a block of stock, then maybe they could share in the wealth too. I do not just *believe* in making somebody rich who makes me richer; I actually say that to each of my employees, and make sure to follow up on it when it is warranted. My reason is not to play the big shot but to limit the demotivating factors and enhance the motivating factors. The important thing is that people seem to take it as I intended, since they seem to take it to heart. When I started showing up every Saturday morning to sort mail, what happened? I'll tell you what happened: All the other executives came in on Saturday morning to do some work! If you want the employee to eat, sleep and drink the company, then you have got to take the lead. An entrepreneur will be driven to that anyway. He just has to figure out how to communicate that same attitude to his employees, and leading by example is probably the best way to do that.

Another great tool is what I call **an open door policy**. Some business executives in major corporations seem to have part of the formula. They will take any phone calls that come in for them and some even answer the phone themselves. Bank presidents are famous for this. They will meet with any potential depositor at any time in any place, but many draw the line at meeting with employees. They are afraid to be seen as second-guessing their supervisors; some do not want to give the impression of being a "spy" and would argue that opening the door to employees might breed a climate of suspicion and mistrust. Well, it might in a mega-corporation or institution where the competition for the top jobs makes honest communication something of a lost, or at least a very Byzantine art.

For an entrepreneur in a start-up company, an open-door

policy is the result of caring about people. It is also a great way to get to know what is *really* going on in your business. When there are only twenty or thirty people around, your door is never shut because you are never in your office anyway; you are out there packing boxes and affixing labels with everyone else. But when the company grows, the entrepreneur becomes loaded down with the more "executive" parts of the job and loses touch somewhat. An open-door policy solves that.

If a lower-level Metpath employee came to see me and told me there was a problem, I could not make the assumption that they were right just because they complained. I would never second-guess my supervisors either. But I had to look into the problem. One of the skills I developed was the ability to look into a report-ed problem without anyone ever knowing who reported it or that I was "looking into" something. I would just show up and noncha-lantly "discover" things, all by myself. I would "notice" that things were being done backwards or that mail was left in a corner some-where. The most important thing was that no employee ever suf-fered from this policy, either the one who reported a problem or the one who was causing it, unless they were creating an insuf-ferable problem for other employees.

I tried to get all the officers to have this same policy but some refused or just could not pull it off. When I hired Bud, who was MetPath's president for several years, he had a totally different attitude. He had come from IBM. My attitude was that an employ-ee who came to see me was innocent until proven guilty. His atti-tude was that the employee who came to him with a problem was guilty and had to be proven innocent. Bud believed that if some-one came to complain, that person was probably wrong and the supervisor or the system was probably right. At least he would look into it, eventually. And eventually, people stopped going in to see Bud.

The employees knew that if they came to me, they would not get on someone's s——t list; but they also knew if they went and talked to Bud, they might wind up on his s——t list. Bob, anoth-er MetPath president, also had a s——t list of employees that he did not like, which he characterized as complainers and whiners, to mention only the less vituperative of his categories. I suggest a kinder, gentler approach. Try as much as possible to treat every-one in the company as an equal, regardless of their position. *Just make them happy!*, because if they are happy, they will work hard and the company will prosper. The ability to adopt such an atti-tude is probably as good a distinction as any between hired exec-utives and entrepreneurs.

Communicating is probably the most difficult thing to get

done in a new business, right up there behind raising *The Money*. It may be *more* difficult, in fact, because you do not have to raise money every day, but you do have to deal with your employees every business day, at least some of them. So it is very helpful and time-saving to **develop more formal methods of communicating with your employees**. Not formal in the sense that everyone comes in dressed to the nines and rigid with fright because they are afraid to say the wrong thing in front of the boss; rather, formal in the sense of regularly occurring, well-organized, and directed toward a single goal.

These meetings are important vehicles to let your employees know what is going on, like making sure they understand that the plan is to cross the river facing slightly upstream, so everyone better row in that direction. They are also good for management to discover just exactly what management has agreed to do and how they have decided to get it done—because management all too frequently says it knows what direction it wants to go, then blithely heads off in at least three different directions at the same time. Or they may head off in one direction, in a perfect example of corporate cooperation. Then they ask, still in unison, "How come the project failed?" Usually, no one communicated to the troops the correct direction in the first place.

There was a standing joke at MetPath that if you really wanted to know what was going on, you needed to talk with Julia, the cleaning woman. We decided that she knew everything because she emptied the wastebaskets in the executive offices. Julia would know things like when the next expansion was going to happen, whether or not there would be a new manager in this or that office, things like that.

"Are we going to open in Kansas this year?"

"I don't know. Go ask Julia."

Instead of relying on such a remarkable but sometimes unreliable source of information, I favor a few formal meetings at different times for different purposes. First comes the proverbial **staff meeting**, a weekly affair where all the top managers get together as a group. I like to hold them on Monday mornings because everyone is rested, relaxed and not involved in the "Problem of the Week" yet. The end of the week is too late, because everyone's ready to go on vacation or to go see their therapist, and they are all mumbling and moaning about whatever their particular "Problem of the Week" was. I also insist on receiving a written memorandum each Friday, prepared that day so that it is the last thing managers do each week. This memo summarizes what happened during the week just passed, divided up into "activities" (what they are doing) and "issues" (things needing decisions). This puts things in a reflective light, away from the glare of the nitty-gritty, and allows managers to step back a few paces and consider the big picture. Then, on Monday, the new computer so urgently needed in the accounting department or the additional space being demanded by the cramped customer service people has already been put in perspective.

All top managers should be expected to attend the staff meetings, except for dire emergencies. No business trips on Monday! Remember, these are people you hired for their brains, people who complement your own business skills. This meeting is a good time to get some of what they know into your head so that you will know what is going on company-wide, become more a part of the team and be better prepared to lead the team. **Monthly corporate policy meetings**, simple one-on-one get-togethers between you and each of your top managers, are excellent opportunities as well. Here the purpose is to find out not so much what the problems are in the interactions from one area to another, but what is going on in each specific area. It also gives some privacy for managers to vent their feelings about personal problems they might be having with other managers. It becomes sort of an open-door policy for top management, in that sense. And since it is formal, happening like clockwork once a month, they cannot get out of it.

Next, it is **lunch with the chairman**, monthly employee pow-wows to which no more than five to ten employees are invited (never more than ten, because too many means that no one will talk). This can start out as a coffee break, breakfast at the donut shop, lunch at the sandwich counter or dinner at the Chinese restaurant across the street. They breed loyalty and productivity. Invite no other top management and do not mix supervisors with department personnel if you expect to get anything out of the meeting. This is an excellent way to find out for yourself what the real world is like, free of management filters. Ask what is going on. Ask them what they see as the company's problems, what they would like to see happen to the company.

These meetings are not the only formal communications vehicles that should be used. Newsletters, through which you get the employees to say something to the company and vice versa, are worthwhile. They travel a two-way street, but other vehicles only go one way, like employee suggestion programs. I try to put a bit of pizzazz into my suggestion boxes, turning them from boxes into programs. One I called *S.T.O.P., Suggestions to Optimize Profits*, which stimulated communications from the employee. Anyone who came up with a way to save the company money got 10 percent of the annual savings from their idea. In several cases, some earned more money than their whole years' salaries. *Formal communications can lead to individual motivation, which builds company morale and a sense of mutual support.* Memos to employees, on the other hand, tend to work in reverse because of their very personal intent delivered in an impersonal manner. Except in critical areas, keep memo writing to a minimum, and e-mail and faxing to a fare-thee-well. **Go talk to somebody** if you have something to say—and don't use the phone! Take the time to walk over and ask a question or to discuss a problem and its possible solution. You can always put a memo through as a follow-up, but present the initial message in person.

Try to get your company executives to do things the way you do them. Keep the meetings short and spread them out over time. Do not turn them into all-day lunches or anything like that. Cover the information quickly, stick to the matters at hand, and then get back to work. The whole point of these meetings is to involve your employees with participating in what is taking place in the company, i.e., *their* company.

What you will find in doing all this is that it is hard to do. Employees often have a difficult time accepting the idea that management realizes there is a problem and intends to do something about it. Once they accept that idea, however, then they have difficulty accepting the fact that their problem may not be taken care of by the time they report for work the next day. Their difficulty seems to revolve around an employee's inability to understand that the problem foremost in his or her mind is not necessarily on the top of management's list of things to do.

But you have to keep trying because all of this is really your fault, isn't it? You started up the company, so it is your responsibility (break that word down and you see it is simply the *ability to respond*) to get your messages across. Wherever you can touch someone, touch them. Walk through the company; visit people on a daily basis.

Communication is your demonstration in the real world that you care about the company, individual employees, and their mutual future, all in one package.

Which leads me to believe that a company should be built with interpersonal glue.

The entrepreneur must provide that glue and, in many instances, *is* that glue.

Just remember what some glue is made of:

The hooves of horses sent away to the glue factory!

* * * * *

The intelligence of the horse has been appraised at widely different levels. Ordinarily the horse ranked fourth among the "lower animals," following the elephant, the ape, and the dog, although some drop it to tenth on that scale. Nevertheless, it is generally agreed to be sensitive in the extreme and possessed of a long memory, with a tendency to form habits difficult to change. Certain instincts are highly developed, such as being able to locate water in arid places, to easily find the way back to favored locations, to be quickly aware of unseen danger, and to discriminate between enemies and friends at close quarters and long range. As an herbivore, it seldom attacks man or other animals, except in the case of a stallion fending off a carnivore from his mate or a mare protecting her nursing foal. When allowed to run wild, particularly in extremes of climate, horses tend to degenerate in size and type.

*   *   *   *   *

3. Terminating Employees

There are two basic reasons for terminating employees:

1. *There is a problem within the company which results in an employee being let go by the company.*

2. *There is a problem with an employee that results in the company firing the employee.*

There are, of course, other reasons besides termination why people leave companies. They may quit for what they think is a better opportunity somewhere else. They may have health reasons or family considerations that force them to move on or out of the workforce. And there are a host of other reasons, from wanting to start their own businesses to just wanting out of business, period. There are also people who have great potential, but they might not be good at a particular point in time. I once hired a young woman away from a manufacturing company. She was a dynamite lab technician but she came to see me soon after we hired her, saying she could not take the pressure, so we let her go back to her old company. She self-guillotined, if you will. But she might have fit in perfectly two years or so later, once the company became more stable.

There are also times, however, when employees reach the level of their maximum ability in a job situation. The company sometimes just outgrows a person's capabilities, and that person more likely than not is someone who had been with the company a long time. So you check to see if they are retrainable, but some will not be. Obviously, you do whatever you can to salvage a good person, but there will be people with specialized skills that cannot be used anywhere else. When that happens, you have an employee problem, and a number of other potential problems as well. But there is really only one question, and one answer,

The question is, "How can you replace someone like that?"

The answer is, "You can't."

There was one woman who worked for me that was the key to the company's survival, as far as I was concerned. Lorraine was the supervisor of the keypunch department, which started with three people. When the company grew to about $70 million in sales, the keypunch department had three shifts of thirty people per shift. Lorraine made the department work because she had developed a relationship with her keypunch operators the same way that I had developed a relationship with Lorraine. She worked for me, not the company, and they worked for Lorraine, not for me. If one day a couple of people did not show up to work in that department, Lorraine would pick up the phone and three employees would come in to cover—for her, not for MetPath—or she would work the shift herself.

She ran the department for nearly eight years until it became obvious that the job had become something way beyond her capability to manage, so I had to let her go and there was nothing else for her to do with the company. She was a keypunch operator when she had started ten years earlier and had been moved into a supervisory position. Everyone in the department loved her and would never understand how such a hardworking, dedicated, and loyal employee could be let go. So how could I replace her? I couldn't, really. Oh, sure, I got someone to take over the supervisor's job of the keypunch department easily enough, but I never even tried to replace Lorraine, because no one could believe she could ever be replaced.

That was the way I felt about it, too, so what I did was give her 100 percent pay for six months, 75 percent pay for the next six months, 50 percent pay for the next six months, and 25 percent pay for the next six months, plus $5,000 a year after that for the rest of her life. She retired and several things happened as a result. Lorraine wound up going into business for herself. Meanwhile, all of the employees in that department knew what had happened, that even though someone had taken over Lorraine's position, she was adequately rewarded and not dumped out on the street. No one could get the feeling that they would get thrown out of the company after ten years if we did all that for Lorraine. I would never do that anyway, but how Lorraine's situation got handled was a stronger testimony than any words I could have used.

And anyone who would suggest that such action was motivated by a guilty conscience or was a waste of company funds is obviously a bean-counting investor, and could never be an entrepreneur. An entrepreneur cares about people and what was done for Lorraine was merely a demonstration of that fact. The lesson is to **bend over backwards for the person that the company has managed to outgrow**. The secondary benefits that the company accrues in terms of goodwill and morale among the employees are of inestimable value, but the real profit is for the entrepreneur. If you are one, you know exactly what I mean.

Rewards, both getting them and giving them, are an integral part of the entrepreneurial profile. But there are also times when you have to give with one hand while getting ready to take it back with the other. If you treat your employees properly, you will be rewarding them with salaries based on their performance, which is part of motivation; but when someone tries blackmail as a means of getting a reward, then it is time to sharpen the guillotine.

We opened an office in Kansas City a couple of years after we opened MetPath. We had hardly any employees then, and we looked around and decided that Steph was the one to send out. We trained her to set up the computer and she went out to install the system in Kansas. She must have taken the wrong flight out and landed in Oz, because a couple of days later she called Guy Seay and delivered this fantastic statement:

"Well, I'm here, the computer is here and everything is ready to go," she said. "But I've been thinking. I'm the only one who can do this, and paying me $12,000 a year hardly seems sufficient for this kind of responsibility. So, if you want me to finish this installation, you'll have to give me a raise immediately to $15,000 or I won't do it."

"Well, I'll have to think about it," Guy replied, fuming, but held off long enough to call me, vent his spleen and ask my advice about what to do.

"It's obvious to me what you should do," I said. "You call her and tell her she's just gotten her raise. Let her complete the installation. But when she returns, there will be no job for her."

And that was what we did. No one likes being blackmailed. Had she gone out there, set it up, got everything running and then came back and said, "Paul, how about a raise? I think I did a really good job out there," she would have gotten her raise. She probably would have gotten a raise without saying a word because we were reward-oriented. So I did not feel bad about taking advantage of the situation and having her put in the system before she left. After all, she tried to take advantage of the situation too, but she lost, that was all. She got paid for what she did and, in fact, got more than what she bargained.

Waste no time in getting rid of someone who makes a major mistake. We all make mistakes in life and those we call learning experiences. But when we make the same mistake twice, then it is a major mistake. And how many major mistakes are we allowed? Well, an employee in a brand new company cannot afford to make even one major mistake, because the whole company might go under. And that is a risk entrepreneurs do not have to take—unless, of course, you still want to learn things the hard way.

We hired one fellow, a supervisor from a major teaching hospital who had been there for fifteen years, and put him in our chemistry department at MetPath. The company had been in business only a short time and he was not there a week before he incorrectly numbered one thousand blood sugar test samples. Had it not been caught and had the reports gone out, the mistake would have meant that one thousand people would have gotten the wrong results. As it was, we had to do all the tests all over again, which was just a waste of time that we really could not afford, but he swore up and down that he had never made a mistake like this in fifteen years, and was probably just overwhelmed with everything being new to him and moving so quickly.

We accepted his explanation, along with his promise that he would never let anything like that happen again. Well, he did not do *that* again, exactly, but two weeks later did the same thing, this time to a cholesterol level test. That was it, I could not wait any longer! I would not take a chance that he would do something else that might bring the whole operation down around our ears. He was in a responsible position and he screwed up, and that was all I cared about. I did not want to get into why he messed those tests up. I was not interested in whether it was his attention span that caused the problem or whatever, I could not put up with it then and I cannot put up with it now. He simply had to go.

There is little to be gained by delaying a decision. **When a person is a problem, that person has to be fired instantly.** No notice, just severance pay and send them out the door. The morale of the rest of the employees must be protected. If the person makes a major mistake, you do not want people to think the company is going to keep them around. You do not reward screwups for screwing up by letting them stay a couple of weeks while they "look for something else." The only thing most of them will be l ooking for is revenge; something else to bungle; a chance to badmouth you and the company; or some sympathy. And nobody needs to go through any of that, especially not the entrepreneur who is trying to build a relationship with employees that is based on honesty and trust.

If communicating with employees is hard, then terminating them can be even harder. Sometimes the offending party is not even aware of the problem that causes their dismissal, but that does not make it any less of a problem. A data processing executive I once hired was terrific at what he did, but he managed to alienate everyone in the office—and he thought he was being funny! It seems Tom was trying to imitate my own sense of humor, which tends to the sarcastic, but is never mean. If I saw a secretary, who probably had been working for ten hours, getting ready to go home, I might say something like, "Gee, leaving so early? Aren't you going to do any work before you go home for the day?" I would get a laugh, or at least a tired smile, but if Tom tried it she would break out into tears. He had the wrong inflection or something, he just could not get it right. And he did it often enough that I had to let him go because everyone was about ready to kill him. He could no longer function properly in his position, even if he never said another word to anybody, which would have made him just as useless to the company.

He was like the first lieutenant in the infantry who leads his platoon to the top of the hill but is just as worried about being shot from behind by his own men as he is about the enemy soldiers in front of him.

And there is too much yet in front of you to be sabotaged by the people with whom you work. But you should be ready now.

Is everyone following your lead? Good!

Keep 'em close! Head 'em up! Move 'em out!

It is time to go deeper into the Business Jungle.

$ECRET$ OF THE WILD HORSE

*An employee's reliability may be worth
more than an employee's experience
to a new business.*

———————

*Nothing motivates an employee more than
owning "a piece of the action."*

———————

*Watch out!
An employee who makes a major mistake
tends to make another.*

Building Ingeniously

Chapter Five
The Beaver: Building Ingeniously

▲ ▲ ▲ ▲ ▲

Beavers (family Castoridae) are aquatic mammals with thickset bodies that may reach six feet in length and weigh more than sixty pounds. The short-legged beaver's five-toed forefeet, used for digging and manipulating objects, are smaller than the large, webbed hind feet which provide most of its propulsion in water and on land. A glossy brown pelt, composed of a dense underfur thickly overlaid with hair, covers a beaver from its small-eared head to the base of its foot-long and distinctively broad, flat and scaly tail. The specialized tail acts as a rudder in the water and serves as a trowel of sorts in the industrious beaver's most significant pursuit: building dams and lodges in rivers and lakes. The diligent beaver spends so much time in this activity that it has been equipped to build at both ends: Its long, sharp front teeth are ever-growing and chisel-like, perfect for munching and crunching wood meant for dinner or for construction.

*　　*　　*　　*　　*

Mark already had started up two businesses—the "coin retrieval from the snow around parking meters" service and the "selling candy bars at school" operation—by the time he was a ninth grader. That year he would add yet another business to the list, however, which eventually proved to be the most successful of all his childhood entrepreneurial ventures.

He even named this one, calling it *The Gleam Team*, an apt name for a car-washing service. But there was no real team in the beginning, just as there was no name to call what Mark looked like when he went out to work, at least none that I could use comfortably. The torn jeans, dirty T-shirt and battered sneakers iden-

tified him more as a refugee from a hippie commune than as a resident of the affluent New Jersey neighborhood where he offered his
services. What made it even worse was the homemade wagon
Mark pulled behind him. That looked to be in just as bad a shape
as he was: the four-wheeled contraption seemed barely held
together with the length of rope that also served as its handle.

I kept these observations to myself as long as I could. Though
Mark generally had not been one to follow the crowd, I thought
that his dress might have something to do with peer approval. He
was, after all, at the age where such things usually became important and it was during the time when the "hippie" look was in
vogue among the young and even the not-so-young. I figured that
at worst it was just a phase that he would grow out of and, at
best—well, to tell you the truth, I really did not see anything good
in it at all. But I was soon disabused of that attitude when I discovered he had a well-considered method behind what I could only
discern as messiness.

Part of the reason I could not appreciate his choice of accou-
terments was that I was his parent. The other part of my concern
stemmed from being a businessman. On the one hand, I hated the
way he looked; on the other, I admired his desire, his obvious hard
work and dedication. He worked after school and on weekends,
initially funding his business from the weekly allowance that I was
happy to afford him when he was between ventures. I particularly appreciated his preparation. Mark's wagon might have looked
like it was on its last legs, but it was in fact quite serviceable.
Everything needed to wash and wax a motor vehicle was neatly
packed into that rickety four-wheeler: detergent, glass and
chrome cleaner, a bucket, a scrub brush for tires and even some
old toothbrushes for tiny crevices, plus a few sponges and a bunch
of clean rags.

Mark was so well-prepared, in fact, that it was all the more difficult for me to understand why he chose to look like one of the
rags he had stuffed in his wagon. Finally, I could not stand it any
longer; I could only hold my tongue in check for so long, so I confronted Mark about his appearance. I caught him one Saturday
morning just as he emerged from the garage on our ten-acre
estate, dressed in his usual ragamuffin disguise.

"Mark, where do you think you're going?"

"You know, Dad," he answered, a little exasperated. "I'm going
to wash cars." His frown told me he did not understand why I was
even asking. After all, he had been doing this just about every
weekend for weeks now.

"What I mean is," I began again, "where are you going dressed
like that?"

"Like I said, I'm going to wash cars, like I always do," he replied. "I mean, it's not like working in an office. I get dirty."

"But is it necessary," I asked, eyeing his outfit with ill-concealed disdain, "to look dirty *before* you wash the cars?"

"Well, yes, it is," he replied without hesitation.

I was the one caught speechless. There I was all prepared for Mark to present a vague and indefensible argument, like "everyone dresses this way" or some such blather, which I quickly would cut to ribbons and get him to change his clothes. But his nonplused reply left me with only a weak response.

"And how can you say that?"

"Easy! It's all part of my plan, Dad."

"Your plan?"

"That's right," he said. "Nobody's going to hire me if I look like I come from around here, so I dress up like this to get people to hire me."

"But everybody knows you around here."

"On this block they do," Mark said, smiling again. "But they don't know me around the corner!"

He had it all covered, coming and going, and proved it over the next few years. Mark earned almost $4,000 from those people "around the corner," plus folks a few blocks away and around some other corners too. He printed up business cards before long and then had to hire other kids to help him service his rapidly growing clientele. *The Gleam Team* lived up to its name, and those boys earned a good deal of money themselves, while Mark additionally earned quite a bit of respect from his father. At least his father became very careful not to be so quick to jump to conclusions! There I was, thinking he would not do well because he was wearing the wrong clothes, when in fact he did great, precisely because of what I thought was all wrong!

Mark grew more through the experience than his income did. After all, he had formed an idea for a business, planned it, and was prepared to see it through. He found out he could pull together the money, equipment, and people needed to start and sustain a business. Mark studied his market and his customer, from which he created and executed a marketing strategy that showed a remarkable understanding of human psychology. And, oh yes... there was one other thing Mark did, without which none of this would have been possible: He did the work. Mark did it the best he knew how, and on top of that trained the people he had hired, got them to work just as hard and to do the best that they could.

I did not realize it at the time, but looking back I can see that the start-up of Mark's business occurred in definitive phases common to all new businesses. Granted, *The Gleam Team* was not a full-fledged business, complete with licensing requirements, tax statements, and employee benefits programs. Mark did not have to worry about the landlord kicking him out on the street if he got behind on his rent—it would have been poor form for his father to ask for rent anyway. He was not forced to perform against impossible timetables; operate under the watchful eyes of investors; deal with strict regulatory criteria; nor meet anyone's financial expectations but his own. Still, no matter its size or its lack of complexity, Mark's *Gleam Team* was at least in principle going through the same stages that every entrepreneurial venture goes through when starting up.

BUILDING A BUSINESS:
THE INITIAL PHASES OF A START-UP

Phase 1: Market Penetration
Phase 2: Systems Development
Phase 3: Initial Profit/Expansion

Now, do not be led astray here and believe that anything at all will happen in your business in simple, 1-2-3 order. The phases can be listed all in a row, but **nothing happens in the business jungle in a neat and orderly fashion**. The reality of a start-up business is that there will be little rhyme or reason to what occurs, and even less order. If anything ever happens just as planned—and it is safe to say that will not happen very often—it will be entirely accidental. The point is that nothing, absolutely nothing, can be counted as certain during the early phases of business development.

Well, that is not entirely true; perhaps it is better put another way. There are three things that are absolutely certain for every entrepreneur starting up a new business: death, taxes and **the lack of enough money**. We can do little about death and taxes. You will learn, however, the way to remedy capital shortfalls and raise more money in *Chapter 7*. But before you get there (which is where you will have to get to in order to expand your business), you are going to have to meet the unforgettable Mr. Murphy in *Chapter 6*, which might mean you will never make it at all. Meanwhile, there is a start-up to get through. So don't just stand there, get going!

Just remember that except for the three things we mentioned above, **nothing is certain in the business jungle** — unless it is that everything else is uncertain, unpredictable, and uncontrollable! Every aspect of your business will seems to require your attention all the time. You write a check to pay for the postage meter in the morning and in the afternoon you're feeding letters through it. That wonderful production manager you hired last week—the one you searched high and low for, wined and dined because of that unexpected increase in orders—called in to say he was taking a job with another company. Now, not only do you have to keep production on schedule but you have to spend a few hours in a delivery truck at the end of the day since you spent so much time hiring the production manager that you forgot to hire the extra driver you needed to deliver the orders to all those new customers that you cannot afford to lose.

When the time comes for business-building to commence, things change so abruptly that entrepreneurs soon wish they were back dreaming on the sunny fringes of the jungle, savoring product and service ideas, chewing on business plans, and hacking out marketing schemes, getting ready for the grand day when the business would open. Only a few weeks or even just a few days in business and even the most uncomfortable memories of that earlier time seem like fun. The tedious testing and fine-tuning of product ideas; the unsuccessful initial forays to locate capital; the time-consuming search for management and staff, all appear almost as idylls compared with running, doing, and staying in business every day. Here and now—once the product or service, the people, and the money for the business are in hand—the dream-time is over and the real-time surely has begun.

Almost as soon as the entrepreneur turns the key in the front lock and opens the business for business, a rude awakening comes. Things begin happening fast, almost too fast, and nothing seems to go as planned. Nearly everything, in fact, feels like a splash and more often a bucketful of cold water in the face. The once sunny field of entrepreneurial dreams is now all dark uproar and storm clouds, thunder, and lightning. The new businessman's carefully conceived business strategies all seem to go out the window and everything starts happening at once.

Those who will survive their start-ups come to understand (perhaps simply by reading this book, but more than likely by learning it the hard way) that the uproar is perfectly normal for a new business. Such an avalanche of activity is the natural state of affairs in the entrepreneurial scheme of things. But it can bury the unwary. The pressure and confusion could be fatal, unless the realization somehow dawns that no step-by-step entrepreneurial plan could possibly have prepared you for what is going on. And what is going on is that **all parts of the business-building process are going on at all times, simultaneously**. The next several levels of the business development process simply crank up without notice or warning just as soon as you, the entrepreneur, make your first business decision.

Think about a little wind-up car, the kind that changes direction automatically when they bump into anything. That is the best example of how entrepreneurial decision-making works during the start-up phases of business development. The car runs along the floor until... SMASH!... it hits a wall, turns this way or that, and then... SMASH!... goes right into a table leg, a chair leg, and the dog in succession, and then... SMASH!... turns into the wall again.

The entrepreneur likewise gets wound up each morning and hits the ground running, only to smash repeatedly into all sorts of problems that require immediate decisions. The business forms are going to come in the wrong color and will have to be changed; the boxes are going to come in opening at the side instead of at the top; the doors will be hung backwards and the counter-top will be a foot too long. Every product or service your operation needs, meanwhile, will be at least a day late. But you really can't complain. You probably will not be able to pay for it anyway, since most of your customers will be a month late and a few dollars short in paying you for your product or service.

True entrepreneurs are well-prepared for the uncertainty of the business jungle, since an entrepreneur operates best on instinct. A gut feeling can automatically deliver all the certainty needed to make a decision. Most start-up decisions tend to be of the seat-of-the-pants variety and will definitely include at least one of the life and death kind on a regular basis, i.e., just about every day, including weekends. This situation will exist for at least the immediate future, which will often seem eternally uninviting and perpetually unstable. Entrepreneurs will even feel as if they have no choice in their decisions, and that will very often be the case. Sometimes only one decision is possible and just needs someone to make it. No matter what happens, however, **the entrepreneur is always the one responsible for all the decisions**, no matter who actually makes them. The buck absolutely, positively stops with the entrepreneur.

That fact takes some getting used to for most entrepreneurs, just as it takes some time to learn how to listen to your own instincts, which can be relied on to help you choose exactly the right course. But it will likely take a long time for you to trust those gut feelings and to become comfortable with your new role and responsibilities—but do not be concerned about any of that. If this is your first adventure in the business jungle, then you will be getting lots and lots of practice at making decisions—right ones and wrong ones. If this is your second or third time around, then you have the voice of experience to rely on as well. But there will be other voices, too, trying to get your attention. No matter how keen your business instincts or how deep your insights, always remember:

WHEN YOU START HEARING OTHER VOICES . . .

1. *Listen carefully, but do not rush to follow anyone's advice.*
2. *Remember that others may lack the facts and may have different agendas than you have.*

This does not mean that you should not listen to anyone and try to do everything yourself, which is a sure foundation for disaster in the business jungle. **You are going to need help**, and lots of it. Your very lack of experience dictates that you listen to someone who has experience. Just be careful! Your lack of experience also makes it difficult for you to gauge the depth and validity of someone else's. Thoroughly investigate the claims and background of anyone whom you are thinking of hiring to help you. Weigh the relevance of their experience and advice against your own strategies and objectives, and that goes double for what consultants say.

Consultants tend to deliver safe, pat answers to your questions, often based on too-limited experience and inflated reputations. To be fair, a consultant's reputation could be based on years and years of hard work, or it could rest simply on being associated with a big and/or very successful company. Be particularly wary of such hot-shots, since they are the most suspect of all—such as the business analyst who told me how to save MetPath when we were going through a tough time. I am not sure which tough time it was, since we went through so many. Anyway, he advised us that the only way to survive was to close the bacteriology, special chemistry, hematology and tissue pathology departments because they were never going to make a lot of money. I did not even need my gut feelings for that one, just half a brain. First of all, we could not afford the loss of even a single revenue dollar. In addition, if we closed down those departments, MetPath would not be able to offer the full range of services necessary to attract physicians in the first place. They certainly were not going to divide up a patient's sample and send us only one piece!

The best advice is really to stay on top of everything, dealing with things as best and as quickly as possible. If nothing else, you will learn that no amount of planning, advice, or money could have prepared you for the startling truth that **everything will happen exactly according to plan and nothing will work out as planned**. If this paradox cannot be accepted, then there is small hope for entrepreneurial success. Don't try too hard to figure it

out if you do not understand it, because nobody can really understand it. It is simply one of those absolute truths that we cannot
understand and probably will not even believe. But that does not
change anything; it is still true, absolutely, and anyone who hopes
to survive the business jungle will come to believe, sooner or later.
Otherwise, they wind up back at their old jobs, grumbling about
working for someone else.

If you would like to avoid that fate, then it is also highly advis-
able that you stop grumbling while you are trying to start your
business and try to accept the above paradox. Now, there may be
no way of knowing what it means but there is a way that will help
you accept it. You, the entrepreneur, must **become the resident
optimist of your company**. Take your problems and grumbling
home with you, if you want, but stay positive every moment you
are behind your office desk.

Maybe you do not understand yet that **being in business
means being in the middle of some kind of a problem most of
the time and not letting it show**. Your employees are looking to
you for leadership in everything, including your attitude, so you
cannot afford to appear crushed by any event short of The End of
The World. Even then, a negative attitude is of no help whatsoever.

Look at it this way: You would make sure to pay your employees before you paid anybody else, wouldn't you? If not, then plan
on being in business only until the first time you run out of
money. Any consultant will tell you that if employees do not get
paid, they will quit. You cannot afford that, and neither can you
afford employees who are disgruntled, unhappy, or nervous. Such
employees are worse than none at all, particularly in key positions. Your business depends more than you realize on your
employees' emotional welfare, which depends to a large degree on
your own. Your vendors will know the real story already, since
they are either getting paid on time or not and your orders are
either increasing or not.

Your positive attitude will show up in your employees. The
maintenance of a positive and yet realistic attitude will also keep
your mind free from fantasies of success or failure that seduce
new entrepreneurs to their doom. Some barely into the start up
become convinced that they have somehow already reached the
destination. Others, already fatigued by the journey, are overwhelmed by the distance yet to travel. A simple reality check
would tell either the degree of their illusions. Those that think
they have covered a lot of ground during the start-up period might
take a look at their constantly declining bank account balance.
Those who feel they have not gotten off square one might take a
look at the small but steady growth in sales since they opened the

doors. The idea is to *try* and maintain emotional balance by not allowing momentary wins and losses to hide or distort your larger entrepreneurial goals.

The focus, of course, still must remain on the day-to-day tasks at hand, for there is much to do. Now is the time for action. The business plan that was written must be implemented and the product must be made or the service delivered. Now the money raised must be spent, by far the easiest task. Facilities need to be occupied; people must be employed at their individual jobs; marketing strategies need to be pursued; administrative systems have to be installed; operations have to be ongoing. These are the tasks that await the entrepreneur during the first several business-building phases, which will mean plenty of work, waiting, change, disappointment, elation, stress, anxiety, happiness, seemingly endless delays, and unexpected, extensive changes.

Then, on the *second* day after your business opens, there will be some *real* challenges to deal with!

Many new businesses—make that most, if statistics are to be believed—do not even make it through the market penetration phase. Sure, a lot do not make it because entrepreneurs in question probably did not plan well enough, raise enough money, or hire the right people. But I would bet just as many were simply not ready for the reality of the business jungle and, therefore, were unable to cope with the problems of their businesses, whatever they were. Someone once said something to the effect that life is a continuous exercise in problem-solving. Be that as it may, I can attest that problem-solving is surely what a business start-up is all about.

There will be plenty of problems, just as there are for a beaver after he has chosen a construction site for a dam. The site looks perfect, the water is deep enough, there is a good supply of timber nearby, and he has plenty of help from his brothers, sisters and cousins—even his mom and dad will help out. But once he starts building, he finds out that the site is close to a swamp that seems to be home for half the mosquitoes in the state; that half the accessible wood is rotten and he will have to travel twice as far to get what he needs; and that most of his relatives are either lazy or undependable.

Things are hardly different for the new entrepreneur. As soon as the first check is written, he realizes that although the financing is in place, there may not be enough cash to see him through the first six months, much less a year. He did not even order enough checks! The business plan that looked so great on paper all of a sudden develops some great big holes. The entrepreneur is dismayed at how many things were left out of the marketing strategy. He is amazed at all the things he never dreamed of needing that all of a sudden he cannot do without when it comes to the physical plant.

It is only during the initial phase of market penetration that business life will be so fast and furious. Later on, during systems development, things will settle down a bit, but not before the entrepreneur develops a strong sense of *deja vu*. As the business grows and matures, the problems seem as if they're on a spinning wheel that stops and starts whenever and wherever it wants. Eventually, things become manageable—until the business makes a profit and it is time to expand, and the cycle begins all over again! Things hopefully will go a little more smoothly if the entrepreneur bounced off enough walls the first time through. The situations and specifics will vary from phase to phase and from business to business, but the entrepreneurial response is always the same: **innovate constantly and replicate success**, and just let the rest fall through the cracks.

When your employees come to you with a problem—and they will—and you say, "Go left" and it turns out to be the wrong way, just change direction again as soon as possible. Don't worry about being wrong or making a mistake. One of my executives at MetPath said I got egg off my face faster than anyone else he had ever seen. If all it takes to make a profit, save a customer relationship, or keep a contract in place is to wipe a little egg off my face, I will do it every time and the sooner, the better.

The attainment of your goals will take years anyway, and it will take everything you have to make that happen, especially those intangible assets we spoke about all the way back in *Chapter 1*. *Common sense, persistence, interpersonal skills, and delusions of grandeur* will most often be the only things that can be relied on to survive the hectic start-up period of a new enterprise. Business success ultimately depends on the entrepreneur's ability to dedicate all faculties towards realizing his or her ultimate vision or destination. Since the specifics will vary according to the type of business—product or service—and hundreds of other variables, the only constants will be the personal qualities the entrepreneur brings to the table. This is particularly true in light of the **three general rules** that apply to all phases of business-building:

The first is that, even though the entrepreneur may have spent a lot of time planning and creating strategies to build the business, **there will be so little time** now that half of them will be forgotten or, if remembered, will never be implemented.

The second is that the other half of those **plans and strategies are subject to change substantially**, more likely sooner than later in the life of a business, and definitely without notice.

The third is that, while an awful lot of things are happening, **almost nothing happens unless it happens out of sequence, at the wrong time, or too late**.

And, finally, the fourth ...

I am sorry! Did I say there were only three?

Well, there is a fourth general rule, which is...

Everything takes effect simultaneously ... immediately!

Ready?

On your mark ...

* * * * *

Ingenious builders, beavers construct lodges in their woodland habitat, either on the shores of forested lakes or in streams and small rivers. In the latter instance, they first raise strong dams made of sticks, stones, and mud across fast-moving water to create pools. These dams take several months to build but may last for many years, impounding water in areas sometimes many acres across until silt fills the ponds and forms a meadow where other wildlife and livestock might graze. Canals are then dug from the pool (or lake shore) which permit the dragging or floating to the lodge of the saplings and even large trees that the beavers have felled and cut into portable lengths. The usually placid beaver works cooperatively with others of the species, spending long hours to keep the dam in excellent repair, which it seems always to require. The industrious worker often can be seen taking care of problems late at night while the rest of the forest creatures sleep.

* * * * *

1. **PHASE 1:** *Market Penetration*

Sit back, take a deep breath and... get to work!

That means get to work at everything, for during the market penetration phase of your business, the most important thing an entrepreneur can do is simply to get through it and on to Phase 2, without causing irreparable damage to the business in the process.

If the business survives, some semblance of control will then be attained during the systems development phase of business-building. Until then, **the business will manage the**

entrepreneur; the entrepreneur will not manage the business. In other words, there might not be a business tomorrow if the entrepreneur does not take care of whatever it is that the business demands be done today.

Many entrepreneurs toil under the erroneous presumption that the main thing they have to do at the outset of a start-up is to build an efficient business organization. These poor souls see themselves primarily as executives, dispensing wisdom and controlling the company from on high, while earning appropriate financial rewards. That, however, puts the cart a bit ahead of the horse. Entrepreneurs may be born and not made, but executives are made in the same way that businesses are built. Nobody gets to be an executive until they prove they can execute things properly and nobody gets rewards unless they stick around long enough to reap them. What is really going on in a start-up is that entrepreneurs simply need to survive the market penetration phase. Hopefully, they will learn enough to get organized enough to eventually make enough money to stay in business—then, maybe, they can think about organization-building.

The intention here is not to minimize the need for organization, but rather to put it in its proper place. No brand new entrepreneurial venture is blessed (or cursed) with the huge bureaucracy of a big corporate environment. If a new business needs to run an ad, it needs that ad right away, not in three months while it is passed around among committees and task forces that are all afraid of making decisions. The pressure cooker of the business jungle demands that new businesses be populated by decision-makers willing to put their necks on the line. They may make mistakes too, but **mistakes can be corrected**. If no decision is made, then there is nothing to correct. If nothing happens at all, then the time for action has passed, probably for good, and with it the opportunity to generate revenues, which is what every new business needs more than anything else.

On the other hand, if the entrepreneur is the only one making decisions, or making them in a vacuum, things will definitely start happening but they might not be doing the company any good. Once "The Boss" starts acting like an eight hundred-pound gorilla, thinking, if not actually saying things like, "There are only two ways in this company: My way, or the highway!", things usually get pretty rough. Such silent or spoken imperatives, demanding that the management of the company be done one way and one way alone, ignore the reasons why managers are hired in the first place. Staff and management people should be sought for their ability to make decisions and for other qualities that complement or fill in for those of the entrepreneur. Employees must make their own decisions and mistakes, and also be allowed the latitude to disagree with "The Boss" from time to time without getting sat on. If the business is to survive, the eight hundred-pound gorilla will have to go away.

The reality is that most entrepreneurs are too busy spending money and making decisions to be bothered with executives. There are always a lot of decisions to make but there usually will not be enough money to hire a staff of executives, which is just as well. Most executives would like to make big decisions commensurate with their big salaries, while most entrepreneurial decisions require consideration of more humble issues, such as, "Do I buy my lunch at the Golden Arches today or do I skip lunch altogether?" Most executives would never eat there anyway, nor would they skip lunch to make one hundred copies needed for a special project. That is not their job! High executive salaries mean even less money available for marketing, which might lead to a decision to reduce the executive staff, starting with whom to fire first.

A new business should spend most of its money on marketing, as the name of this phase implies. Money will be spent on many other things, of course, and the first in line will be landlords and contractors for facilities in which to operate, followed closely by vendors, those suppliers of goods and services without which the new business cannot operate. But even there, spending on those other things should be kept to an absolute minimum, which for brand new businesses means as close to zero as possible.

Saving money is a great idea in any phase of business building but close to impossible during market penetration. The most pressing need is to generate increasing revenues *month by month*, otherwise, there will be no facilities or vendors and anything else. Obviously, the only way for any business to eventually make a profit is by selling a product or service and figuring out how to successfully bring a product to market is the entrepreneur's biggest challenge. *Marketing is without a doubt the most cost-, time- and attention-consuming focus for the entrepreneur during the start-up.* Marketing strategies usually have more angles than the fun house at an amusement park. Only your financial projections will be farther off the mark than your first attempts at marketing. But as difficult and complicated as marketing strategies get, there are only three cardinal rules for successful start-up marketing:

DOCTOR BROWN'S RULES
FOR SUCCESSFUL START-UP MARKETING

1. *Do not try to sell any product or service before it is ready.*
2. *Talk to your customers and find out what they really need and want.*
3. *Do not hesitate to scrap any marketing strategy that does not work.*

I do not want to waste any of your time—since you do not have very much—so let me just give you examples of what might happen if you do not follow those rules.

Kinetix was a company with a great product and great market potential, which never was able to penetrate the market. The concept around which Kinetix was built, a hand-held device called a Pulmometer for the measurement of lung function in patients with asthma, bronchitis or emphysema, started out as a single-product idea. We bounced the idea off some researchers, and their reactions were positive, so we built one. It worked, and there seemed to be no problem with replication. The market was there—about 20 million people—and we priced it realistically at $100 per unit. That equaled a $2 billion marketplace, and this was a proprietary technology. But it was only a single-product concept. Remember, it is not easy to build a company around a single product; but with some creative analysis, we came up with another product called the Respirometer for all the joggers and others trying to get themselves into condition. Then we took that same product and added a printer so a doctor could use it in his office.

We had expanded from a single technology and were now into huge potential market numbers in three different markets—consumer, sports, and medical professionals—and a national marketing program was initiated, with a few new wrinkles. Originally, the units came with only two plastic mouthpieces, meant to be thrown away and reordered. But the thought occurred that if there were only two, no one would think they were disposable; people would merely wash them out and put them back in the carrying case. But if we put twenty in a plastic bag, people would use them, throw them away, and then buy replacements—just like the proverbial razor blade.

Everything looked perfect and orders were beginning to increase daily, so we decided to go ahead and step up production. We were certain the business would be a winner.

Well, it could have been, had we not overlooked . . . *The Woofer.*

I got involved in managing Kinetix after raising some capital so that the fledgling business could get off the ground. One day, while walking through the factory and watching production, I noticed that the product runs were very small. I was impatient and wanted to see if there was anything I could do to speed up the manufacturing process. I discovered nothing unusual until, just before turning a corner near the end of the assembly line, I heard an oddly punctuated sound:

"Ahhhhhh... *Woof!* Ahhhhh... *Woof!*"

A few more steps and I discovered the source of the sounds. There, sitting behind the machine with two boxes of products at his feet, a gentleman sat taking products off the conveyor and making those absurd noises with each one.

"Ahhhhhh... *Woof!* Ahhhhh... *Woof!*"

I had no idea who he was or what he was doing, so I watched him for awhile before I interrupted his strange ritual. Turned out that he was our product tester, nicknamed *The Woofer* because he "woofed" or blew into each apparatus to test it as it came off the assembly line. He would "woof" each machine, and if it did not register within the parameters of his predetermined lung function measurement, he would put it into the box at his feet marked "Rejects." If it did, then it passed quality control and it went into the other box which was marked "O.K."

The entire procedure had to be rejected, finally, because "woofing" was anything but O.K., for two reasons: First, the manufacturing process was so precise and the testing procedure so time-consuming that the combination of the two meant we were able to turn out only about one hundred products per week. That meant a year's production would total just a little over five thousand devices, which does not even come close to satisfying a market of twenty million people. The second problem was that if *The Woofer* came down with a cold; if he smoked too many cigarettes; if there was too much pollution outside; or if he just was having a bad day, he might "whiff" instead of "woof." No one had recognized that if *The Woofer* had a change in lung function and became *The Whiffer*, then the accuracy of the testing procedure would vary from day to day and likely from hour to hour.

Kinetix therefore became and will likely remain the only business I ever heard of that failed due to the whiff of *The Woofer*. The idea of a product intended for the mass market that cannot be produced in quantity is not worth very much—an apt extension of the Business Vision Test in *Chapter 2*. Had we thought beforehand to test the replicability of the quality control system on the production line before investing, we might have saved ourselves from a significant tax write-off. Because we did not, we broke the first rule of successful start-up marketing and tried to sell a product before it was ready. The penalty for breaking the rule was that we ran out of money before we could find a way to solve that problem and still bring the product to market.

I have not given up on that company yet (something to do with a bulldog mentality), and if I get back into it I will have the advantage of knowing what I learned the first time through. Which brings us to the second rule for successful marketing: Talk to your customers in order to learn just exactly what it is they want and need your product or service to do. Choose not to talk to them and you court disaster, as I found out with the Dermabrador (a dermatologist's skin-abrasion machine), we were making at Permark (see *Chapter 2*). We thought the prototypes were so terrific that we made a tactical decision to begin a national marketing campaign. We came out of nowhere with the product, and our competitors were caught unawares; we got a great customer response, and, as usual for entrepreneurs, thought we would make a fortune.

Then we found out that the machine developed a hot handle after about forty-five minutes of use. Worst of all, the news came not from our design department, but from a customer. No one at Permark had ever tested the machine for that long. We had no idea how long such a procedure took. We had a hot product with a hot handle that we could not deliver—which made us hot under the collar. It took us another year to fix the handle and by then interest had cooled and we lost our customer base, as well as all **The Money** we spent on our initial marketing strategy. The company survived, although it took years to recover from that setback. It could very quickly have become a much bigger and more profitable company if someone had only bothered to see how our customers actually used the machines and then tested them accordingly.

Obviously, a big part of the rules of successful start-up marketing is product design and engineering. If you bring a product to market before it is ready, then you will fail. So the engineers must have enough time to make things work properly. The problem is that engineers are *never* finished designing *anything*! "No, you can't have it yet," almost any engineer will say, no matter when you ask. "Just wait until I add one more clabber-knocker to the left side of the faffen-baffle, and then it will be perfect" ... which, of course, it never is. Therefore, the rules for successful start-up marketing have a corollary:

If you ever want to get a product to market, shoot the engineer once you are satisfied with the product. You can always make a second generation, improved product. Just make sure, before pulling the trigger, that the engineer has done the job; the results otherwise could be costly.

Which brings us to another important corollary to the rules of successful start-up marketing: **Innovation is not worth any-thing unless it is targeted precisely towards customers' real needs and wants.** If we pause for a moment—just a moment, mind you; I know how busy you are—and reflect on the old Roman saying, *Mater artium necessitas*, we might come to see the con-nection between the customer and innovation. For, if "Necessity is the Mother of Invention," then it can also be said that "Innovation is the Father of Worry" and that "Worry is the Grandfather of Successful Start-Up Marketing." We do not have the time to go through the philosophical underpinnings of these connections, so you will just have to trust me. What it all means, in less ponder-ous fashion, is: **Worry about what your customer wants and you will build a better product**.

So, worry! That's the ticket!

You need specifics? *Don't worry, you'll worry!* Market penetra-tion is a very, very stressful period, and worry will be your con-stant companion. Not only will you worry about what your cus-tomers want, but everything you think of will bring with it some worry. I believe my hair began falling out during the time that MetPath was in the market penetration phase. I may even have had an early case of ulcers when HEARx was in that same phase. But I lived through it all, and you probably will, too. You will have more than a few sleepless nights, though; quite a few, if you eat, sleep and drink the business like most entrepreneurs. Every morning during this phase at MetPath, the sample-receiving room would get a call from me at 5:00 A.M. I was so concerned with what was going on that I could not wait to find out how many urine samples or blood samples or whatever had come in the night before. No matter what the number of samples was, I would worry about them: if there were too few or the same number, I would worry about sales; if there were more than anticipated, I would worry about whether or not we would be able to process them.

What I call "worrying," others might call "paying attention," "staying informed," or "taking care of business." Whatever you call it, it is something that every entrepreneur does, and it is crucial to being successful. This is particularly true in a service-oriented business because then an entrepreneur hardly ever gets to shoot the engineer. Think about it: The success or failure of a service business depends on constant innovation, so in a very real way the entrepreneur is the engineer. An entrepreneur running a ser-vice business never leaves the drawing board and, therefore, never stops worrying.

Unlike a product business, where only a single innovation is necessary to get started, the service business must constantly be coming up with new and different ways of doing things because the competition is always catching up. This is especially true when a successful start-up represents a radical departure from traditional methods. When McDonald's pioneered the national fast-food franchise concept, for example, they had to worry about keeping the French fries warm and crispy because they knew that their customers liked them that way. Once they figured it out, however, competitors who followed later on, like Burger King or Wendy's, did not have to do very much. They merely had to send a spy or two over to McDonald's.

"How did they keep the French fries warm and crispy?"

"Oh, easy. They use an infrared bulb and put it over the French-fry tray."

After that, all the competition had to do was find out the wattage of the bulbs, where to get them, and how much they cost. If McDonald's had not been successful, no one would have bothered to imitate its innovations; but it was, and everyone did. MetPath was like that, as discussed in *Chapter 2*. There were thousands of medical testing laboratories, but MetPath was a very big laboratory, working on a national basis. No one had ever done anything like that before, so we had to come up with new things all the time. New methods of delivery, of testing—you name it, and we at least thought of some better, more cost-effective and customer-satisfying ways to do it.

All this innovation invited imitation from our competition. One of our biggest creative challenges (i.e., one of our biggest *worries*) was how to keep our people from getting hired away. With as many as 3,600 employees working throughout the company at several locations, it was no easy task, and we were never entirely successful at stopping that flow. I am not sure it mattered much anyway, since everyone eventually seemed to copy just about everything we did at MetPath no matter what we did to try and stop them. We certainly did not let it stop us from worrying about how to keep on innovating. We had to, because we were never as well-heeled financially as our competitors. We needed whatever advantage doing things first gave us, for however long it did, in order to stay competitive.

Starting up HEARx was quite different, but the need for innovation and worry was no less acute. HEARx is a multiple-unit retail system that does not depend on a central facility. Although it is a service business, it sells non-proprietary products—hearing aids—while providing the service of hearing testing. The innovation that initially made HEARx stand out to investors was our goal to create a medical business with retail overtones rather than a retail business with medical overtones. Our marketing plan expects that each hearing center will produce $2 million in annual sales. To build a big business out of that there would have to be a lot of HEARx centers, which means that the market potential would have to be pretty large, and it is: Approximately $1.2 billion is spent annually on hearing aids in the U.S. To achieve my goal of $500 million in sales will mean that HEARx will need about 250 to 300 centers nationwide.

What made it most attractive as an investment was that those figures assumed no growth in the market whatsoever and no proprietary HEARx products in the future. To realize my latest delusion of grandeur, HEARx only had to penetrate the market locally and then replicate the successful formula nationally. That was the plan and, of course, it did not go smoothly. We had to solve a number of problems and are still solving some of them at this writing. Our facility size had to be changed; we had to refigure our staffing requirements and compensation programs; our computer systems had to be revamped; we had to almost entirely redesign our marketing strategy ... and that was just the short list! Was there anything that we did not change? Probably not.

Which, neatly enough, brings us to our third rule for start-up marketing success: **Be ready to change any part of your marketing strategy at the moment you notice that it is not working**. Even more neatly, the illustration for rule number three also sheds more light on rule number two, since it concerns a marketing puzzle that could not be solved. Remember Medex? (If not, see *Chapter 2*) One of its products, the Web-Guard, never even got to market due to a failure to properly evaluate the product idea. But the company had two products and the second one did make it to market—and then the whole company failed! That second product, an exercise device for the fingers and hands of arthritics, the Hand-A-Cizer was based on the well-known fact that exercise is good for arthritic joints. It looked like a little wishbone, it had three different resistance levels, and you could carry it in your pocket. We planned to sell it in sets of three, which cost $1.65 to produce, for $19.95.

Everything seemed perfect from a product standpoint. Where did we go wrong? Well, one rule of thumb for making money on a product in the consumer market—which, for your information, is the toughest of all markets to crack—is to sell it for five times what it costs to make it, and we were trying to sell it for more than twelve times the manufacturing cost. We were a little greedy, besides not realizing then that the "five-times-cost" rule does not apply for brand new products, but only for more mature ones. The idea in the beginning is not to try to recoup the cost of developing the product and make a profit all at once (unless you have a "fad" product like a Pet Rock) but to build up to that once the product has proven itself in the marketplace.

Overpricing the Hand-A-Cizer—with the result that not very many people would buy it—was only one of the marketing gaffes that would cause the demise of Medex. The single most damaging event was during the kickoff of our marketing campaign for the Hand-A-Cizer. We chose St. Petersburg, Florida, as the initial market because of its high percentage in the general population of senior citizens. We spent most of our marketing budget, which was most of the money we had left after developing the product, on a television advertising blitz that was scheduled to saturate the area over a weekend.

We did not bother with radio or newspapers, but that was not the problem. In fact, there was not even a hint of a problem. The ads were made, and they were great ads, scheduled for perfect time slots. We had plenty of product and the money was spent; all we needed were the orders. Everybody was going to see our ads on television. All the ads ran when and where they were supposed to, and they were great... and we did not sell a single Hand-A-Cizer!

The lack of sales was not attributable to anything we had done or failed to do, but rather to something totally out of our control: The great, big hurricane that hit the west coast of Florida on the same day as our ads!

We should have quit right there, but my partner, the inventor of the Hand-A-Cizer, was still sure we had the next Pet Rock on our hands, so we kept trying. Unfortunately, we could not get it to sell like the Pet Rock did, although there were other ways the comparison was valid. The price, for example, started dropping like a stone: We lowered it to $14.95, then down to $10.95 and then finally to $7.95. We should have started low and raised our price later on, but we had gone for the quick kill. By the time we got down to an affordable price, we were the ones who got killed, as by then no one wanted the product. We had made too many mistakes already and saw too many problems we could not solve. The level of sales fell like a stone too, and seemed impossible to lift. After a few months, the drag became so heavy that the company simply dropped from sight, out of existence into that bottomless lake where all failed Pet Rock-like ventures go in the business jungle. Nothing we could do would bring it back up.

Ah, experience! How clearly one sees one's mistakes after one makes them. Getting a product ready for market is one thing; pricing it, selling it, and making a profit are quite another. Our main problem at Medex—not counting natural disaster, poor timing, and the negative Pet Rock syndrome—was one that no amount of trying would solve: We had not raised enough money. We never dreamed we would not be successful, so we raised just enough money to see us through the initial marketing campaign. Then, when our sales performance proved abysmal, we could not raise any more money from anyone, and that meant we could not afford another marketing campaign. Never forget that, early on, the interest in your business, which may be translated into more investment money, is directly related to the growth of your sales. No one expects you to be profitable anytime soon, but rising sales figures are a must.

The chances of successfully going back to the well early are normally very slim. The well may dry up completely, too, if the entrepreneur spends the initial start-up capital frivolously.

"What's frivolous," you would like to know?

Frivolous is anything that is not going to help get the business off the ground. *Frivolous* is particularly obvious when it comes to **facilities, the first place an entrepreneur usually gets a chance to spend money unwisely.** It means spending it on things like extra-plush carpet, gold-plated toilet fixtures, and a twelve-foot desk. It is better to have stark space than something that looks like the Taj Mahal. When investors see opulence, they start thinking unhappy thoughts such as, "This guy's going to be out of business in less than a year," or "She's not getting another cent until the business performs as well as her office looks."

Remember, investors are only worried about losing their money and want to see it spent wisely. The least savvy among them recognize that a new company will only survive if there is enough money to make it work. ***The Money***, therefore, should not be used to deliver "wants" in a start up—like enhancing your entrepreneurial ego or your personal working conditions. It should be conserved, as we said before, to satisfy the most pressing needs of the new business, which during market penetration will be expenditures almost entirely for the sales and marketing effort. Otherwise, it would be better spent on more office or manufacturing space with less expensive appointments.

MetPath, when it came to facilities, needed a lot of space but had very little money in 1969. After all, a medical testing laboratory that wanted to do business nationally required a lot more space than a two-room apartment in uptown Manhattan. And since no one had ever done what we intended to do, we needed the space designed in a way that no one had ever done. Only problem was, MetPath could hardly afford to rent space, much less pay for specialized construction. Business survival, however, often demands that we settle for less than what we want in order to get what we need. That truth was first driven home when we started looking at facilities at a time when there was a great gap between what we needed and what we desired.

We settled on a storefront in Teaneck, New Jersey, for our first space, which we then converted into a lab. It did not take us long to learn that a business cannot be efficient in too little space, and that moving every few months tends to traumatize the operating efficiency of a business organization. (We will expand on that more in our discussion of the next phase, since businesses during Phase 1 are barely operating, much less operating efficiently.) During market penetration, the important thing is to **arrange for enough space to get up and keep running**. MetPath did not have enough space in Teaneck, so we wound up getting additional space across the street, and within a year had to expand again and convert an old warehouse in Hackensack into an automated laboratory.

Though the Hackensack warehouse was not very pretty, a large, inexpensive, ugly facility is much better than a small, pricey and luxurious one. First of all, it was bigger than we needed at that moment, so there was **room for expansion**. A small and expensive office might have made me feel more important, but the dollar drain it created would have prevented the business from growing. It was much better to delay gratification and wait until we could afford a nice big luxurious space—which leads into the second reason why an ugly building can be attractive: **the price was right**. The price was, in fact, close to zero: $1.25 per square foot. That allowed MetPath enough money to lease the space and construct the lab—but only because the contractor who built the first lab in the storefront had taken a block of MetPath stock in payment. I simply extended that arrangement to cover a partial payment for building the second lab in the warehouse.

The point is, situations controlled management rather than the other way around. When a business requires something, entrepreneurs respond to that need the best way they can. Their decisions are based on what they are given and, lacking much in the way of capital, the choice of facilities is driven more by that lack than by any other factor. Granted, a place to do business is something that you cannot do without. But generally speaking, a new business lacks everything, so avoid focusing on what you lack and just accept that something always will be missing for a while. It is a lot easier to figure out how to make more out of less, or even the best out of what looks like the worst.

The worst, by the way, might just be vendors when it comes to the phenomena of lack. Everybody needs somebody, and entrepreneurs starting up companies of any size need vendors; unfortunately, that equation often does not work the other way around. **Vendors love money** and seem to love you when you have some. But they seldom trust you and, if you do not have a big enough bank account, they seem not to love you as much as when you did. Only the banks never even *seem* to love or trust you, even when you have money and they are holding it for you.

Banks and other moneylenders are very short on those human commodities of love and trust, as Guy Seay discovered when he went to buy a desk one day at a furniture store in Teaneck. We had just moved into our first facility and needed office furniture and, since we had put $250,000 into an account at the National Community Bank, Guy figured we could afford $165 to buy him a desk. So he went to the furniture store to get his desk and open an account. The store manager naturally asked for a bank reference, and we gave him the National Community Bank. The furniture store manager called the bank manager to verify the information, and the bank manager said that he was sorry, but that they did not give out references for new accounts. It was hardly coincidental that MetPath revised its own banking policies within moments on that very same day; i.e., we refused to do business with any bank that took our money and refused to acknowledge our existence. Guy may have lost his desk momentarily but National Community Bank lost our account forever.

That same $250,000 came into play one other time but in less unusual circumstances. Scientific Products was the major vendor of supplies to clinical laboratories, and when we called them at the beginning, they worked with us very diligently and competently. They were aware that we had raised $250,000 to start the company, so they gleefully sold us that amount of supplies. Their eyes gazed lovingly on our account when they found out we intended to be a really big laboratory doing business on a national and even an international level. But they chose to look away when the money ran out and we were running around trying to raise more. The love was gone from their gaze and they would not deal with us, refusing to advance us any credit. Scientific Products just abruptly cut off the relationship, so I likewise spurned them for a long time.

These experiences, as bad as they seemed at the time, had a good side to them, too. They taught us early on that **it is critical not to be dependent on one vendor** for love or money, or anything else. Those and other similar situations forced us to go out and develop relationships with alternate suppliers. With more than one vendor of a particular commodity or service, there was always someplace else to go for what we needed. If one supplier was out of test tubes and MetPath needed them fast, then one of the other vendors we had taken on would be happy to oblige. The same would be true with credit if I happened to run into financial problems again and needed some time to go raise some more money—which, as has already been mentioned, I did rather often.

As far as Scientific Products was concerned, however, the outcome was not very good for a long time. When they came back to me—after they saw the company had survived and was growing again—I refused to deal with them. The break in our relationship lasted ten years, after which I let them sell to us. We had grown so large by then that not to take advantage of their volume discounts would have been a case of cutting off my nose to spite my face. It was then my choice about whom to deal with, once I had gained some management control over the business.

But even though they got back in the door, standing outside had cost them a bundle. The year before we let them back in, MetPath's revenues were about $80 million; the cost for supplies, assuming an average annual rate of 15 percent of revenues, was approximately $12 million. So, Scientific Products lost out on potential business of something close to $1 million a month, just in that one year. The same thing happened when HEARx started up. One of our early suppliers (Starkey) cut us off and now no longer shares in the $8 million we spend each year in purchasing hearing aids. All of which just goes to prove what playwright William Congrieve said back in 1697 about hell having no fury like an entrepreneur scorned—or something like that!

I was not, by the way, particularly interested in being vindictive with either the bank or the product suppliers. It just did not make good business sense to deal with someone who had run out on me when I needed them most. I have always tried to manage any company in conformance with what I believed were the best interests of the company at any given time. If I was unable to find alternative suppliers, I probably would have had to deal with them, since without them I could not stay in business. But working with someone who only wanted to do business on their own terms could hardly be in the best interests of my company and I would have gone with someone else as soon as I had the chance.

It would not surprise me if the market penetration phase reminds you of the boy who stops the leak in the dike with his finger—until another leak pops up, then another and then another! The reality of it is, however, much worse than that. I often felt that even if everyone used all ten fingers and toes simultaneously to plug the leaks, and anyone else's who happened to be nearby, that still would not have been enough.

But was I worried?

I should say so! And if I were you I would worry, too. Then maybe you will survive. Perhaps years later, the market penetration phase will end and most of the leaks will get repaired. You will begin gaining some semblance of control over your business, and eventually the day will come when you will be able to say to your vice president, "All we have to do is plug that last leak. Then we'll be ready...."

"Mr. President," he'll interrupt. "I hate to say this, but where's all that water coming from?"

"What water ...?"

Oh, well! Here we go again!

Ready?

On your mark!

Get set . . .

* * * * *

The next phase of a beaver's dam-building project involves the construction of a dome-shaped lodge, often with a six-foot-high interior. The lodge, situated on an island surrounded by water, is made of sticks plastered with mud. When the mud freezes in winter the lodge, with all its entrances below the icy surface of the water, is impenetrable from predatory attacks. This construction feature fits the beaver's instinct to seek safety in the water when alarmed, for even in frigid temperatures a beaver can dive and swim with ease. Nose and ears provided with watertight valves, the beaver alone can gain access to its lodge—entering the water through holes in the ice or tunnels burrowed into the water from along the shorelines.

* * * * *

2. Systems Development

The time has come.

It may indeed take years, as it did at MetPath, where it took us until the fifth and sixth years of operation to enter the systems development phase. Sales had grown to about $4.5 million in 1973, when we began to get a handle on how to actually run the business. We had not done too badly up until then, but we began to realize that the business had been running us.

Once we began to take control, however, things got better—in fact, very much better. By 1975, we had grown to $8.5 million and made a profit for the first time. As we gained more control and were able to fine-tune the systems that we put in to help us run the business, things got even better. The company expanded nearly fourteen-fold over the next five years, and MetPath had

$110 million in sales by 1981. HEARx, after ten years, is still wait-ing to make a profit for the year, despite sales approaching $25 million. If you study HEARx, you will find out why: We did not follow the rule. We expanded before we made a profit, even a *paper profit*, a phenomenon we address later on.

Whatever the size or type of business, **a period of systems development is the key to growth**. This is when management becomes proactive rather than reactive, when creating or fine-tun-ing systems becomes a priority in all areas of the business.

Up until then, there simply was no time. It is not that the entre-preneur did not know that they needed doing or did not want to do them. It is just that getting the systems organized that allow a business to function *smoothly* are only important after you get the business to function.

The lack of well-defined administrative and management sys-tems is not unusual in start-up businesses. Even financial sys-tems, which one would expect would be among the most well-organized fall far short of anything approaching perfection. Personnel systems—including records of payroll, time worked, vacation time taken, employment applications, personnel inter-views, work histories, dismissal slips—are likely the least orga-nized. Yet every business needs records and the systems that keep them, not the least because of the increasing governmental scruti-ny for reasons ranging from taxation to environmental issues. But the priorities during market penetration do not include any allowance for the design and maintenance of such systems. It is not that entrepreneurs do not want to get those things done or that they do not know that they need to get them done. There is just never enough time during market penetration to take care of any of those things. It is simply a matter of choice: Sales and mar-keting matters always get attended to first.

"Guy," I might have asked once during the first few years of MetPath's existence, "do you want to develop the personnel record-keeping system this afternoon?"

"Well, Paul," he might have answered, "since payroll's due today and we don't have any money in the bank, I think I'd better work on something that will continue to afford us the luxury of having employees."

But when systems-development time comes, all of a sudden there will be some time for entrepreneurs to pay some attention to all those other things that fell through the crack for all those years. You know the time has come when the sales and marketing effort is probably somewhat stable and producing some halfway decent revenues; when the major bugs are out of the plant and equipment; when production is at least keeping pace with sales;

and when none of your vendors and few of your employees are threatening to leave. Then comes the chance to expand, repair, increase, or improve all the things in the business that need attention.

What you will do will be governed by what you know and if you want your business to move on to the next business-building phase, you had better know a lot. Entrepreneurs must know their businesses better than anyone else. Now, that does not mean that you are going to become the world's foremost authority on marketing men's clothing, manufacturing home pregnancy test kits or whatever. That would be wonderful if you could, but that is not what we are talking about here. What it means is that you should already be well on your way to **becoming the world's foremost authority on how your own company does whatever it is your company does**.

You must know the workings of your business better than anyone who works for you, because you must. That does not make your business some kind of giant do-it-yourself project, by any means. But it does mean that you will be glad that you had to participate at least once in everything that went on in your company during market penetration, or however long it took you to learn how to do it or what it involved. I have seen too many entrepreneurs try to set up businesses by delegating everything without understanding how anything works, then wind up wondering how they got bamboozled and lost control of their companies.

Understand that this generally has nothing to do with trusting the ability or honesty of the people who work for you. I implicitly trusted Guy Seay with everything, but he still could make mistakes. And if I did not know enough to be able to recognize and point them out to him, who would? While I was still in the Navy and starting up MetPath, Guy called me at the naval base in New Hampshire with the revenue total for the month of November, 1969.

"$62,000," he said.

"That's not possible," I said immediately.

"What do you mean, that's not possible? I've checked and double-checked the figures," Guy replied adamantly. "We had $62,000 in sales last month."

"Guy, listen. Am I incorrect in saying that we did tests on a little more than ten thousand specimens last month?"

"No, you're correct. That's exactly how many tests we did: 10,163 specimens."

"Then we didn't do $62,000 worth of business, we did over $100,000 in business. There's a mistake somewhere, someone missed something. Go back and find out what the problem is."

Disgruntled, Guy agreed to go back over the figures. He called me later that day to tell me that he was absolutely sure the

$62,000 figure he had given me earlier was correct. Patiently, I further explained my reasoning.

"Guy, we've been in business now since April, and we're talking about November sales. That's eight months. During that time our average revenue per specimen has been $10.02. What you're telling me is that our average revenue all of a sudden has dropped nearly four dollars to $6.20, and I'm telling you that's not possible! Something's wrong, so go back and check it again."

Guy went back and called me from New Jersey the next day, once more swearing up and down that he was correct. By now, I was a little more than upset. Something like $40,000 was unaccounted for in my brand new business in New Jersey, and I was sitting in New Hampshire in midwinter, unable to go find the error and solve the problem myself. To make a long and rather uncomfortable conversation short, I told Guy in no uncertain terms to go back again and find out what was wrong, and not to call me again until he had. That afternoon, a very sheepish voice spoke to me over the phone.

"You were right," Guy admitted. "Revenues actually were $102,000 in November."

What had happened was that a couple of boxes of keypunch cards never got to the billing department and instead had been sitting in the trunk of someone's car for several days. Our lab was in Teaneck at that time but our computer processing was being done in Hackensack. This was before the days of on-line systems; our lab medical reports were produced daily but billing was done separately, in batches at the end of each month. I figured that some of the cards might have been lost or misplaced. How did I know? Because I had delivered the cards myself more than once and it had occurred to me that could happen. I just did not expect that it would.

It would be a few more years before we could straighten out our financial systems, not to mention our entire computer situation (for more on that, see *Chapter 6*). But the problems and potential shortfalls were obvious to me right from the beginning because I took the time to learn and understand them during the market penetration phase. I also knew how long it took to label specimens too, because I worked at that for many hours. Trained as a pathologist, I started out by necessity doing much of the testing in certain areas myself. I also knew things like how long it took for a driver to make runs to Manhattan from New Jersey, thanks to my wife: Cynthia was the company's first driver. These activities made the difference between cost-effective operations and wasting money during market penetration, and the future of the business eventually rode on the insights gained from them.

Eventually, I had to delegate responsibility for such things when the company had become too big for me to do otherwise. As time went on, some things simply demanded more of my attention; plus, I discovered I was more interested in and/or was better at doing some things than I was at others. So I tended to focus on fundraising, marketing, and deal-making, while delegating most of the other areas—but not until I learned those others well enough so that I could not be hoodwinked or miss any serious mistakes.

Knowing all about your business—aside from saving you embarrassment if anyone asks a question and you do not know the answer—is the only way you can make it better during systems development. At MetPath, we were up against huge, well-heeled competitors who had come into the business after us, like Bristol-Myers and Hoffman-LaRoche. We were doing nicely, but we had to do something with our production systems to consolidate our gains and keep competitive. So we decided to push one-day turnaround of laboratory test reports to our customers, something no one else had ever done, and it enhanced our business tremendously. How it happened was that we knew our limitations and our strengths. We had a computerized system, but so did they, and a bigger and better one at that. If we were going to compete, all we could do was to work faster, smarter and make the most of our limited resources.

The way we began was by adding a second shift. Now, most employees do not want to work nights, even the committed, hard-working types that I generally managed to hire. But after calling everyone in and explaining that our growth, their company (remember, they all owned or could own stock), their jobs and our mutual future depended on it, all but three of the three dozen people required for the night shift agreed. But once we had a second shift, things did not automatically run by themselves; the work was hard and demanding, and we needed to help sustain the employees' commitment to the double-shift arrangement. Before long I had at least one top management executive on duty every night and developed an executive rotation schedule so that they would have to be there only once or twice a month. I was included in the rotation, since **it is very poor management to expect people to do things that you will not do yourself**.

The effect on morale was tremendous and without it we would not have succeeded. It was tangible proof to the employees that we were indeed all in this thing together. There were other benefits, too: getting all management personnel involved in the business at a very basic level, smoother operations, and always having someone in the plant who could make big decisions. We had to fine-tune the system, of course, as we went along. One of the interesting things we found out was that if we stayed on the night shift until 1:00 A.M., or showed up for the day shift at 6:00 A.M., the effect on employee morale was negligible, hardly worth the effort. But if we stayed until 2:00 A.M., or showed up at 4:00 A.M., the effect was positive and noticeable.

It was as if there was an unwritten code among the employees that said: "*Anyone* can come in a little early or stay a little late. You have to do better than that to get credit from us." I remembered all those things later on when we had multiple locations and started up a European operation. We had several shifts and by then had empowered shift supervisors to oversee the work. I had to go to Europe quite often, so I changed my time zones by coming in and working during the night shift for an entire week before I left for London or wherever else I was heading. Since 7 A.M. there was 2 A.M. here, I would show up at odd hours of the morning. The fact that the CEO was in the building at 3 A.M. generated a certain amount of excitement, which was heightened by the understanding that business was expanding and Dr. Brown had to go to Europe again.

This is the stuff that successful systems developments are made of. As the company grows and the entrepreneur begins to gain control of the business, many things just start falling into place. They don't always, however, and it is good to remember that some of the most valuable lessons are learned when things do not work out. Mistakes are a natural part of doing business, and are the best teachers—the potential ship-sinkers being the most instructive. This is not to advise a foolhardy attitude, however, since only a few bad management decisions in a row can inflict serious damage. If you pay the price for the mistakes you do make and you are still around, then do not forget the cost. That should help you avoid getting into a persistent spiral of bad decisions.

The most difficult mistakes to make (and possibly the more instructive) are the ones where you are sure that you have the knowledge. One such mistake I made at MetPath was so outstanding that it was named "Brown's Folly" by my managers. I went ahead and spent $25,000 on a piece of laboratory equipment that would do a certain type of blood testing that I was sure would become a major part of our business. But I was wrong; the market never developed. The machine, instead of making us a lot of money, got covered with a canvas tarpaulin after about nine months. It sat there in the middle of the lab collecting nothing but dust for three more years, a constant reminder of my fallibility. Finally, we gave up and it was sold for the grand sum of $1,000.

What that should tell you is that **managing a business most closely resembles trying to hit a moving target that is**

constantly changing shape, speed, and direction. That is why it is so important to never stop learning, and to start as soon as possible. Entrepreneurs must begin even in the planning stage, realizing that their instruction will continue until after the business is sold and they become consultants to their own companies (see *Chapter 9*). Just like a child learns more in the first ten years of life than at any other time, entrepreneurs learn the most during the start-up period, when the instruction is most necessary. That knowledge will not begin to be effectively applied, however, until the crucial systems development phase. Once you learn the ropes and begin to manage the business, things will start to get settled in your business.

There are some things, it must be noted, that will not get settled no matter what you do, for whatever reasons. With MetPath, it was in facilities, because the company was just growing so fast. Right from the start—even when I thought I had gotten more than enough space as was mentioned earlier—we would no sooner settle down and we would have to move. During the thirteen years I owned the company, right up until the last year when we decided to build a second national laboratory in Chicago in 1981, we moved our original lab facility and administrative offices ten times—the last move not actually completed until 1982, a year after we had sold the company!

These constant moves created a number of problems. Not only did operating efficiency fall drastically every time we moved a department, but **it is very difficult to manage multiple locations**. One of the biggest management problems was overcoming the "us versus them" mentality that grew with each move. Upstairs versus downstairs, original site versus cross-town, headquarters versus satellite building, this town versus that town—everyone was worried about the goings-on at wherever they were not. They were afraid they would miss out on something, lose some privilege they had or not get something they wanted because they were not where the action was—which they translated as wherever top management's attention was focused at any one time.

Employee systems were another particularly troublesome area. After a few years in business, several employees came to us and asked if they could get paid for the vacations they had not taken since they had been with us instead of taking the time off. They all were more or less talking about three months' worth of time. Gratified that they had obviously taken my "put the company first" speech to heart, I was not so gratified later on when I found out that we had no records to verify their claims. Our personnel records showed how much we had paid them overall, but there was no indication of whether or not they had taken a vacation. So we had no choice but to believe whatever they told us and make good on the vacation pay, and in at least one case that cost as much as $9,600. Overall, tens of thousands of dollars went out the door, just like that.

Later on, there was the time in MetPath's San Francisco office that we got sued by a black person and a white person, each claiming race discrimination over the same job. The white person said we had favored the black person, and vice versa. Then there was the time in Philadelphia that we were sued by a driver who said he had been dismissed for reading a religious magazine. Now, had we been acting like a real business from the beginning and had things like employee application forms; job performance records; salary histories; a track of all job-related interviews and actions with employees; a sick roll; records of all vacation pay schedules and rules; non-compete agreements; and other necessary personnel files, things like that would not have created the problems they did.

The reasons why we had these problems were not because I was just a medical doctor who never went to business school, but because we were only capable of putting in very rudimentary employee, financial and other administrative systems during the market penetration phase. This is simply because most start-up companies are concentrating on sales, sales, sales—not systems. Most entrepreneurs simply cannot afford to think of such things until after a business is on its feet. There might be computerized systems available, but the computer hardware and software to run them—not to mention the expertise and time necessary for installation, training and maintenance—is beyond reach at the outset for most businesses. Only large, well-established companies can transport their personnel systems wherever they go. Entrepreneurs, who as a rule are almost entirely market-driven, do not have that luxury.

The luxury of well-designed **financial systems** becomes a necessity, however, during systems development. As the business grows they become more valuable, since all of a sudden there is something to lose, where before there was nothing. The cracks in the foundation that were unavoidable and acceptable during market penetration can no longer be ignored. The lifeblood of the business, in many ways, could leak out without effective systems. MetPath had one employee who worked a couple of years in the chemistry department, for example. He left for two and one-half years, then reapplied for his job—bringing with him all the weekly paychecks we had been sending him while he had been gone for about forty-two months! I tried to hire loyal, reliable and hardworking people. Arnold was one, so he had never cashed them. That was amazing enough; but what was really amazing to me was that no one at MetPath had found the mistake in all that time.

We reviewed and improved that system pronto, I can tell you! Had we been able to take a good look at the system earlier, we might have figured out the problem before the company had been in business for five years. But it was more likely that systems analysis would not have happened until there was a problem such as that to force a look, as it did in so many areas. When the telephone bill was very high for four straight months, for instance, we looked into it to see if someone was making unauthorized calls or if it was time for us to put in a WATS line, or something like that.

And that is how it goes. Not only are entrepreneurs market-driven, they remain problem-solvers for a very long time. Part of the reason is that entrepreneurs want to believe that all the bases are covered, the same way that they want to believe that everything will go according to plan. The other big reason is that the business jungle is full of problems. The only way to minimize the effects of those problems is to **start reviewing all systems on a regular basis as soon as sufficient time and resources are available**.

That means *all* systems, since even good systems can develop holes in them. I will never forget our check-writing machine at MetPath which used a signature plate rather than requiring individually signed checks. We kept the machine in a locked room: What could be better? Then one day I noticed the door to the room standing open and the signature plate in place on the machine. All anyone had to do was type in a name and date, run off a check for any amount, and head for the border!

Needless to say, we fixed that problem pretty quick, too. But these are only the more memorable among the multitude of day-in, day-out management decisions that had to be faced during the early stages of business-building. All of this not only builds a business, it also builds a lot of pressure. It is there right from the beginning but often is not noticed until later on. The market penetration phase has a built-in pressure-relieving mechanism known as ignorance, and ignorance is bliss. Managing by default, merely putting out fires and plugging leaks, is wonderfully ego-enhancing if the entrepreneur survives. Once things slow down to a mild roar and the management of the business becomes steady and more designed, the pressure to perform becomes more noticeable and the entrepreneur, believe it or not, may miss all the excitement! To draw an imperfect but instructive comparison between business and medicine, it is one thing to work in an emergency room and quite another to work in a long-term chronic-care ward—especially if you love to be where the action is.

On the other hand, the shock of the market penetration phase may have been so unexpected that some may want to stop once things begin to quiet down. The heavy and constant pressure of running a business may first be felt during the systems development phase, creating a seductive sense of emotional security that can fade even the most vibrant of grand delusions. Once there is a comfortable level of business and the company's finally making a little profit, there is a strong pull on some entrepreneurs to just keep things running smoothly and stay right where they are. Oh, they might want to improve their profit margin a little more and will look for leaks at all times, but the desire that initially drove them on may not burn so brightly when they start to gain some control over things.

Entrepreneurs need to remain flexible if they expect to survive the business jungle. Few entrepreneurs will stay the course unless they learn to go with the flow, and the systems development phase requires such flexibility. Business is full of situations where the entrepreneur much change: change gears, direction, suppliers, location, banks, managers, and who knows what else.

Success very often comes down to the ability of the entrepreneur to manage all that change, and the systems development phase of the start-up is the first mark of his or her ability to do just that.

Ready?

On your mark!

Get set ...

Grow!

*　　*　　*　　*　　*

Once the lodge is complete, beavers set up housekeeping and start looking to the future. Breeding takes place in midwinter, resulting in two to eight, but most often four young, born approximately four months later. Living in colonies of perhaps several family groups to a lodge, beaver families usually consist of a mated pair and two sets of offspring. They subsist on tender bark, cambium, and buds—mainly of aspens, willows, and alders—but also consume a great variety of vegetation types. Branches, twigs, and small logs are cached for winter food, anchored in the bottom mud in deep water.

*　　*　　*　　*　　*

3. *Initial Profitmaking/Expansion*

If an entrepreneur gets through market penetration and some-how manages to survive systems development, somewhere along the way an unusual phenomenon will take place.

One day, the bookkeeper will begin using black ink instead of red on the monthly P and L sheet. When the quarterly results come out, the same thing happens: A profit! Somehow the losses have stopped and the company actually made some money, at least on paper.

If this situation continues, entrepreneurs face a very basic choice: Do they stop where they are and take a long and well-earned vacation, then come back and maybe increase their salaries a little? Or are they willing to put the profits back into the business and put off the rewards until later on? I do not know about you, but there is no vacation long enough that I would con-sider to be reward enough at such a time. But that's me. Perhaps the prospect of continuing to grow does not impress you, that it seems better to just maintain the business at what seems a com-fortable level.

Now, I think that is just fine, if that is what you want to do. I guess you won't mind having to replace all the key people in your organization who helped the business grow as well as it has. The good ones, sooner or later (maybe even while you're on vacation), will probably want to go where there is a greater opportunity for growth and bigger salaries. You will probably have to settle for less-talented, less-aggressive people, but ... that is up to you. I know that no one who helped MetPath eventually become a giant corporation or who expect to help HEARx reach its $500 million goal would have agreed to work for me in the first place if my delu-sions of grandeur for the future had not existed. In fact, when I hired them I deliberately did not paint them a picture of content-ment. They thrived on excitement, as I do, but then ... maybe you are not like that.

I guess, too, that you will not mind having to explain to your investors why you have decided to lie in the sun and start taking money out of the company. You will not be able to satisfy them if you plan to tread water and they know that but ... hey! That is entirely up to you! I guess you don't mind having to deal with them. It will not be easy and you might even have a fight on your hands for control of the company, but listen! You just do whatev-er you think is right!

Most entrepreneurs want more. They're not particularly inter-ested in playing it safe. The only kind of safety with any kind of appeal to them is safety in numbers, particularly numbers fol-

lowed by multiple zeros and preceded by dollar signs. An entrepreneur sees this not as a time for profit-taking but as a chance
to realize even better profit-making down the road. This is no time
to take a vacation! If you put off gratifying yourself even for just a
little while, the rewards could be much greater. Expansion, as far
as I'm concerned, is the natural result of a successful start-up.
Entrepreneurs want to grow things, to make them bigger, better,
higher, wider, stronger and prettier. They may want to do it for the
sake of money, or achievement, or power, or whatever. The point
is that to an entrepreneur, the only point of a start-up is to get the
business to the point where it can really soar.

I'm glad you agree! Now, if you're ready, let's finish expanding
the themes already advanced in this chapter. First, we talked
about pure survival in the market penetration phase, with an eye
to building sales. The question then was:

"How *can* we ever survive?"

Next, everything came under close scrutiny during the systems
development phase, with the vision of gaining control. Since the
dollars, systems, people, facilities, marketing plan, equipment,
and everything else that we put in place to start up the company
were so poorly utilized, the question had changed slightly. Then
we asked:

"How *will* we ever survive?"

When initial expansion is in order, the key focus will shift away
from survival. Entrepreneurs will no longer be worried about
doing better with what they have once they realize that they could
do a lot better if they simply had more of everything. Their primary concern, now that the business has gotten off to a good start,
is whether or not the elements of the business will be adequate to
support expansion. The question, therefore, now becomes:

"Where can I get some more money?"

Now, haven't you heard something like that before?

More accurately, the question is: **"Are there enough dollars to
provide an adequate supply of quality systems, supplies, people, facilities, marketing support, equipment and everything
else needed for expansion?"** Expansion, not survival, is now the
focus. What it really comes down to is raising money once again,
but this time to provide the wherewithal for the business to grow.
There are two absolutes in this final start-up phase. They are:

THE SINGLE MOST IMPORTANT RULE OF EXPANSION

There are only two sources of capital.

These are **internally generated capital** or **profit**, and our old friend **externally generated capital** or ***The Money***. The other absolute is equally as important:

THE SECOND SINGLE MOST IMPORTANT RULE OF EXPANSION

Paper profits cannot buy anything.

Expansion could actually be called "starting all over again" because that is really what happens—more of the same that went on in the start-up, just "getting ready" on a bigger and better scale. There is even more money to raise; better planning to do; more people to hire; better systems to install; larger offices and production facilities to arrange; more locations over a wider geographic area to establish; better service levels to develop—constant growth and improvement in all areas. Certainly, there is more to learn, too, but all a variation on the same theme as the start-up: *Get ready, because here it comes!*

Successfully starting up a business in the treacherous waters of the business jungle, in the final analysis, is great training. The entrepreneur by now should be ready for anything. Surviving a start-up is great for one's self-esteem and it has the additional advantage of teaching the entrepreneur all the basic skills needed for success. Eventually, a start-up may get so much bigger and better that it could be considered as the biggest and best. But do not start counting on that just yet. It will take a while longer for your new business to get to that point. Until then, just keep getting ready and raising more money, all the while listening for opportunity's knock.

You know, I think I hear someone knocking right now. Could it be opportunity? I'll just go and answer the door ... Hello! Who are you?

"Hi! My name is Murphy."

Uh-oh... are you ready?

If not, get set.

It's time to get going!

$ECRET$ OF THE BEAVER

Never begin marketing
until sure that you can "deliver."

—————

An entrepreneur does not manage
a start-up business—
the entrepreneur is managed by the business.

—————

If you want to be "The Boss"
then you must know as much
about "The Business" as your employees.

Surviving the Tight Squeeze

Chapter Six
The Snake: Surviving the Tight Squeeze

▲ ▲ ▲ ▲ ▲

Snakes (order Serpentes) are elongated reptiles and among the most unusual of all animals. They are as a group best described by what they lack rather than what they have, starting with the fact that they have no limbs. Snakes also are without external eyelids or ears, and do not possess vocal chords. Moreover, though there are more than two thousand different species of snakes throughout the world, they generally lack a friendly environment wherever they are found, which is often in the most desolate and inaccessible places. Many face extinction daily in arid deserts, dense jungles and the deepest oceans. Even those fortunate enough to inhabit more temperate climes are almost universally feared by mankind, often loathed, and as quickly killed as seen. Yet they survive this antagonism from what seems all the rest of creation, despite their lack of ears and eyelids, limbs, and larynxes. The miraculous thing is that they survive rather well: along with their cousins the lizards, snakes form one of the planet's dominant groups of reptiles.

*   *   *   *   *

The problem started with a phone call.

"This is Dr. O'Brien."

"Ah, yes," said the voice on the other end of the phone, rather distractedly. "Is this Dr. O'Brien?"

"Right," Joe said, almost sarcastically. Dr. Joseph O'Brien, the head of MetPath's laboratory, was not by nature a sarcastic man. But it had been an especially long and trying day and he was in no mood for unnecessary conversations. Still, this was a client, so he quickly added, "How can I help you?

"Well, Dr. O'Brien, I'm from the 'Boston Teaching Hospital'. How are you this afternoon?"

"I'm fine, thank you." Joe recognized that the call was from a brand new client. He did not even need to know the name; he could tell automatically from the speaker's very uncertain manner. The new ones always sounded like that and usually asked a lot of questions. Most doctors had no idea what pathologists did in clinical laboratories or did not care, and it was more than likely this one was no different. Joe sighed resignedly, politely asking, "What can we do for you?" He was prepared to answer questions but it had been a *very* long day; he hoped there would not be a problem.

"Well, we have a bit of a problem."

"Right," Joe said, sighing almost inaudibly. Why did *he* always have to be the one to get these calls? "What's the problem?"

"Well," the doctor began with obvious displeasure, "we have got this twenty-four-hour stool sample that we want to send down to find out how much fat is in it. How do you want us to handle it?"

Several suggestions jumped immediately into Joe's mind but he suppressed them. He just knew that he was in no mood to take a bunch of stool from anybody, especially twenty-four-hours' worth sitting in a pail. Besides not needing that much for the test, MetPath was not set up to handle any sample that large. Still, he breathed a smile of relief; he simply had to explain that everything the doctor had to do was all spelled out very clearly in our literature outlining our procedures, which every client received when they signed up.

"Literature. . . procedures?" came the uncertain reply.

Now, Joe is normally a very kind and straightforward man; but, as I said, it had been an *extremely* long and trying day. He could just see the doctor, sitting at a desk with the stool sample in front of him, with no idea of what to do with it. Joe knew that all the doctor wanted was to just get it out of the office and on its way.

Not even Joe knows for sure what got into him, but he could not resist having a little fun with the Boston Teaching Hospital, new client or not.

"You don't have a copy of our procedures for shipping samples?"

"No, I'm afraid I don't. I'm sorry."

"Oh, no need to apologize," Joe said, smiling broadly. "I'll just tell you what to do. Why don't you write this down?"

"Fine," said the voice at the other end, after a pause. "Go ahead!"

"What you do, Doctor," Joe explained in as matter-of-fact a manner as he could muster, "is weigh the whole sample."

"Weigh it, right," repeated the doctor. "No problem."

"Right," Joe agreed, grinning to himself. "Then mix it well."

"M-m-ix it?" The voice on the other end quavered just the

slightest bit.

"Rrrriiight!" Joe knew he almost sounded like a game-show host, but he could not help himself. "Then you have to measure out ten grams of it..."

"M-m-easure it?"

"...right," Joe went on quickly, "and then put it in a small container and call for our courier to come pick it up." He gave the doctor the phone number without missing a beat. "Then just send that off to us, along with how much it weighs. That's all you have to do, and we'll be able to calculate exactly what the fat percentage is. We can have the answer back to you in a day or two, all right? Just send that up here right away," Joe continued cheerfully, "and we'll take care of it for you as quickly as we can.

"Thank you for calling," Joe added, "and have a nice day!" He hung up the phone without giving the caller a chance to ask any more questions.

Joe later admitted that a slight smirk remained on his face all the way home that day, thinking about the horrible assignment he had just arranged for somebody. Joe could just see the doctor, sitting with the now silent phone receiver in his hand and staring dumbfounded at the sample, saying to himself, "Weigh it? Mix it well? Measure out ten grams? He's got to be kidding! No way!" It was more than likely the doctor would pass on the dirty work to someone else, a thought which spoiled Joe's fun just a little bit. But he consoled himself with the further thought that now at least one doctor at the "Boston Teaching Hospital" would have a greater respect for clinical pathologists.

The fact was that the doctor was so affected by Joe's hasty instructions that he did not pass the job on to anyone at all—he just decided to put the twenty-four-hour stool sample in a brand new, tightly sealed paint can, and shipped the whole mess to MetPath! Our courier made his rounds and picked up the paint can, putting it with the many other samples collected in the Boston area that day. Then the entire collection was brought to Logan Airport in Boston, put on an Eastern Airlines plane and flown to Newark Airport, where another courier would pick up the shipment and bring it to the lab.

Now, what do *you* think happened?

As fate would have it, the paint can, with no special instructions on its label, wound up in the unpressurized baggage compartment of the airplane with all the other samples. And before too long ...

KA-KA ... KA-BOOM!!!

The volatile gases produced by the stool sample, assisted by the lowered air pressure in the baggage compartment, resulted in an explosion. When the plane landed, I am sure no one could figure out where that terrible odor was coming from; and you can bet that when the ground crew opened up the baggage compartment, no one wanted to go in and get anything out either. Needless to say, we were not very popular with Eastern Airlines for awhile, but we eventually got back into their good graces. And, of course, we quickly changed the packaging instructions in our marketing materials and the language in our contracts!

But why did the paint can have to explode when it did? Why did it happen when no one could have done anything to prevent it? Those fumes were certainly volatile enough to blow the lid off the can at any time—before we picked it up; or while it was being jostled in our courier's truck in Boston or in Newark; or at the airport before or after it was on the plane; or when it got to us at MetPath. Things at least would not have been so bad at those times, but as it was, we were powerless. Despite everyone's precautions, *the worst possible thing that could have happened, did happen, at absolutely the worst possible time for it to happen.*

The more astute readers among you will recognize that last statement as **Murphy's Law**, the bane of businessmen the world over. True, the story just presented to illustrate the workings of that law was about as unusual an incident as you could imagine, one that would not happen to very many businesses. But lest you think it was an isolated case, let me assure you that **Murphy's Law operates at all times**, in all kinds of situations, in as many ways as there are businesses, entrepreneurs and things.

Mr. Murphy can cause all kinds of problems and any one of them could sink your business. He will get key employees to quit at exactly the wrong time and he will create labor problems. While he has convinced one supplier not to deliver your components, he will have another deliver someone else's parts to your loading dock—a fact that you will not discover until the parts are on the assembly line. He will have your customers calling and placing orders that you cannot deliver. He will create production problems, administrative problems, management problems, restroom problems ... and on and on! All of your neatly conceived plans will appear to be in shambles, money will be disappearing from your bank account, and an amazing number of the other resources so painstakingly amassed to help build your business will have run out or turned out to be faulty, too late or the wrong size.

The things that happen as a result of *Murphy's Law*, in short, can threaten the very life and future of your business.

Do you require further proof?

Then please consider the following true story:

Guy Seay and I just happened to be upstairs in MetPath's

laboratory at our Teaneck, New Jersey, location when the supervisor of our couriers burst in on us.

"Dr. Brown!" Gene nearly shrieked. "Come quick! It's raining in the chemistry department!"

I looked at him as if he were slightly crazy! The likelihood of such an event was way outside the law of probability, and even the law of possibility, as far as I was concerned. We were certain that Gene—a very resourceful and organized man who kept our growing number of specimens and test results flowing smoothly to and from our clients—was playing some kind of a joke on us with his supposedly dire pronouncement.

Dire indeed it would be, if it were true! The company at that time still was struggling to establish itself. Metpath was little more than two years old and really much younger than that as a full-fledged company. The eight thousand-square-foot space we were occupying in Teaneck was our first address after we raised enough money to move out of the apartment in uptown Manhattan where we began. We had been in residence at Teaneck only a few months and it was a struggle to stay there from the beginning. If a disaster of any magnitude were to hit us, we were sure to be goners.

The last place we expected any trouble was from the building, originally intended to house three or four retail occupants. We had combined it all into one space and had just finished renovating it to house our fledgling laboratory. We were worried about the rest of the business, but not the facility. It was all we could do to market our laboratory testing service and keep increasing our revenues, just so we could pay our employees, keep current with our vendors, and meet the monthly rent. Merely getting used to being a company was about all the pressure we could bear just then, so we were more than a little sensitive about anything that threatened our survival—even jokes, no matter how funny.

Given those circumstances, our first reaction was that if what Gene said was true, then we were in for even more trouble than we had already and that was no laughing matter. His words brought a parade of misfortunes marching before our eyes: We would lose all kinds of time in processing the work we had, our reputation would suffer, we might have to move, we could lose customers—it would be, in short, a disaster of the highest magnitude. Not only didn't we believe Gene, we did not *want* to believe him because we could not *afford* to believe him.

What shored up this disbelief was that the facts were on our side. Now, it is true that executives are sometimes guilty of not knowing enough to come in out of the rain, but they generally can tell whether or not it is raining. One look out the window and even we could see that there was not a cloud to be seen that day.

Chapter Six: The Snake

▲ ▲ ▲ ▲ ▲

"Now, Gene," Guy began with a strained laugh, pointing up at the slice of blue sky that came with the window. "Who do you think you're trying to kid? Just look at that sky!"

"No, really," Gene replied, not bothering to look out the window. Instead he reaffirmed his pronouncement, now waving his arms up and down. "There's water all over the place down there! Maybe there's a leak in the roof."

Guy and I exchanged glances, both thinking that perhaps Gene had missed his calling, given his obvious talent as an actor. Despite his excellent performance and highly agitated state, we remained unconvinced. There were, after all, several other good reasons to think that he, not the chemistry department, was all wet. Aside from the lack of any rain at that particular moment, not a drop had fallen for at least a week. Furthermore, there was no water tower, no air conditioning or any other equipment installed on the roof that might leak. There was no way that any standing water could have collected that would cause the kind of artificial cloudburst Gene was claiming. Even an executive could see that, and one look at the roof would verify the fact. So Guy patiently got up and took Gene over to where they could see the roof of the rest of the laboratory, housed in the single story that was attached to and beneath our second-story perch.

"Look, Gene," Guy said, with only the slightest edge of exasperation in his voice as he and our erstwhile comedian-courier surveyed the roof below. "There's no water anywhere on the roof." Then, as Gene stared with a most convincing expression of disbelief at the bone-dry tar, Guy added in good humor, "Gene, it was a nice try, but you can't fool us. Just give it up!"

"But I'm not trying to fool you," Gene retorted with more than a little consternation, his brow knitted into a genuinely puzzled look. "It's really pouring down there. I honestly do not understand how it's happening, but the water's got to be coming from somewhere. Maybe a pipe burst, or something!"

That last remark brought him past credibility, though the ingenuous look on his face came close to convincing us otherwise. His dogged persistence notwithstanding, he had finally gone too far. It was now obvious to both Guy and myself that Gene's report had to be some sort of gag, and we exchanged knowing glances as Guy clapped Gene on the shoulder. In a rather clipped but still good-natured fashion, Guy explained that there was not a pipe or a hose carrying water or anything else between the drop ceiling and the roof, anywhere across the entire first floor. We executives knew that because we had seen the place gutted before the laboratory was built and the drop ceiling was installed.

Even confronted with those facts, Gene still refused to recant his obviously tall tale. Yet, straining our already well-tried patience, he remained so anxious and insistent that we finally agreed to go downstairs with him and see for ourselves, expecting only some further comic developments, likely at our expense. But when we got there, things were exactly as Gene had said: Water was pouring down in the chemistry department. There was water all over the place! There was water dripping everywhere from the drop ceiling, a good deal of it collecting in large puddles on the floor, and it felt as if you could cut the humidity with a knife.

Gene, now vindicated and with perhaps a slight smugness, stood beside us as Guy and I drank in what was a decidedly unbelievable scene.

"See, I told you . . ." Gene's next words were cut short as he leaned against the wall—and promptly fell right through it!

No one, least of all Guy and myself, had any idea at that moment how any of what we had just observed possibly could have happened. Yet, there it was, complete with a slightly wet, disgruntled and now wounded employee, struggling to regain his feet, who soon would be heading to a hospital emergency room to assess and repair the scrapes and bruises caused by his fall through the wall (not to mention the stitches he needed on his arm). The repair of the damage to the laboratory would take somewhat longer (about a month, in fact), but it did not take much time at all to assess what had happened there.

Guy and I inspected the hole in the wall and found that all the plasterboard was damp where Gene had fallen through. The entire wall was wet and very warm to the touch, no doubt caused by the thick billows of steam that were steadily and profusely escaping from the hole in the wall. The steam had been rising long enough to get absorbed even in the ceiling tiles, which explained the rain. But where was the steam coming from? That was not too tough to figure out either, even for executives. There were no pipes visible in the walls, and the steam seemed to be rising from the floor. So we figured correctly that the problem must be somewhere underneath us.

Our surmise soon was proven by the brave descent of an employee into the building's four-foot-high crawl space. He waded some distance through the several inches of hot water flooding the crawl space before we had our answer. Some of the hot water pipes supplying the building were broken and pouring out incredible amounts of hot water—hence the steam, soggy walls and unauthorized ceiling sprinkler system.

When the plumbers showed up, they soon exposed the evidence that allowed us to trace the cause of the leaking pipes. It seemed that our growing volume of business was to blame.

Chapter Six: The Snake

▲ ▲ ▲ ▲ ▲

Since we were one of the only national labs at that time, we were doing many more sophisticated tests than any other laboratory did in those days, which meant using much higher volumes of chemicals. Those chemicals, even though properly diluted with water and flushed down the sink drains in the chemistry department, still contained large enough concentrations of certain acids to eat holes in the pipes. The drainpipes were just above the hot water pipes, and it was not long before the chemicals dripped down and ate holes in them, too. That told us how the rains came, but did not answer a much more difficult question: Why did something like this happen at one of the worst times possible for the business, just as we were beginning to get on our feet?

This was quite different from the case of the exploding stool sample. Or was it? When that paint can exploded in the baggage compartment, the event caused only a momentary, albeit extremely unpleasant, halt in our march. The effects of the laboratory cloudburst, however, were much more severe. When it rained indoors at MetPath, our worst fears were indeed realized, and then some. We not only had to pay to repair the plumbing, we had to go to the extra expense of installing stronger pipes, draining the crawl space, and replacing the walls and ceiling. Not only did we lose customers because they did not get their test results back on time; we lost some for good and missed out on others because of the upset. As we struggled to catch up we got farther behind and almost went out of business.

Yet on a different level, the way both events came about was exactly the same, in principle. Who, after all, could trace beforehand the sequence of events related in either of the stories above? And if those things could have been anticipated, was it reasonable to assume they would both be missed or averted? Even then, could the stool sample have exploded at a better time to be unobserved and therefore unstoppable? Could it have rained in the lab at a time that was worse for the business? The answer to all these questions is: Of course not! The sense of helplessness that accompanies that answer is increased by the knowledge that there is nothing that can be done to undo the effects either. What it boils down to is you just have to take it and hope that your business survives the attacks.

How we survived such events as well as we did is a miracle, as inexplicable as the mystery of why they happened when they did. Many would simply call them "strokes of bad luck," a statement which holds water just about as well as that broken pipe—or stool as effectively as that paint can.

I say, *Mr. Murphy did it.*

Now, you may not believe that there is some person—or being, or entity, or whatever he or she or, God forbid, *they* might be—called *Murphy* that bounces around the globe wreaking havoc among entrepreneurs. I am not so sure I do either; but if Achilles had his Heel and Holmes his Moriarity, then every entrepreneur could have a Murphy! The fact that he might be mere fiction only serves to heighten the unavoidable reality that there are things miraculous and mysterious in life that are hard to account for rationally. So even if Murphy is a fiction (and I am not saying he is, mind you!) strange things still happen in this world.

Many entirely rational business people do not hesitate to lay the blame for certain types of events squarely at the feet of an individual they call Murphy. I will call him that, too, if you don't mind, although I have never met him. No one else that I have ever heard of has met him either, so there is no way to describe what he looks like. But his presence, at least, is easy to spot.

HOW TO RECOGNIZE IF MR. MURPHY IS AROUND—MAYBE

1. *Some major disaster suddenly threatens your business—but you will never see it coming.*
2. *It will always come at an inappropriate time—usually the worst possible time.*
3. *Whatever it is and whenever it happens—there is nothing you can do about it.*

The above are always true, no matter what the specifics of the occurrence are, and there are many different types of Murphy-caused disasters. He can affect every aspect of your operation, from production to administration, and is equally capable of attacking you with your own equipment, systems and even your vendors. And you can be sure that he will attack anything that has to do with your money. These disasters can come at any time during any phase of the business-building process, from market penetration all the way to the time when you are getting ready to sell your business—but each occurrence will be at an absolutely critical moment. Even though Murphy may not follow through completely with his mayhem, it will still take some small miracle to mitigate or cancel the possible ill effects. Whatever starts happening may suddenly stop before it ever really gets rolling, but nothing that you can say or do will make any difference whatsoever.

"Why," one of you, I am sure, is just dying to ask, "*is it important to know about Murphy? He probably doesn't exist, and even if he does, you're telling us there's nothing that can be done about him anyway.*"

Right! And if you know about him, at least you will not be surprised when these things happen—and they will happen, trust me!

"Well, if they're anything like the story you just told, then they're so weird that the chances of them happening again, or to anyone else, has got to be close to absolute zero!" Is that what you think?

Well, you may be right. I cannot say for sure. But if you do not get told about them, then you will complain you were not warned. Come to think of it, since I have told you about them, they are no longer unexpected, are they? So if the exact same things start happening to you, don't go blaming them on Mr. Murphy!

The truth is that most entrepreneurial problems can be anticipated, and something usually can be done about them once they occur. There was more than one problem with the building in Teaneck but none of the others could be traced to Mr. Murphy. When, for example, we had to run extension cords out the windows of the first floor, up the outside of the building, and in through the windows of the second floor, that was a problem. But it was not a Murphy-problem. The contractor just neglected to put outlets on the second floor. It is reasonable to expect that contractors will forget things or put them in wrong (which they always do, in my experience) and no matter what they do, the building will never be finished on time. But these are things that can be expected to happen, things that have answers. If the building is not finished, either you do not move from where you are or you find someplace else temporarily. Not being able to use any laboratory equipment on the second floor was a pain in the neck, sure, but the extension cords fixed that—even though they looked a little ridiculous hanging out of the windows!

Business life is full of such difficulties and, just like we told you in *Chapter 5*, the only answer is to react to them, doing whatever you have to that will keep your business intact. None of the events recorded in that chapter were Murphy-inspired, by the way, including the disasters. Kinetix did not deflate because Mr. Murphy planted the Woofer on our production line and he did not send the hurricane (natural disasters obviously are not directed by Mr. Murphy) that wound up destroying our marketing plan and blowing away Medex. Most production problems, marketing setbacks and other operational dilemmas—even those caused by acts of God—are things that should be anticipated, or at least could be expected to occur, in the normal course of doing business.

This is particularly true of the highly annoying but less serious difficulties that go on all the time. The wrong size, color or number of things will be delivered regularly; and if not wrong, the delivery's at least going to be late. Count yourself extremely fortunate when most of the shipment of almost exactly what you ordered ever arrives on schedule—which to most vendors seems to mean just after closing time on the date it was promised to arrive. Disastrous or not, such shortfalls are usually not the domain of Mr. Murphy. The business jungle is pockmarked with more than enough pitfalls without him.

Remember when we told you that things are always going to take twice as long as expected, and cost twice as much? (That was so long ago that I am not going to even bother going back to look it up. If you want to know where it was, do it yourself!) Mr. Murphy has nothing to do with that either.

He will not be in town on the fifteenth of the month for the grand opening of your pizzeria that you planned, since he already knows that things will get all screwed up anyway and it will not open until a month later. Mr. Murphy will not be lurking behind the pinball machine in the corner when you come in on the big day and the ovens are broken. He will not be smiling crookedly when you find out that the repairs that took a week to start and another to complete did not fix the problem. Neither will he be there to laugh at your colorful reaction when you find out that the warranty is expired and you have to order new ovens, which of course have gone up in price since you bought the old ones. He will not be snickering when you find out that, not only will it take an extra week for the ovens to be delivered, but the installers will not be there for a week beyond that. And when the second grand opening is delayed because the cheese you got in a week early goes sour because the refrigerator broke down over the weekend, you will not hear Murphy's mocking laughter.

Mr. Murphy will not even care that you had to reorder more cheese and get a new refrigerator. Even if you ran out of money and never could set that third grand opening date, he will not be there. All of those things should be expected to happen, because they often do—and especially because we told you so! Mr. Murphy will not be around to tell you, however, that nobody ever has a grand opening unless they have already been open for at least a month. He would not even tell you he told you so, since he has it in for you. Do not take it personally; he has it in for every other entrepreneur, too. That is why **Mr. Murphy specializes in disasters which are impossible to foresee and to fix**—the unexpected event at the most inappropriate time.

Now, you may or may not believe in Mr. Murphy, which is your choice, of course.

You might even believe that what you are reading here is a bunch of horsefeathers. Certainly, that is your prerogative.

I only suggest, whether you believe in Mr. Murphy or not, that you remember Gene when something disastrous unexpectedly befalls your business.

He literally had to fall through a wall before Guy and I believed him ... and he was telling the truth!

*   *   *   *   *

It is surprising that any legless creatures, so beset by the general animosity of both man and nature, could survive such a variety of hostile environments as snakes do. One key to the scaly serpents' survival is their uncanny mobility. Even without legs, agility and speed are their most valuable attributes. What motivates a snake is a series of oversized and overlapping scales (as many as three hundred for some) on their undersides. Each of these plates is attached to a pair of movable ribs which, when moved back and forth, create a wave along the length of the snake's body. This wave creates the snake's many-curved sideways or "sidewinder" form of locomotion. The forward wave of this serpentine motion smooths out the plates, offering no resistance to whatever surface is being traveled over. The reverse wave exposes the edges of the plates downward at an angle which allows the snake to push against even the slightest irregularity of the surface and thus propel itself in any direction.

*   *   *   *   *

1. Basic Murphy

Any believer will tell you that all people, places and things connected to an entrepreneurial venture are fair game for Mr. Murphy.

The more advanced Murphy aficionados know through bitter experience that what he can do to a laboratory, manufacturing plant, office building, or other place of business is only the beginning. His worst and more frequent attacks, they will tell you, are reserved for the people and things in those places.

Your people are his prime targets, since Mr. Murphy seems incapable of doing anything without the assistance of some human agent. Coupled with the fact that you never see him coming, this gives strong support to the widespread belief that he is some type of invisible spirit or force. Whatever he is, he is most likely to make his presence felt through someone's unwitting assistance, which does not mean good intentions. Mr. Murphy could care less if your employees mean well or whether they are good, bad or indifferent. He will use anyone, anywhere, at any time to attain his malicious ends.

Every employee screw-up, however, is not the fault of Mr. Murphy. Many of an entrepreneur's people problems come from simply hiring the wrong employees, no matter how carefully they are screened (see *Chapter 4*). Some employees will take a job, only to find out later that it was not the right job for them. Some will feel they are not getting paid enough. Some absolutely cannot perform in the atmosphere of constant pressure and change so basic to the risky environment within which entrepreneurs thrive. Some simply will not be able to handle the uncertainty of a start-up.

Whatever the reasons, some employees will cause problems, sooner or later, and often very big problems, but most of the problems they cause will not be Murphy problems, even though they may be disasters. Human history offers copious and undeniable proof that people seldom need help from Mr. Murphy or anyone else to create incredibly bad situations! It is the same in business and entrepreneurs should expect to have some of these problems. Fortunately, most of the people who cause them will leave the company, one way or the other.

Things are a bit different when Mr. Murphy strikes. The intentions or talents of the people involved seem to have little bearing on the event itself. Moreover, the ramifications generally are so unusually complicated, unbelievable, incredible, and even outrageously comic, that to fire someone in their wake seems hardly relevant and even unfair. It even plays into his hands, since Murphy certainly would consider a firing or two as a fitting finish to his unworthy designs. One of his primary satisfactions must come from getting people into trouble, especially good employees. When he sees you have hired a good-intentioned person who is willing to go overboard to help the company, he is only too happy to help—help them get a leg up on the railing to jump, that is, or even push them overboard himself! Of course, when he happens upon a person functioning in complete disregard of the company, he will gladly pitch in there too, only to make sure that the ill effects of that employee's actions will be as unsettling and far-reaching as possible.

A perfect example of the latter case occurred in 1973 when MetPath was beginning to expand. We had moved our entire laboratory into a brand new thirty-thousand-square-foot building in Hackensack. It was our second building on that site and we were poised for growth. This was the first time since the very beginning that everything was in one location, and we had just expanded our lab to include drug testing and other specialties. We had recently hired several people with masters degrees in chemistry who were doing drug tests and analysis for city employees, government agencies, and things like that. So it was particularly distressing when, one Monday morning, I was in my office, working at my desk, and my secretary Joyce told me I had some visitors.

"There are some people here who would like to see you," she reported. "They say they're from the Hackensack Police Department, the Drug Enforcement Agency and the Federal Bureau of Investigation."

"Oh, I see," I said, hardly looking up from my work. The incongruity of having the police, the DEA *and* the FBI in my waiting room did not strike me as strange at all. "What do they want? Are they interested in our new drug-testing service?"

"Well, maybe," Joyce said calmly. "They say there is some kind of a problem that they need to talk with you about. Do you want to see them?"

"Joyce," I said, her words starting to sink in, "you're kidding me, right?"

"No, Dr. Brown," she replied quite matter-of-factly, "I'm not kidding. Shall I show them in?"

"Do you really think there's a choice, Joyce?" I was sure at that point that either Joyce was made of sterner stuff than I had ever imagined or I had entered the *Twilight Zone*. "Yes, of course, show them in. I will be glad to see them."

So these three people came into my office. One was right out of the *Miami Vice* television show, replete with sunglasses, a beard, torn jeans and a jaunty little cap—easily twice as bad as my son Mark ever looked when he went out to wash cars on Saturdays. Obviously an undercover cop, he was accompanied by two well-dressed men in suits and ties. All three looked as if they meant business, but not my kind of business at all. Meanwhile, I was having trouble breathing.

"Doctor," one of the suits said, "do you know Mr. So-and-So?"

"Yes, I know that name," I said, surprised that my voice hardly quavered at all. "I believe he works in our chemistry department."

"Well," said *Miami Vice*, "that same Mr. So-and-So sold me eight pounds of raw opium in your parking lot on Friday night."

"Excuse me?" Those were the only words I could manage, since I was otherwise occupied, trying to breathe.

"That's right, Dr. Brown," said the other suit. "We arrested Mr. So-and-So on the spot and he's now in jail. But he didn't have all the opium with him. We've searched his car, his apartment and everyplace else that we could think of, but came up empty. Obviously, we would like to know where it is, but he's not talking. We have a search warrant for this building, and we need to ask you a few questions about him. What can you tell us?"

"J-O-Y-Y-Y-C-C-E," I bellowed, not knowing whether to be indignant, scared, angry or relieved, all the while fighting off the hyperventilation that I was sure would begin any moment, followed by an anxiety attack or a coronary. When Joyce (completely calm, I might add) showed up at the doorway, I asked her to "Call Joe O'Brien. Tell him to come up here *immediately.*"

The three gentlemen interrogated Dr. O'Brien to learn what they could about Mr. So-and-So. Over the next several days, they searched the entire building for opium, beginning with the area in the lab where he had been performing, what else? Drug testing. They came up empty there, so they spread out into the rest of the building. When they failed to find the opium, they left, not bothering to question any of the other employees or even to find out who was friendly with him. I did not speak much with them during that time, but they seemed to be everywhere, and I expected they would leave no stone unturned. Apparently, they did not turn up much and hit a deadend without getting anywhere at all.

They left on a Friday morning but were back on Monday morning. Seems someone had a brainstorm and all three of them showed up in my outer office once again. Hardly waiting for Joyce to open the door, in they marched.

"Dr. Brown," one of the suits asked, "can we see Mr. So-and-So's employee file?"

"J-O-Y-Y-Y-C-C-E," I again bellowed, perhaps a bit less breathless this time, and asked her to get Mr. So-and-So's file. We would have done it sooner, but we had only recently put together our employee files (see *Chapter 5*), and I frankly did not even think about it! But I do remember wondering why it took them so long to ask in the first place. Anyway, when Joyce returned and stuck her head into my office, it turned out that probably would not have mattered.

"I'm sorry," Joyce said coolly. "It seems they can't find Mr. So-and-So's employee file."

"WHAT? IT'S MISSING?" Perhaps I spoke a bit too loud.

"Well, they can't find it," Joyce responded, still as cool as ever, although sounding a bit hurt at my overreaction.

The three drug investigators seemed unwilling to accept another deadend and asked to see Dr. O'Brien again, who promptly showed up in my office. They explained their thinking: Mr. So-and-So was in jail, the drugs were missing, and now his personnel file, which might offer them some leads, was nowhere to be found. How could this be? He did not have the time to ditch the opium anywhere since he was supposed to deliver it at the time of the drug deal in the parking lot. They were almost 100 percent sure that the opium would be hidden somewhere nearby on the premises but they had not been able to find it. It was unlikely he would have bothered to steal or destroy his personnel file since he certainly did not know he would be arrested.

Chapter Six: The Snake
▲ ▲ ▲ ▲ ▲

"So, where's the opium," Miami Vice wanted to know, "and where is his personnel file?"

"Did you check his locker?" Dr. O'Brien asked.

Eureka! That was it, they were sure! Their excitement was visible as the three simultaneously asked to be shown Mr. So-and-So's employee locker. However, the locker was empty and showed signs of a forced entry. By the time they returned to my office, they had a new theory. They reasoned that Mr. So-and-So must have had an accomplice who had access to his locker and could have taken his personnel file, and with that pronouncement they looked squarely at Dr. O'Brien.

"Who could that be?"

"Ah, I've been meaning to call you," Joe said, seeming to squirm uncomfortably in his chair, "but you got here before I had the chance to tell you."

"WHAT!" My tone this time was only a decibel or two below the pain threshold. I could not believe my ears! Was Dr. O'Brien, one of my trusted managers, Mr. So-and-So's accomplice? Joe looked at me in surprise, and then started laughing.

"No, no," Joe said. "Not me! His cousin!"

"His cousin?" asked one of the suits. "He works here, too?"

"Well, he has done a little work for us, part-time."

"Why didn't you tell us about this before?"

"I just found out myself on Friday, after you had gone," Joe confessed. "Let me explain. Thursday, I was going over the time cards for last weekend and saw Mr. So-and-So's name on one of them. I figured our weekend shift supervisor had made a mistake or had forgotten to enter the name of whomever he found to fill in when Mr. So-and-So did not show up on Saturday. I asked the shift supervisor about it late Friday, when he normally comes in. I guess you missed him. Anyway, he told me that the name on the time card was of Mr. So-and-So's cousin. It seems he had called early Saturday morning saying that Mr. So-and-So wouldn't be in—he did not say why—but, not to worry, he would come in and take care of things.

"And I guess he did," Joe added, a little sheepishly.

It was now obvious to us all what had happened. Not only had the cousin done Mr. So-and-So's work that Saturday, he also came in and cleaned out his locker and took the personnel file. The detectives in fact had not spoken with the weekend shift supervisor, since he had not been in since their investigation started. Not immediately suspecting an accomplice, they did not expect anything that might have happened after the arrest would have any bearing on the case—until it was too late. So they got Mr. So-and-So, but the opium disappeared along with the cousin and with him all chances of recovering it.

Likewise absent (but not that you would have noticed it; no more than you could have detected his presence) was Mr. Murphy, who probably left town with the other So-and-So. But before he left he must have made sure that the media got hold of the story, since it made all the newspapers. He probably enjoyed the irony— how a laboratory that was doing drug testing to help prevent abuse had also hired a drug dealer who was helping to cause it. Murphy knew the last thing MetPath needed right then was bad publicity, so he hit us in a young company's worst spot—its reputation—at a time when we could least afford it.

Though the company was blameless, any hint of impropriety could affect our image before existing and potential customers and investors. It certainly gave our competition a chuckle or two, as well as the opportunity for some implication and innuendo. It is hard to say how much business or money we lost, since a company's reputation is one of those difficult to gauge intangibles, but suffer it did. All we could do was ride out the storm. Certainly the whole affair delayed us, disrupting our operations directly for a week and indirectly for much longer than that. Joe O'Brien thought about it at least once a year for the next three, every time he received Mr. So-and-So's Christmas card from federal prison.

Come to think of it, maybe Murphy sent the cards, just to rub it in!

I would not put anything past him, especially after what had already happened to MetPath, something which also bore Mr. Murphy's unmistakable stamp. A few years earlier, I learned that it is not on only the malicious employee that he may manipulate; even the most conscientious might fall prey to his machinations. The event was totally unexpected and ill-timed, just as its effects were indefensible, surely qualifying as a Murphy-visit, but I will leave you to draw your own conclusions.

It happened just after Metpath went public. We did that at a very early stage, when we were still a small little business. All the employees could own stock, but most of them knew less about stocks than I did at the time, which really was not very much. They wanted to know everything and among the first things they asked about were how the stock's value got decided, and what the price-earnings multiple was. (*If you don't know already, or if you have forgotten, go back to Chapter 3.*) So we called a general employee meeting and I explained to them how those things work and that, since we were not earning any money yet, our multiple was boundless.

The important thing, I stressed, was that everyone who worked for the company could have a say in the price of the stock. If they could help us make more money, then our earnings per share would go up and the P/E multiple would stay the same. That would give our stock a higher price and then the stocks they owned would be worth more. I explained that there were two ways to help the company make more money: either increase revenues or reduce expenses. It is a lot easier to reduce expenses than it is to get new revenue. If a company is making ten cents on the dollar, every ten cents that someone saves is equivalent to the marketing department going out and getting us a dollar of new sales, without having to spend any more money to get the extra sales. Since our multiple was infinite, I added, there was no telling how high the price of the stock might go. So I told everyone to go out and try to save money.

Well, I never thought any more about my speech, until one day a trucker came into our just-renovated, ten-thousand-square-foot building in Hackensack and inquired, "Where do you want us to put your boxes?"

"What boxes?" Guy Seay had no idea what he was talking about. He just happened to be at the door when the trucker showed up.

"The boxes that you ordered." And Guy looks out at the not one, but three ten-ton trailer trucks sitting in the parking lot. At which point he called Joyce, my secretary, who then was functioning as the purchasing agent for the company.

"Joyce, there are trucks here with some boxes."

"Oh, the boxes have come!" she said, very excitedly, not yet the cool customer she was in Hackensack in 1973.

"What boxes, Joyce?"

"Oh, you know," she explained. "The boxes that we send supplies out to the doctors in. You know how Dr. Brown wanted us all to save money? Well," she went on to admit, with no small show of satisfaction, "I saved us a fortune! We were paying seventeen cents a box and I was able to get us a price of eleven cents a box. All I had to do was buy a large quantity."

"Joyce," Guy said rather quietly. "Come out here and see what you've bought."

No one had any idea of what Joyce had bought, including Joyce. Once they unloaded the shipment of flat, two-foot-squares of cardboard, they filled the entire length of our one hundred-foot-long, eight-foot-wide corridor from floor to ceiling. They left us three feet of walking room and space to get through the doors that let out from the corridor. The lounges in men's and ladies' rooms, as well as a large storeroom, were filled with boxes—and they needed more room! We wound up having to rent a dilapidated ten-ton trailer, put it in the back of the parking lot, and filled that with boxes, too.

Joyce was mortified after she realized what she had done, although she did not lose her job over it. Still, she was miserable for weeks after and there is no doubt she had a twinge of conscience every time she saw one of those boxes. But there was nothing she or anybody else could do. The shipping cost to send back the boxes alone would have been prohibitive, even if we could have returned them. About the only good thing was that we did not have to order that type of box again for about five years. Balancing what was saved against what things cost, Joyce's well-intentioned box-buying spree wound up costing us quite a bit, not only in terms of a big cash outlay that we did not have the money for, but also in terms of years of disruption. Think of the upset! Other office and laboratory supplies had to be stored elsewhere, we had no rest room lounges for a long time, and there was barely enough corridor space to walk in. Had we ever been inspected by the fire department, we would have been in really deep trouble.

MetPath survived that attack and many others besides, but there was never a specific antidote to any of them. The most frustrating thing about such situations was that there was really nothing we could do. All we ever could do was try to make the best out of a bad situation, not allowing Mr. Murphy to bring us so far down that we would be out, unable to get up again. We somehow managed to stay on our feet, even when things got worse than you can imagine... and things got much, much worse than that, as you will see later in this chapter.

Well, then, what's your verdict? Was the fiasco with the boxes the work of Mr. Murphy? I do not know for sure, but it easily could have started with Murphy getting that price list for the boxes into Joyce's hands right after my little speech.

And can't you just imagine him showing up later, just to laugh up his sleeve as he watched us cringe with every box that got delivered? I can see him there, standing behind one of the stacks of cardboard that he would knock over as he left.

Now, this is not to say that Mr. Murphy did those things.

I am just suggesting that he could have.

If he exists at all, of course!

* * * * *

If there is a space between a rock and a hard place, then it is likely to find a snake occupying or inhabiting it. Most snakes survive their difficult living arrangements by adapting their bodies to fit the situations they find themselves in. Whether setting up housekeeping and laying eggs; hiding or escaping from natural

*enemies like the mongoose; laying in wait to surprise
mice and other prey—or just to get in out of the hot
sun—cold-blooded snakes will stretch and coil themselves into the most impossible spaces. Ensconced
there, even a deaf, dumb, and blind snake would be
secure, but it has still a further advantage. All snakes,
from bushmasters to boomslangs, make good use of
their tongues. When not testing for vibrations or "tast-
ing" the air through a complicated biochemical
process, the snake's slender, forked tongue fits neatly
into a sheath at its base. Exposed and accompanied by
an unfriendly hiss of escaping air, however, a snake's
tongue is also one of the most effective visual deter-
rents to any aggressor.*

*   *   *   *   *

2. Advanced Murphy

Mr. Murphy seems attracted to anything new.

Perhaps that is part of his diabolical strategy, since it is unlikely that new business people will be ready for him—not that they
ever could be, of course, even when they become old business people. It is equally likely, however, that his attraction to new businesses is because that is where he can get maximum mileage from
his mayhem.

It is not just the new business itself that seems to lure Mr.
Murphy, but everything new within the business as well. This
does not imply that he will stay his hand from sabotaging old
things but he does seem partial to the new. So not only **new facilities**, as we related above, but **new equipment and new systems
are particularly vulnerable targets**. Every new idea you have,
every innovation that you install, is the most likely place for Mr.
Murphy to gain entry into your business, again and again. How
does he do it? Well, this is where Murphy really gets sneaky,
because not only does he involve you and your own people in his
dastardly plots against your operations, but many others as well.

**Murphy will try to get as many people as possible to work
against you.** You can expect your competitors to be working
against you, but hardly your vendors and your customers. Yet Mr.
Murphy will involve all of them as often as possible in his plots,
and they will seem to be the ones responsible for screwing up your
equipment and your systems. He seems especially fond of using
the legal system and governmental agencies to assist in these
attacks. None of these people are out to get you, of course, no

more than your employees are, so don't go blaming them or getting paranoid. But Mr. Murphy does seem to be out to get anyone who runs a business, so trust that he will go to any lengths and employ anything or anyone to advance his unholy cause.

You can do any number of things to try and protect yourself. Unless you have to, for example, do not be the first to try a new piece of equipment or install a new system. Use what is tried and true, and make sure it works before you buy it. Find out about others who own one and try to benefit from their experience. Give the manufacturers some time to get the bugs out, just like you need time to get the bugs out of your own production system or marketing strategy. Such precautions might narrow the field for Mr. Murphy a bit, but it does not guarantee that he will not show up anyway. Remember, no matter how much care you take, Mr. Murphy can show up anywhere, at any time.

Mr. Murphy seems particularly fond of any machines or systems that have anything to do with numbers, especially when the numbers indicate that your company is growing. Now, it is not Mr. Murphy's fault if you try to get too big, too fast—like the building products business that tried to open in sixty-five cities simultaneously. It did not work, which is simply an example of the entrepreneur's great potential for automatic self-destruction, requiring no help from Mr. Murphy whatsoever. He probably ignores any numbers that indicate a company is trying to grow too fast, since he already knows what will happen. Apparently, there is no challenge for him in that. But let a company build a solid foundation, get through market penetration and start to consolidate, and he must begin to sit up and take notice. As the revenues build and the numbers begin indicating that a company is on the verge of expansion, then Mr. Murphy is more than likely to devote a good deal of unwanted attention to the business.

One memorable Murphy-attack came just after we had signed a contract with the City of New York to do a massive testing program in the fall of 1973, involving fifty thousand people over a ten-week period. Among other things, we were going to be processing about one thousand urine samples every day. We were trying to figure out how we were going to run those through our lab and Ames Laboratories was sure they had just the machine for us. Ames had developed an automated urinalysis machine that they claimed could do 140 urine samples per hour. The machine was brought in and, sure enough, it worked exactly as advertised. It worked so perfectly, in fact, that we ordered one on the spot, convinced now that we easily could do one thousand urine samples in about seven hours—truly a piece of cake!

The day came for our first run and Ames sent a lot of senior people along to observe. This was the first real-time test of their machine, so when the first samples started trickling in, anticipation was high. We knew that it would be slow at the beginning, since the city agencies would not send much until the end of the work day. Still, we were all there early, anxious to see the system work. Ames was well aware they had to make it work, so they even sent in a back-up machine so nothing could go wrong. As the first batch dribbled in, a labeling machine assigned numbers and prepared labels for each sample. The samples were then put into racks, ready to be brought out to the automated urinalysis machine. It was dark before we had 140 samples, which we quickly loaded into the machine and it deftly churned out the urine samples in an hour. The operation was a success, or so it seemed.

After we finished congratulating one another, we went to load the second batch into the urinalysis machine, but there were only twenty samples numbered, labeled and ready to process. Had someone merely forgotten to move the next batch from the labeling machine over to the urinalysis machine? We went back to the delivery area to check and what we found was much worse than we imagined. There were about 250 samples that our couriers had since brought in, but only a handful of them had been labeled and numbered. The problem was that, while Ames' urinalysis machine could process 140 samples in an hour, its numbering machine only operated at the rate of twenty per hour—and they had only brought one of those. Even running twenty-four hours a day, it could produce only about four hundred labels a day. At that rate, it would take us about two and one-half days to process the first day's worth of urine samples.

It is hard to express just what happened next. All the people from Ames were going absolutely berserk, for starters. Here they had come to help and it was their oversight that caused the problem. Now they began rushing around trying to get things labeled faster but there was little we or they could do. It seemed the harder anyone tried, the worse things got. We were already an hour behind when the samples started arriving in earnest. The poor numbering machine could not work any faster and the next thing we knew there were eight hundred samples waiting to be processed. Meanwhile, the urinalysis machine was only working on processing the second batch of 140. Before long we had all of that day's one thousand urine samples, some numbered and some not, plus all our other regular business, all over the lab. It was all we could do just to keep track of what we had, since we could hardly process any of it. We were stymied.

The next day, we were in real trouble with another one thousand samples on their way. We knew it would be impossible for the city to suspend and re-coordinate the collection of samples—and we were not about to ask them either, and let them know about our problem. We would just have to fix things ourselves and get back on schedule, or drown in urine! Ames arranged to fly in six additional numbering machines—all they could get their hands on— and decided to press the back-up urinalysis machine into service. But there was not enough machinery to solve anything.

The upshot of all this was that, three days after the beginning of the testing, we had processed significantly less than half of the three thousand urine samples we had already collected (and that was only accomplished by working round the clock) and we knew there were yet another one thousand samples on the way. It took us several days to come up with a solution: We had to create an additional bar coded label number to add to the existing numbers so that we could use all the numbering machines simultaneously. It was a couple of weeks before everything returned to normal.

Even so, the laboratory staff was highly stressed. It was a miracle that most of them did not quit right then and there. The greater miracle was that the City of New York did not dump MetPath. Now, I really cannot explain why we did not lose the contract as well as our lab technicians, unless it is to say that Mr. Murphy lost interest or that miracles are the only known Murphy-antidote. This is particularly true when your competition gets into the act, for they have about as much mercy as Mr. Murphy and are just as interested in seeing you go down as he might be. They, at least, have good reason to be concerned when they see numbers that say your company is getting too big for their liking—and that does not have to be very big at all, just threatening to get bigger. What happens is that Mr. Murphy is only too happy to accommodate them, somehow putting the law at their disposal to help do you in.

We had been operating out of our Teaneck facility for perhaps two months when we got a call from one of our drivers, saying that he had been arrested crossing the George Washington Bridge.

We asked the obvious question: "What were you doing wrong?"

"I wasn't doing anything wrong," he said, although he was already down in jail.

So we asked the next obvious question: "What do you mean, you weren't doing anything wrong? If that's the truth, why did they arrest you?"

"They arrested me for coming into New York City and picking up blood."

Since that was exactly what he was supposed to be doing—the very thing we had sent him across the bridge to do—we could not understand any of this. We were soon disabused of our ignorance. It turned out that New York City had a law permitting only licensed laboratories to process samples from patients in New York. When our competitors found out that this upstart MetPath from New Jersey was trying to take their business away, they told the police and got one of our drivers arrested. We got him out of jail and the next day called the city bureau responsible for professional licensing to find out what we could do about the situation. What we got was a speech about the law saying we had to be licensed to work on the citizens of the City of New York.

"Fine," I said. "Send us an application and we'll be happy to become a licensed New York City laboratory."

"We're very sorry," the replied, "but the law does not permit out-of-state laboratories to have a New York City license."

"Wait a second! You're telling me I can't come into the city to pick up blood or samples because my laboratory doesn't have a New York City license?"

"That's right."

"And, number two, you're telling me I can't have a New York license because I am located out of state?"

"Yes, that's right, too."

Well, that did not add up at all and it was obvious, to me anyway, that they were in restraint of trade. Meanwhile, we could not ignore the customers we were already servicing and they arrested two more drivers over the next week to make their point. Then we had to sue them to make our point! We had no choice; we were backed into a corner and had to fight. If we were going to be a national laboratory, laws like this would have to fall. Now, we were not exactly wealthy to start with and this lawsuit made it even worse. Not only did we spend about $200,000 in legal bills over the next three years we were fighting the lawsuit, but probably at least as much in terms of our own time and effort. It seemed we were meeting with somebody's lawyers every week and testifying all the time. There were injunctions brought against us, then we would have to file for counter-injunctions. It went back and forth constantly and got so complicated that our case made all the law journals. Finally, we won and that forced New York to license labs all over the country. But we were out at least two years' worth of growth and development, several hundred thousand dollars, and all the lost business besides.

Legislation that works against you is an obvious point of entry for Mr. Murphy. There can be little doubt that he had something to do with the FDA and the mouse's fallopian tube that we talked about back in *Chapter 2*. Legislation that is supposed to be working for you, however, is seldom suspect. The unhappy truth is that even there, Mr. Murphy's influence knows no bounds. Whenever Murphy hears through his nefarious grapevine that your business might be getting ahead, he will show up and try to ruin it. It seems that as the numbers get bigger, Mr. Murphy tries harder; the more promise and potential something holds, the more serious his attack becomes.

What got Mr. Murphy's attention at MetPath one other time was the patient billing law that was passed in New York State in 1970. We thought we were really going to grow as a result of this law, which mandated that medical laboratories bill patients directly, rather than bill the physicians (as explained in *Chapter 2*). This prompted physicians to start looking for labs that did a good job at a good price, rather than on the basis of how much money they could make off the tests. It turned out that the company did indeed benefit and grow—but not before Mr. Murphy had tried to do his worst.

Probably attracted again by the numbers, he hit us right where they resided—in the brand new computer system we had installed. **If Murphy likes numbers, then he loves computers,** which are often called number-crunchers. (Need I say that he, more than anyone else, would take that literally?) Anyway, the computer system we put in was called the Berkeley System. We had looked around very carefully before we decided to get it. Our consultants had gotten involved, and everybody's feeling was that it was absolutely state of the art for a clinical lab at that time. It not only generated all the documents for everything we needed on the laboratory side of the business—worksheets for the lab, report forms and the like—but took all the data we generated from the tests and filled them in, as well.

The system really looked like God's gift to us after the patient billing law was passed. We quickly got a lot of phone calls from physicians, many of whom stated that they had been watching our lab closely for the last year, and now were ready to change to us because of our reputation for quality and service. (We will not comment upon why it took them a year and a new law to suddenly realize we were there.) Whatever their motivation, we got some six hundred new clients over a four-day period, a huge jump in processing volume. But we were ready for them with our brand-new computer system ... until we discovered that it didn't work.

It seems the Berkeley people had never seen or heard of a lab that processed more than a few hundred samples a day, so they decided that two thousand would be more than enough for their numbering system to stop at. (Is this starting to sound familiar?) When we put the computer in and were processing about 150-200 samples a day, there was no problem. The numbers could not get confused in the lab: Number 1 would not repeat for about ten days, and by then the previous Number 1 would have been long gone. When the patient billing law went into effect and we all of a sudden jumped up to about seven hundred samples a day, things started getting confusing. We started reusing the same numbers about every three days, which meant that different samples with identical numbers would both be in the building on the same day! When we started processing more than one thousand samples a day, it got even worse.

This may not sound like a problem, unless you have ever tried to tell a computer that is ready to print out a report:

"No, no, no! It's not Monday's #1, it's Tuesday's #1.

The simple fact is, you cannot. Our computer had no way of knowing that because we never told it to. I would wager Mr. Murphy realized it, because not only was the system limited in numbering only two thousand samples, there was only enough processing power to handle one thousand accounts. Just to give you an idea of how far off it was, MetPath wound up with better than twenty-five thousand clients and processed thirty-two thousand specimens per day at the peak of my tenure there. We had nowhere near that many in 1970, of course, and the system would have been adequate for our needs even at the first rush of new customers that came with the law's passage. But we and the Berkeley people managed to make things worse, perhaps with a little misdirection from Mr. Murphy.

The system allowed only four characters to identify clients and we compounded that limitation by the scheme we came up with. We first broke down the clients by the first letter of their last names (A = 01 through Z = 26), which took care of the first two characters. Then we assigned each client a separate number with the second two characters. This meant that we could have only ninety-nine hospital or clinic or doctor accounts in each name-letter group—actually less, since the computer was limited to handling one thousand accounts anyway.

Now, we obviously did not think this out too clearly. Of course, both we and the Berkeley folks were smart enough to know that there would be a lot of "M" clients, but very few "Xs". But it seems impossible in retrospect that we missed the simple fact that, even if we doubled-up some letter categories (combining "I and J," or "X, Y and Z," for example) we still would be severely limited. Plus, we seemed to ignore the reality that there were only two thousand possible sample numbers, which meant that if a clinic sent us a large batch of samples, we would be even more limited. We found out just how limited, very quickly: Once the floodgates opened with the patient billing law, we could not deny the complete inadequacy of the numbering system.

Barely more than a week following a threefold increase in our client base, the computer drowned in a confusing sea of numbers and we were left to swim for our lives in very deep water. Now we had to process close to one thousand samples a day from a huge number of new clients who had come to us "because of our reputation for quality and service"—all without a computer. The lack of processing power also made it extremely difficult to take on any new clients or do any new processing, even for existing ones. Had all that happened gradually, we could have made provision and absolutely vacuum-cleaned up the market. At the rate we had started to get new clients, we would have enjoyed a period of incredible growth. Instead, it happened incredibly quickly and we could not possibly handle it without a computer.

Words cannot express the magnitude of the disaster that befell us. I will never forget walking in the day after the computer went down and seeing seven and eight-year-old kids scurrying between floors, clutching pieces of paper in their hands. Just about every employee brought in their children who were old enough to walk and they had set up a "war room" on the second floor of the building, plus another in the room on the first floor where the now useless computers stood idle. It was bedlam. There were people sitting at desks and tables, and on and under them, cross-legged and prone on the floor, and paper seeming to fly everywhere.

"O.K., Billy," advised one mother to an adorable little moppet, talking loudly above the din of adult conversation, children's patter, and the frequent wails of both. "You have to go upstairs and find out about specimen 4369."

"Right," Billy squeaked enthusiastically. "4639!"

"No, Billy," she corrected. "That's 4369."

"Right, that's what I said," Billy replied. "4369."

"Good, Billy," said his mother supportively. "That specimen needs a hematology," she explained, checking her clipboard.

"A hema ... wha ...?"

"Never mind. I want you to go downstairs and see if you can find out if 4369 is finished. Ask the technician..."

"The tech... nittin'...?"

"Just look for a man in a white jacket," Mom patiently explained, "and ask him if 4369 is finished, and bring back the papers he'll give you."

And off went Billy, saying under his breath, "4369, 4369, 43 ... or was it 4936?," getting halfway downstairs and then running back to ask, "Mommy, did you say ... "

Besides locating the samples, the children made copies of those little slips of paper, delivered hand-prepared worksheets to the lab—many of which some distraught adult would later find on the floor. It might not have been so bad had there been a manual system in place before we were swamped. But we were a brand new company and we had nothing to fall back on. We had to create the manual system in the middle of our biggest disaster. Each sample required several tests, each test result had to be collected and matched with the proper specimen, the paperwork had to be prepared, the reports had to be assembled and written, the client's original order form had to be located, and all of this stapled together in an unsightly collection and mailed to the client.

This situation lasted for thirty days and we should have gone out of business in the meantime. If it were not for the families participating, we would have. Even so, we had nowhere near enough employees or children to keep up with what we had to do. What saved us was calling in a new computer company. We asked Honeywell to help us out of the mess we were in and they were dynamite. The Honeywell contingent and one of our computer people worked twenty-four hours a day, around the clock. I do not know if any of them ever slept but in a month they designed, tested (believe me, I made sure they tested it first!), and installed a completely new system.

They saved the company but we still lost a lot of clients, since we lost their tests or could not even do them. By the time the new computer system was ready, we had hundreds of requisition forms with strange and hastily scrawled numbers on them and no corresponding test results strewn about upstairs; downstairs, there were hundreds of samples that could not be properly identified, not to mention the hundreds that were nowhere to be found! I had to make a very tough decision, one I am sure made Mr. Murphy very happy: I decided to start from scratch. Everyone was horrified when I told them to get a big barrel and throw everything out, saying that if clients had not gotten their results by then, they never would.

Not only did we lose clients, but we lost them for a long time; there were some who complained about what had happened even three years later.

"Oh, I remember you guys at MetPath," a doctor might say to one of our marketing representatives. "Sure, I'll be glad to use you—as soon as you find Mrs. Schwartz's protein analysis test results from 1970!"

It was like the story about the man who went to a restaurant for dinner and wound up with ptomaine poisoning. Years later, no matter that the restaurant subsequently got a clean bill from the Board of Health, changed hands, and won awards for its culinary perfection, he still had never gone back. All he could remember was, "That's where I got ptomaine poisoning."

MetPath's reputation was similarly damaged, and we had lost

much: an incredible opportunity to market our service, a large number of customers, and a lot of time that could have been spent getting new customers. If I needed any more than that experience to convince me of Mr. Murphy's existence, or that he really loved computers, I did not have to look far. Significantly, every single company that came up after us in the volume-oriented clinical lab business ended up with a computer failure of a similar sort and we all wound up losing lots of business and a small fortune. If there is another way to explain it all, other than the intercession of Mr. Murphy, I did not find it then and I have not found it yet.

What I did find was that Mr. Murphy was not finished, even then! We soon discovered that he is capable of spinning off one trouble from another the same way some entrepreneurs can create spin-off companies. But there was something else this miserable event showed me that is worth mentioning: **There is some good that comes out of Mr. Murphy's visits.** You just have to be willing to look past the immediate disaster to see what it is. Murphy did not intend it, of course, but the Berkeley experience not only taught the people at MetPath that computers can cause a lot of trouble, but also taught them **the importance of a good reputation**. After the aspirin and antacids kicked in and gave us a little relief, we also found out about **the importance of developing good relationships with vendors** who will bring help when it is needed.

That point was driven home as Mr. Murphy picked up where he left off and the saga continued. Any rational person would have expected that our troubles were over once we installed the new computer system. But Murphy was not quite finished with us. When we switched over to the Honeywell system, we had to change our computerized paper forms—worksheets, report forms and the like. At first, there was no problem. We properly anticipated how many of the different types of forms we would need and ordered them in sufficient quantity. What no one can understand to this day is the following: How, after a few months, did everyone connected with ordering forms think that there were plenty of report forms in the warehouse, when in fact there were none at all? If this was not a case of Murphy whispering lies in people's ears, well, you will just have to decide for yourself.

Everything had calmed down, the business was running smoothly and the computer was running fine—until someone came in and told us there was no more report paper. This is where we learned that if you do not put paper in the printer, you do not get reports back, no matter how well your computer is running! We did not know what to do, so we called our forms supplier (it was UARCO at the time) and told them of our discovery.

"No problem. We will have them to you in two weeks."

"Two weeks? If it takes that long," our purchasing agent said, "the boxes will be coming back to you unopened, since we'll be out of business." But there was nothing they could do.

When I heard about it, I felt I could almost hear Mr. Murphy saying, "Oh, think everything's better now, do you? Well, here! Let's see how you handle this!" It turned out to be something we could fix—almost a non-problem, after all. I called our distributor salesman, whom months earlier I had convinced to become a shareholder in the company.

"John, I've got bad news for you. Our stock's going to zero."

"What do you mean," he said a little excitedly, "the stock's going to zero? I thought things were going so well!"

"Yep! They were," I said, "But in a few days, we're going to zero, and all because we ran out of report paper."

Well, John somehow found a way to get us report paper over the weekend instead of in a couple of weeks, and saved us. No one ever knew we were on the verge of going out of business. Had we not had John as a shareholder, we definitely would have; just as management will not tolerate employees who screw up twice, neither will customers tolerate a company that fails to deliver twice.

We survived and maybe outsmarted Mr. Murphy that time. It rather seemed to me that he figured he had already hurt us enough, but I definitely cannot be sure about that. I can say that the whole episode with our computer taught us that we should **never be complacent** and not accept everything at face value in any aspect of business. Vendors often do not deliver what they say they are going to deliver and, even when they do, things seldom work the way you expect them to.

The Berkeley computer system was one perfect example of how Murphy can exploit the tendency towards imperfection of the mechanical world. Most often, he attacks things after a machine is in operation, not before. What can possibly go wrong with a machine that is only on order? You haven't even got it, right? I could have asked those same questions if I had not learned that **Murphy will go anywhere and do anything to make trouble**, even before equipment is delivered and installed. We found this out the first time Mr. Murphy showed up in Hackensack, long before he had convinced Joyce to send MetPath all those boxes. We had only begun renovating the building, getting it ready for the Autochemists, two brand new Swedish-built machines that were going to put us in the big leagues of laboratory testing. Each machine was huge—thirteen feet long, nine feet high and seven feet wide—and weighed two tons apiece. One machine could do nine hundred tests an hour, hundreds more than we could do manually, and it could keep doing them as long as we could feed it electricity.

Once the manufacturer gave us a delivery date, we had to go and get the building and start remodeling it. The manufacturer was saying that the building had to be ready by September and the contractor was trying as hard as he could to get it built when the construction delays started. That was when Murphy must have sneaked in, but so quietly that we did not realize that anything was afoot. We were ready for an attack on the facility, remembering what he had done to our plumbing in Teaneck. We figured that the attack would not come from that direction, since Mr. Murphy specializes in the unexpected. In fact, we did not get very upset when the contractor missed several deadlines, nor when he was late finishing the building. We were ready for that, so he just sneaked by our defenses and ignored the facility. Instead, he sabotaged the equipment before it ever arrived.

It was not anything straightforward, like the machine breaking down or throwing a gear, or anything so simple as that. No, it was quite a bit more imaginative than that. And if there is one thing Mr. Murphy does not lack, it is imagination, warped though it may be. The manufacturers just could not get the Autochemist finished! First, they pushed back the delivery about two weeks. The builder heaved a sigh of relief because he was still far from completion. After two weeks he was not much closer, but neither was the Autochemist. Delivery got delayed again. The contractor kept building and the delivery kept getting delayed until the space was finally finished, but by then the contractor was angry at us because he broke his back trying to get the building done and the machine was still several weeks away from delivery.

The delays had already cost us the opportunity to begin stepping up our marketing and therefore to experience some growth, but that was only the beginning. When the day finally came and the Autochemists arrived in two huge tractor-trailers, they showed up just after 5:00 P.M., of course! But it did not matter since it was New Year's Eve!

Guy Seay was the only person in the building. He just got the short straw and agreed to stay until the end of the day. Can you imagine what to do with two huge pieces of equipment that weigh two tons each when there is no one else around? The truckers who brought them, of course, wanted them unloaded (probably so they could go get loaded themselves for New Year's Eve). What Guy somehow managed to arrange was to get both trucks into storage (both entire trucks, mind you, with the machines still on them) that was heated, weatherproofed and secure. Then he had to find somewhere to buy a million dollar insurance policy for the machines because, once the truckers had arrived at their destination, they would no longer be responsible for them.

Guy gave up the bulk of his New Year's Eve, obviously, in trying to get that done. Was that enough for Mr. Murphy? No, he had to come and give us one more little zing after he zapped us. A few days later, the trucks were brought over to get the Autochemists unloaded. The men had to use special forklifts to get them across the building and they were doing just fine—until one of the tires went flat. So, while Guy toiled and worried for the entire holiday, Mr. Murphy went off and probably had a few relaxing days off. Then he came back, just in time to give us a little more grief.

If Mr. Murphy keeps a scrapbook, I am sure my companies are in it several times each. The net result of this particular escapade of his was that our breakthrough machines nearly broke us, before they ever got in the door!

Once they were finally in place, we heaved a sigh of relief.

We thought we had seen the last of Mr. Murphy.

Truth was, he never left.

How do I know?

It took another two years to get the machines to work!

* * * * *

Snakes possess many other means to ensure their survival besides mobility, agility and their tongues. Most have deceptive markings and colorings, like rattlesnakes. Many possess the intimidation of fangs and venom, as do most vipers. Even a few, such as boa constrictors and anacondas, are endowed with great size and strength. But adaptability remains the most important attribute of the whole family, from sea snakes to tree snakes. This is perhaps best expressed in the way snakes eat. All snakes ingest their prey whole and most eat them alive, although some might first crush or poison them. Snakes' curved teeth, besides injecting venom, are designed to hold fast the prey—quite a necessity for any animal without arms or legs, claws or paws. The teeth also allow them to begin "swallowing," which for a snake means pulling their bodies over their meals. Even more amazing, the bones in their lower jaws are not one piece, but the two sides are joined in the middle by an elastic ligament. When snakes swallow, they do not just open their mouths—they literally open their faces!

*   *   *   *   *

3. *The Recurring Murphy*

The fish tank in my office was really beautiful.

It was really big, too.

After all, what entrepreneur with delusions of grandeur would settle for anything less than a three hundred-gallon fish tank in a new, sixty thousand square-foot office building that his company was building?

A decade after MetPath had begun, we were able to afford to build our own office building in Teterboro, N.J. The company was doing very well. Our profits finally were growing as well as our revenues, the market was expanding, our stock was riding high, and so were we. Everyone connected with the company was positive about the future, especially me. It was gratifying in several ways that the company was doing so well and not the least on a personal level. At last I felt comfortable enough that I could perhaps begin enjoying the fruits of my labor and indulge a few of my entrepreneurial prerogatives that I had put off for so long.

One of those indulgences was to finally have a big office—with a fish tank, of course. The thought of having a fish tank in my office was very exciting, especially since I had just become an avid scuba diver shortly before we began the building. But it could not be just any old fish tank; besides wanting it to be large, I wanted a saltwater tank so I could stock it with fish from the Caribbean. There was no problem with justifying it, either: There had been some interesting studies done that discovered when there was a fish tank in a physician's waiting room, it had a calming effect and patients' blood pressure levels went down.

Isn't that fantastic, I thought. *This will bring a big calming effect in my office. It will keep my blood pressure down, too, every time a disaster befalls us.*

So in went a six-foot by four-foot by three-foot fish tank, which needed three hundred gallons of salt water to fill it—creating an incredible load factor on the floor of about two thousand pounds-per-square-inch. That necessitated putting special steel in the corner of the building. The building cost a little more that way, but that's a privilege you get when it is your company and your company is making money. As soon as we moved in, I brought in some big tropical fish, as well as some undersea formations and things from shipwrecks that I had gotten during my scuba diving trips to the Caribbean. And it was just spectacular, really a gorgeous environment. The fish prospered and my blood pressure was never better from then on—right up until the time we started thinking about selling the company.

Chapter Six: The Snake
▲ ▲ ▲ ▲ ▲

If there was ever an inappropriate time for the fish tank to break, that would have been it, so I was more than half-expecting a visit from Mr. Murphy, but I never dreamed what was in store for us this time. I came into my office one day and the fish tank was only about half-full of water. All the fish seemed fine, however, and there was no water on the floor and the walls were dry.

Where had the water gone?

I opened the door to the bathroom next to the fish tank, slowly and with great trepidation, but everything was dry in there, too. There was a closet between the bathroom and the fish tank, and I stood back and opened that door too, expecting water to start flooding out and ... surprise! No water! I was really puzzled. I knew that no one would have stolen the water. I did not think it could ever get hot enough in my office for 150 gallons of water to evaporate overnight. Could it? Even as I told myself it was an absurd thought, I put my hand on the tank, only to find it cool and dry. I was really confused by then and, afraid I would lose *my* cool, I sat down at my desk at the other end of the room and just stared at the fish tank. I was not there long when my secretary rushed in.

"What are we doing about the water?"

As far as I knew, she had not been in my office yet. I wondered for a moment if she was psychic.

"What water?"

"It's raining downstairs in the accounts-receivable department."

"WHAT..." I started to yell, but then caught myself and continued as evenly as I could, "are you talking about?" I was looking at her as if she were crazy. A strong sense of *deja vu* came over me as I looked out the window at a cloudless blue sky.

"They just called and said there was water dripping from the ceiling," she advised me. "There are hundreds of gallons of water on the floor down there."

"No," I told her. "There's only about 150 gallons down there."

Then she looked at me as if I were psychic, or crazy—or both—until I pointed to the half-empty fish tank.

An investigation proved that one of the back seams of the tank mysteriously had sprung a leak about halfway up. Because the concrete floor was tilted toward the walls, the water did not flood my office area. Instead, the water found a channel and ran into the space between floors. After we calmed everybody down, assuring them that the deluge was over, we started cleaning up the mess downstairs. Then we began on my office, taking the fish out of the tank, putting them in storage in plastic bags, and draining the remaining water. Then I had a choice: Rebuild the tank (which was past the warranty period, of course) or sell the company.

I sold the company.

Now, the more observant reader will have noticed that the above story has brought us full circle. We are right back where we started, talking about water damage to a business facility. The very observant reader will also have recognized that the other anecdotes related in this chapter also seem to have something in common, although it may be hard to put a finger on exactly what that is—unless it is that they were all caused by a certain Mr. Murphy. On the surface, it is certainly a bit of a stretch to say that the water problems in the facility in Teaneck had any connection with the water problems of the facility in Teterboro. And yet, is it not strange that it would rain indoors in two different laboratory facilities separated by so much time and space? Strange, indeed, unless there was someone, or something, responsible for both occurrences, which brings us now to discuss:

THE RECURRENT MURPHY SYNDROME

Non-recurring events tend to recur—
but they will not necessarily recur as the same thing.

A rainstorm indoors, in your laboratory, certainly would be considered a once-in-a-lifetime, non-recurring event—until you have a rainstorm indoors in your accounts-receivable department. No one would ever try to send us anything like the stool sample that the Boston Teaching Hospital sent us in a paint can again, would they? No ... but a hospital in the South would send us a radical mastectomy in a mayonnaise jar. That time, we processed the sample but called them to explain that was the wrong kind of a sample to send us. The warning came too late, however. It seems their pathologist had quit and they just thought they would send us all their samples, which included a descending colon (i.e., a large intestine) that was also winging its way to us, packed in a mayonnaise jar.

If these were the only such events in my entrepreneurial experience, then I would never even consider the existence of some malfeasant personage like Murphy. But then, why do things recur all the time that are not supposed to recur?

As we related earlier, for example, we had a legal fight on our hands with the City of New York in order to get legislation changed so that we could get a license to do business there as an out-of-state company from New Jersey. Years later, HEARx got embroiled in a legal battle with the State of New Jersey over legislation that required all promotional material to include the name and state license number of the supervising audiologist of a hearing center.

(Do you have any idea what it is like to try and get all that information, along with our logo and whatever else we want to say, on a ball-point pen or a refrigerator magnet?)

Then there were our recurring party problems at MetPath. The company was known for its parties. We had a lot of them: going-away parties, people being transferred parties, company picnics—you name it and we were ready to have a party! Well, it happened that, after one of our company picnics in Teaneck in 1971, all of our typewriters had been stolen by some thieves who had broken into the building. Then in Hackensack in 1974, we came back after a company picnic to discover that all the telephones had been stolen—by one of our own security guards!

These things may sound at least laughable and even unbelievable. But believe me, they are entirely too real and not at all funny while they are happening—except, of course, to Mr. Murphy, who probably laughs from the beginning to the end of each episode. No one I have ever known has admitted to hearing him laugh, however, so I cannot be definite about that. But if anyone ever does hear him laugh, I am sure it will be a time when he is screwing up somebody's bank account, or stock offering, or anything that has to do with money.

If I believe anything about Mr. Murphy at all, I suppose it is that **there is absolutely nothing Murphy likes to mess with more than your money** and that he will come back and mess with it as often as possible.

"Can you please tell me," I have more than once asked my financial people, "why the profits are down this month? Last month you told me you expected profits to be up."

"Well, Dr. Brown," they invariably began, "the reason why the profits are down, is because we neglected to pay the phone bill last month. So we had to pay for two months this month; so that extra $20,000 we thought we'd have was spent on the phone bill. But that's not going to happen again," they would invariably promise, "so we expect to show a profit next month."

Then, when the next month came, I'd have a meeting with the financial people and ask them the same question. This time, I got an answer that seemed quite different on the surface, but actually was very similar to the one I had gotten the month before.

"Well, Dr. Brown," they would begin again. "It seems as though we forgot the rent for the entire mid-west region last month, so we had to double-up on our payments there. But that's a non-recurring expense, so don't worry about it."

Well, that was different, but the result was the same—no profits. And invariably, whenever something like that happened, they would end by saying:

"Next month we'll have it all cleaned up." And every once in a while, they did. Murphy, however, always seems to be at least one step ahead in money matters—since money matters so much to most entrepreneurs. He is, for that reason, even farther out in front of everyone when it comes to raising money, particularly when it comes to the stock market.

MetPath was scheduled to go public in March of 1970. Approximately thirty days before our public stock offering was to take place, the Securities and Exchange Commission came out with a new ruling that stated that a company could not go public if, without the money they would raise, they would in fact be out of business. The SEC did that so entrepreneurs could not use a public offering to stave off bankruptcy and ... guess what we were planning to do with the proceeds from our stock offering?

When the SEC dropped that little bombshell, we had already printed up our prospectus. We had already gone through everything we needed to get the company ready for a public offering. We were all ready to go, just waiting for SEC clearance, which of course did not come. Instead, we were apprised of this change in the regulations, which came very close to destroying the company. It was only after many, many conferences between us and the SEC, including our accountants, attorneys, and auditors, that we were able to go ahead with the offering. So we just squeaked by, and went public on March 4, 1970. We were safe, right? Well, we thought so—until the next day, when the stock market started heading into a major, unexpected tailspin. We were among the last of the new offerings for start-up businesses that year—a drought which lasted well into the following year.

Fast-forward now to 1987, when we likewise took HEARx public at a very early stage, in circumstances only slightly more auspicious than the MetPath offering seventeen years earlier. HEARx had only $15,000 in revenue for the year and a million dollar loss. Wall Street, however, is a strange place and chose to ignore those things. Instead, on the basis of my track record and MetPath's success, it was willing to take the company public. We went around the country with our "dog and pony show" (see *Chapter 3*) and ended up with a total of almost $7 million of indications from investors. All we were trying to sell was $3.3 million worth, so it looked like it would be a dynamite deal. Couldn't be better, right? Sure, except for one thing: The day we got our SEC clearance was for a certain Friday in October 1987, the last business day before the stock market would experience one of its worst downturns in recent history. By the time the market opened on Black Monday, the whole deal went down the drain. (You can find the full story in *Chapter 7*.)

The SEC must be one of Mr. Murphy's favorite tools, at least in my experience. In fact, when the agency showed up again at HEARx, I was tempted to see how many people they had working for them that went by the name of Murphy. Just as we were about to complete a $30 million private placement, they insisted that we adhere to an unwritten, not-yet-promulgated policy and write off $9 million on paper. There was only one catch: The SEC said we could not allow the write-off to have a significant effect on our balance sheet. If you can figure that out, then you are better than our accountants and lawyers. You should probably be looking for a job with the SEC! No matter that the instructions were unintelligible; we had no choice but to comply.

Mr. Murphy also seems partial to messing with your money around banks, probably because banks have so much of it. Put the two together and he appears, eager to play one or more of his dirtier tricks. Maybe he likes the idea of killing two birds with one stone, as almost happened when MetPath arranged for a $1.2 million revolving credit line with the First National Bank of Boston. Everything was set, and Guy and I traveled up to Boston to close the deal. As is typical, we sat down in a conference room with about nine other people around this big table and nothing was ready. Things got passed back and forth to get signed in duplicate and triplicate, paper was flying all over the place, half-finished cups of coffee were staining the table ... complete mayhem! Then, about two hours later, it was all over. The table was whisked clean and everybody congratulated everybody on how well it all went. A little tired but entirely satisfied, we rose to head for home. Safely on an elevator, Guy turned to the banker, Don, and said:

"Well, that went great! Thanks again," Guy said for what seemed the thirtieth time, grinning at Don, the banker. "Can I have the check now?"

"What do you mean?" Don answered, smiling back at Guy, assuming he was kidding. A look at Guy's expression, however, and it was obvious he was not. "What check?"

"The check for $1.2 million," Guy said. "I'd like the check. We've signed everything, haven't we?"

"Yes, but we ...," Don was struggling for words right then. "We gave you the check upstairs."

"I never got a check," Guy said.

"I never did either," I chimed in.

Don stood there looking very unhappy.

We had to stop and get off the elevator, get another one, and go back upstairs. By the time we returned, the room was quite empty, and there was nothing at all on the table. No one could figure out what had happened to the check—until somebody decided to take a look in the wastebasket. There, with all the thrown-away extra documents, torn-up papers and empty coffee cups, was our check for $1.2 million. By the time we left, the credit line was not the only things revolving; you can bet a lot of heads were spinning, and probably a few flying!

That was a close call. Mr. Murphy obviously missed a cue somewhere and was not quite able to turn it into a complete disaster. I am sure that he would have liked it much better if, having gotten back to New Jersey before we discovered that we were as broke as when we left and called the bank, the line of credit would be canceled. As it was, Mr. Murphy managed to raise some blood pressure and must have had a good laugh. Many of the things he does seem to be like that: Little needles to let you know that he can get to you any time he wants to.

Once, and only once, mind you, I thought that Mr. Murphy had made a mistake and tried to do something nice for us, crazy as that seems. We had requested $60,000 to be wired to us by the First National Bank of Boston, which was to be transferred immediately into our account—and they promptly wired us $600,000! Was Murphy attempting to compensate us for all the trouble he had caused over the years? I doubt it, given his track record. More than likely, he was just trying to screw up things at the Bank of Boston and we just happened to be involved.

If this chapter has depressed you, loaded as it is with accounts of dark days and black humor, let me encourage you. I tend to look on these events as some of the most hopeful in all my entrepreneurial career.

I survived, after all.

So, if you notice strange things happening in your business that you can do nothing about, take heart. After all, nothing would be happening at all if you were not doing something right! Murphy does not have to knock you down if you are already on the canvas. Despite the horrible things that happen to you in your business, in spite of Mr. Murphy and all his shenanigans, your natural entrepreneurial ability will likely save you.

You will more than likely come out in one piece from between that rock and that hard place.

So, let's pick up where we left off last chapter and talk about how you are going to get more money to expand your business.

The miracle is ...

You might even get it!

▲ ▲ ▲ ▲ ▲

$ECRET$ OF THE SNAKE

Murphy's Law repeatedly affects a start-up business.

----

*No area of your business
is immune from Mr. Murphy's attention.*

----

*To guarantee a visit by Mr. Murphy,
just be the first business on your block
to install anything new.*

Negotiating for Security

Chapter Seven
The Kangaroo: Negotiating for Security

▲ ▲ ▲ ▲ ▲

Kangaroos (order Marsupalia) are marsupials belonging to the family Macropodidae ("big-footed"), found only in Australia, New Guinea, Indonesia, Tasmania and neighboring islands. Also known as "roos," the family includes many large and small cousins: wallabies, bettongs, pademelons, quokkas, and wallaroos are only a few. The biggest are the red and gray kangaroos. Reds can grow to seven feet tall and weigh over two hundred pounds; the more numerous grays are the largest living forms, averaging seven feet in height. The smallest, the musk kangaroos, stand under a foot high and weigh only ounces. Whatever their size, these mammals have numerous and unusual physical characteristics—the most intriguing, the pouch on females' bellies designed to carry, nurture and protect their young. Yet it seems little protection against a perilous existence. Aborigines have hunted roos for meat and fur since their time began, while dingos and farm dogs kill as many as eighty to ninety percent of the young born each year. Numerous kangaroo species, including a ten-foot-tall model with a head the size of a Shetland pony, are already extinct and known only as Pleistocene fossils.

*   *   *   *   *

It was our sixth year in business and we were ready to go. MetPath's sales had grown sufficiently to attract Corning as a corporate partner. The company seemed (and was, as it turned out) on the verge of profitability for the first time, rather than on the brink of extinction, which had been our usual position over the previous six summers.

Not only had Corning invested $1 million in our little company that spring but, to make things even finer, MetPath had just been awarded a large contract from the City of New York that was partly funded by the federal government. We had to arrange complete physicals for fifty thousand women with dependent children, all within a ten-week period. It was far beyond the capabilities of MetPath to do that, so we had to run around the city, arranging for subcontractors. Since that contract was such a big one, we were getting a lot of publicity, and finding the subcontractors was no sweat. In fact, they often found us, although some of them sent us into a cold sweat.

Like the fellow we will call "Frank," who called one day that summer and said he ran a number of health care facilities in New York City. He had heard about our contract, and he wanted his clinics to participate in performing the physicals on the women. We spoke briefly and I explained that I would have to meet with him, inspect each facility, and talk to all the owners. Frank did not have a problem with that, so we arranged to meet at his Elizabeth, New Jersey, office the next morning.

It was already a very hot day by the time I arrived at his office. My car's air conditioner kept me cool enough on the drive over, but I started sweating the moment I drove up to the address Frank had given me. I began to think I had made a mistake when I found myself in front of a rather old and seedy-looking office building on a not-exactly-booming back street in an industrial section of the city. But the address was right, as wrong as it seemed. I found no building directory in the un-air-conditioned lobby either, but he had given me his office number: 504. Presuming that was on the fifth floor, I went up in the odd-smelling elevator, which let me out into a dim hallway.

It was not hard to find Frank's office. The door was right off the elevator and just about glowed in the dark! It was emblazoned with at least a half-dozen company names in stark, black letters, outlined in gold leaf, but none of them said anything about health care. All the names seemed similar: "American ... National ... Worldwide ... Regional ... Global ... or XYZ Management ... Leasing ... Investment ... Company." The collection nearly filled the opaque industrial safety-glass window that made up most of the front door.

Despite the little voice that by now was yelling at me not to, I went in. The door was heavy, and I had to push hard to walk into the reception area of the two-room office. A receptionist informed me that Frank would be glad to see me in just a few minutes. I nervously took a seat and waited, surprised that I had worked up quite a sweat in such a short time. But I hardly had enough time to take out my handkerchief to wipe my brow; in a moment, I was ushered into Frank's office.

The first thing I noticed as I entered the large, thickly carpeted, knotty-pine-paneled room was the near-freezing temperature that iced over my perspiration, thanks to a large wall-unit air conditioner pumping BTUs for all it was worth. The next thing I noticed was a television hanging from the ceiling on a platform suspended by chains, looking just like those in hospitals. Unlike a hospital, however, the smell of rather acrid cigar smoke permeated the chill air.

Then, as the large leather chair behind the large wooden desk turned dramatically towards me, I could not help but notice all the gold hanging off the very dapper little man who now faced me in his rust-brown polyester leisure suit. There were more gold chains, medals and whatnots hanging from Frank's open-collared neck than I had ever seen on one person in my entire life. It was then I was sure I had made a mistake. If I could have, I would have really started sweating.

"Ah! Dr. Brown," Frank began, offering to shake my now clammy digits with a cool hand decorated by several heavy gold rings. "Glad you made it! Please, sit down," he said, motioning with his other hand that held an oddly shaped cigar. It looked like a thin, black, wooden stick with knots all over it. Though entirely polite, his invitation to sit seemed more a command, so I wasted no time in filling the seat he indicated in front of his desk.

As I nervously arranged myself in the straight-back chair (I never did get comfortable) Frank again expressed his desire to have his clinics participate in the contract MetPath had won. He was all business and very direct, although he hardly looked like any businessman I had ever done business with, nor wanted to! As he explained his operations, I was soon convinced that he was running what were then known as "Medicare mills," clinics that regularly ripped off the government and the people they were supposed to be caring for.

After spending a few moments listening and trying to figure out which of the puffs emanating from Frank's mouth were cigar smoke and which were hot air condensed by the cold, I decided to be just as direct. Swallowing hard, I explained to him that both city and federal officials would be scrutinizing the multimillion dollar program.

"So if there is any reason," I told him as discreetly as I could manage, "that anyone shouldn't be looked at closely, then it might not be a good idea for them to participate."

"Oh, of course," Frank replied easily, flashing a toothy and totally insincere grin. "I don't see any reason why my clinics should not participate."

"Fine," I said, although I was sure it really was not. "But I still have to investigate each one very carefully." I was hoping that would put him off but he seemed hardly to have heard what I said.

"That's fine," he said, puffing on his cigar a little absently. "But I really wanted to talk to you on another subject," he continued, leaning forward through a cloud of smoke as he spoke.

"Fine, fine," I replied, but I was lying. I must have started sweating again, too, because now I noticed wisps of steam rising around me in the cold air. I was unsure if Frank could see them but I was absolutely certain that I wanted nothing more to do with this guy. In fact, all I wanted to do was figure out how to end the interview as quickly as possible and get safely out of his frigid office (an uncomfortable comparison with a meat locker came to my mind) with my honor and body parts intact. "What else do you want to talk about?"

"I've been following your company," he said, his black cheroot in one corner of his mouth. "Your company is growing very rapidly. You know, a company that grows as rapidly as your company is going to have increasing receivables. That means you will have increasing cash flow problems. Yes, you will have a definite money problem." Then Frank paused, took the crooked cigar out of his mouth and looked straight at me, gauging the effect of his words.

He leaned forward and added pointedly:

"Maybe you need a partner. Maybe I'm it!"

"Well, that would be fine," I replied without missing a beat, although my heart skipped one. "Thank you very much for the offer, but we just got a partner who put $1 million into the company a couple of months ago."

"Well, that's fine," Frank said, but he was not about to give up. "But I mean a real partner! It's like this: You want to do a deal? Fine! Then you pick up the phone and call your partner and he brings you over the money for the deal, right away, that same day." And with that he opened his bottom desk drawer, motioning me over. My perspiration-damp pants' legs, stuck to the varnished chair seat by the cold, made a surprising noise when I stood up. But my embarrassment turned to amazement when I looked inside the drawer.

My jaw dropped, allowing about a quart of steam to escape from my mouth at the sight of what was probably two hundred thousand dollars in cash, all neatly wrapped and stacked, filling the deep drawer.

"That's something to consider," I managed, a little weakly.

"Y'know, if you want to buy somebody," Frank continued, "just call me! We don't have to go through a lot of legal work, a lot of paperwork." I never sat back down and, as nonchalantly as I could, started backing towards the door as he went on.

"Well, that would be fine," I answered, hardly knowing what I was saying. Frank obviously was not the type to take no for an answer, so I figured it would be best to try and put him off. I looked at my watch. "Whoops! Look at the time! I really have to get going to my next appointment—with some Federal people," I said, hoping he noticed. "I definitely will remember your offer, though, believe me! And if you think you want to participate in this program," I added as I turned the doorknob, "just call me so we all can visit your facilities."

"Fine! And when you need money," he called as I retreated, "you just call me!"

"Fine, fine!" I called back, smiling and nodding as I went, but I never stopped moving. I just about flew past the receptionist and out the front door (which seemed much lighter), into the hallway (which seemed much brighter) and onto the elevator (which still smelled bad, but I hardly noticed). It was still hot out, too, but for some reason I opened the car windows wide instead of putting on the air conditioning as I drove away.

Later, I laughed when I got home and my wife Cynthia sniffed at me, asking if I had taken up smoking cigars. The suit needed cleaning, of course. But that was a small price to pay to avoid getting into the money-laundering business!

We never heard a word from Frank again, thank God, and that really has been just fine with me. But he has remained a chilling reminder for me that not everyone who wants to give you money for your business has your best interests at heart.

I sure will never forget the lesson.

Remember ...

You can always get what you need ... whether you like it, or not!

* * * * *

Kangaroos grow for their entire lives, which average between eight and twelve years, although some may reach the age of twenty. Offspring of either sex are called "joeys," and live a surprisingly long time in their mothers' pouches. The joey of the grey kanga is pink, hairless, blind, and the size of a lima bean at birth, perhaps three-quarters-of-an-inch long and weighing only a gram. Just prior to birth, the mother goes off to a quiet place and licks the outside of her pouch; during birth, which takes about three minutes, she sits completely still. When the joey emerges from the birth canal, it uses strong forelegs to pull its way up the wet fur on the outside of the pouch. A scent, possibly from

▲ ▲ ▲ ▲ ▲

the milk accessible from four teats covered by the
pouch, guides the joey into its new home. It latches
onto one of those teats, which enlarges during suck-
ling, and does not let go for about three months.

*   *   *   *   *

1. Growing Pains

Remember when you had no money and really did not have
anything except a great idea and a lot of potential? When all you
had to do was look good and be able to tell a good story to get the
start-up capital needed for your business?

Since then, a not so subtle metamorphosis has taken place:
Performance has replaced potential as the deciding factor among
the moneylenders and investors you already know, as well as
among a few others you have not had access to or perhaps did not
even know about. You still have to look and sound as good as you
did when you were chasing **The Money** to start up your business.
But now that you need **More Money** (and you will, no matter what)
you must be as good as you look to get the best deals and to
avoid getting eaten by the more predatory capital sources in the
business jungle.

Since profit and loss have become matters of record and not
reflection in your business, capital sources from here on will
gauge their participation primarily on the ebb and flow of your
business fortunes. Meanwhile, those sources we looked at in-
depth back in *Chapter 3*—banks, private investors, professional
investors, or venture capitalists—also will look more or less attractive to entrepreneurs looking for **More Money** than they did in the
search for **The Money**. None of these capital sources, of course,
have changed their stripes or lost their spots just because your
business needs some additional capital. They still have the same
more or less greedy characteristics with the same more or less
fearful attitudes towards taking risks as when you started out.
What has changed is the relative position of your business.

The view from here and now will be so different that some capital sources will even seem diametrically opposed to their previous
positions during your start up. Banks, for example, may see your
growing company in a more benign light and might even be willing to make you a loan. Private investors may now seem strange-
ly distant, although professional investors or venture capitalists
may look much more appealing. And other capital sources all but
invisible before to most entrepreneurs—namely finance and leasing companies, corporate partners and public offerings—will
suddenly pop into view on the horizon, heading into your future.

As existing capital sources are revisited and new ones met in the entrepreneur's search for additional capital, there is one constant amid all these shifting perspectives. No matter who is looking at the business from whatever vantage point, what they see will be highly colored by the reasons why the entrepreneur needs **More Money**.

DR. BROWN'S INDEX OF CHANGING FORTUNES

Entrepreneurs always need More Money because:

1. *The company is not growing as fast as planned and . . .*
   The Money has run out.

2. *The company is growing faster than expected but still is*
   not profitable and . . .
   The Money has run out.

3. *The company is growing, just made a profit and . . .*
   The Money has run out.

Once again, you need to run out and get some money, whether you overestimated your potential income, underestimated your expenses, or even if you have made a profit. In all cases, **More Money** will probably have to be found. But you knew deep down, of course, that your start-up capital would not last very long, since business plan projections seldom track the reality of doing business. Likewise, you know that if you want to start or keep making a profit, you had better go and get some **More Money** to expand your business. Or did you forget the cardinal rule? *It will cost twice as much and take at least twice as long to accomplish about half of what you thought you could.* The rules do not change just because your business has survived the start-up, or just because you have either. The rules especially do not change for experienced and successful entrepreneurs, particularly for successful ones. Yet entrepreneurs tend to forget that a start-up is always a start-up, no matter how many they have been through, and that they are always going to need **More Money**.

Entrepreneurs who start out with **Too Much Money** are just as likely to need **More Money** as those have too little, believe it or not. But you never hear an entrepreneur whose business has flopped say, "We could have made it, but we just had too much money." What you usually hear, over and over, is something like, "We could have made it, if only we had just *a little more money.*" More than likely, they could have used a *lot* more, not just a little.

Entrepreneurs never seem to complain of having raised too much, yet the rule remains: **Having *Too Much Money* at the wrong time can ruin a business as sure as having too little**. And while it is true generally that many marketing and operational problems can be overcome with enough money, that is seldom true during either the market penetration or the systems development phases.

What happens when most entrepreneurs start up businesses and raise *The Money*, they think they are rich! Not very many of them ever had a bank account of six or seven figures. Even if they say they are going to be careful and frugal, they just are not. Not that they intentionally waste money, although some might. Rather, entrepreneurs just do not believe that *The Money* is going to run out, or that the business is managing them, even if they have gone through it before. If they do anticipate those things, and manage to raise twice as much money as they think will be needed, they will just find some way to spend it at least twice as fast as originally expected.

Give an entrepreneur *Too Much Money* at just about any time during the life of a business and the tendency is toward over-building, over-supplying, and over-spending on everything. I must have known that instinctively when Corning first wanted to provide MetPath with some money. They were ready to pay something like $5 million for a share of the business. I would have had to give up more equity than I wanted to for a $5 million investment, but that was not the only reason I only let them invest $1 million. I told them I would not know what to do with $5 million, and it was true: I was more comfortable spending $1 million, but not $5 million.

Yet, by the next decade, I somehow lost that simple insight. I was, after all, hardly an unsophisticated novice when I did my cash flows and projections to start up HEARx. I had started up MetPath with only $500 and succeeded, and I had $7 million of capital at my disposal during the first year at HEARx—$4 million in private capital (a good chunk of that my own, thanks to MetPath) plus $3 million from a public offering. How could I possibly screw up with that much money and such a great track record?

Well, it was pretty easy. For starters, an ad campaign too costly for any start up, put together by one of the biggest and most expensive advertising agencies in the world, all of a sudden did not seem so expensive. Then there was the beautiful and unbelievably expensive retail store design that we just had to have. What happened, of course, is that the ad campaign got scrapped and the stores got redesigned because we found out those things did not work. Unfortunately, we only found that out after we spent all *The Money* and needed *More Money* to fix it.

Now, understand that an entrepreneur easily can overdo things even without **Too Much Money** (*like buy equipment in anticipation of a market that never comes, as I did with "Brown's Folly" back in Chapter 5*). Over-expansive decisions can come from being bullish and over-confident, or even from being worried about the company losing what it has gained. Our most profitable quarter at MetPath, for example, was when the size of our lab facility totaled six thousand square feet. Once we started operating at capacity, we enjoyed a 21 percent pre-tax profit, figured as a percentage of revenue. But we were still a small company and I got worried that the competition would eat our lunch, so we moved to a new thirty thousand-square-foot facility. Now, it is better to have more space than needed because you can operate more efficiently and there is room to easily expand. But in another sense it is also possible to have too much space. After adding all that space, we never made as much money (percentage-wise) ever again because we never operated at capacity again. The maximum profit we realized after that was 14 percent, at the pre-tax level.

A better decision at that time might have been to use **The Money** we were making to hire a few more employees and expand the number of shifts, rather than adding all that space. Most entrepreneurial vision, sad to say, is only a perfect 20-20 in hindsight. Looking back, however, I know that if I had **Too Much Money** at MetPath, things probably would have been much worse. Not only would I have had too much space but I would probably have hired too many managers to handle the larger facility and spent too much on pricey designer office furniture for them, as well. My misadventure with **Too Much Money** at HEARx tends to bear that out. It was a classic case of how a full bank account can be a dangerous weapon to someone full of confidence and delusions of grandeur!

An entrepreneur with a big bank account normally will spend all **The Money** in the account, every penny. No matter how much money is in there, it will all be gone before anyone can stop it. That money will be spent as if business projections already had come true, which they seldom, if ever, do. The reason why is because *entrepreneurs basically do not believe the cardinal rule* (need we repeat it?) that everything in business is going to take *at least* twice as long as planned and cost twice as much. **Entrepreneurs, experienced or not, always believe that everything is going to happen *exactly* according to their projections**. Therefore, they reason that a lot of money will make their plan happen faster ... *Not!*

I believed that the $7 million we had for the start-up at HEARx was more than enough for the company to become profitable in about half the seven years' time it took for MetPath to get there. Yet the company has needed and will continue to need a lot **More**

Money for us to achieve profitability and meet our financial projections. Though sales have grown consistently, it was only during year five at HEARx that we met our business plan's first-year financial projections. The business, moreover, will consume more than five times that $7 million before it gets to be profitable— which, of course, looks like it will now take about three times as long as expected! Even though I had been through it all before, even though I had my own money to invest and was experienced at raising capital, even though sales were increasing, none of that made any difference. What it all boiled down to was that, with **Too Much Money** to spend, we spent **Too Much Money** and we needed **More Money**.

Just as the supply of milk for the baby joey is ever-present and available in its mother's pouch for it to latch onto, so must the entrepreneur's money pouch be filled from this point forward for the business to draw from and, lest we forget, for the entrepreneur to eventually take a few nips from as well. Your business certainly will not long survive without it and must be fed so it can grow healthy and strong enough to stand on its own in the business jungle. And what about you? Have you forgotten that you started up this business with a dream of being successful? Didn't you? The motivator and measure of that dream was to make money and, preferably, a whole lot of money. Wasn't it? Failure and bankruptcy were not what your delusions of grandeur were all about. Were they? Well, then, when it comes time for business expansion, it is also time to get back to the future with a little fast-forward to the past.

What is needed here is a little entrepreneurial mind expansion, a total recall of those dreams of being successful and making a lot of money. If your goal all along has been to own a big piece of something small, then the rest of this book can be read for enjoyment. That dream has already been accomplished if you have made it to this point. Read on with careful attention, however, if your dream is to own a little piece of something really big and make a lot of money. That dream is yet to come, so dream on.

Your dreams may have been all but forgotten in the tooth and nail struggle for survival that most start-ups must endure. When you started the business, your mind was filled with visions of the success that lay ahead. It is just that along the way in the business jungle, your vision may have gotten clouded, especially if you feel that you have been trying to survive in the dark all alone. Subtly, worry might have overwhelmed your dreams, your delusions of grandeur lost in the struggle for survival.

Whatever your mindset, profitability marks the end of the start-up and the beginning of the future—the first day of the rest of your business, so to speak. Market penetration and systems development have been accomplished. Profitability *requires* that you bring your dreams once more to the fore. Look at how far you have come, after all, and remember where you are heading! You may still be on the brink of disaster after years in business—or is it that you are on the verge of success? Your glass may seem half-empty—or is it half-full? It is your choice how to view it, but you have survived the test.

Remember (get used to remembering, by the way, since you will need to do a lot of it in this chapter and throughout your business life) when I introduced you to Mr. Murphy, how we were waiting for opportunity to knock? Well, it's knocking now! Just like Mr. Murphy, it probably has shown up at a most unexpected time. But that should not bother you. When a woman gives birth, the baby does not ask, "Mom, is it okay for me to come out now? Is this a good time for you? Would you rather I wait until the pain stops and you can get off the floor of this taxi and into the hospital before I make my entrance?"

When it's time, it's time!

Even if you have only barely survived, even if Mr. Murphy has made things very difficult, your business has grown to the point where it is now profitable, which is where you have been heading all along. The idea is to concern yourself about maintaining that profitability. And for that, you are going to need your delusions of grandeur, a positive attitude and ...

Do you remember?

That's right!

You are going to need **More Money!**

No problem, as long as you are ready ... and willing to go and get it.

* * * * *

Kangaroos are chiefly grass-eaters and prefer feeding at night. They inhabit every kind of terrain, including open plains, dry river bottoms, swamps, deserts, rocky cliffs, forests—some even live in trees and one, the bur- rowing boodie, goes underground. Most species travel in congregations called "mobs," the groups larger when- ever there is ample food and water. All kangaroos share some physical characteristics, most notably small forelegs, large hind limbs and thick, muscular tails. The tail is imperative to balance any kangaroo, at rest or in full hop, and keep it from tipping forward. A six-foot-tall roo is more than half tail. Though usually timid, adult male grays box with their two-foot-long forelegs, leaning back on their tails to deliver devastating kicks with their hind legs and eighteen-inch-long feet, which are powerful enough to kick holes in fences. Propelled by those huge hind limbs, which are three-quarters of their weight, adult grays can ricochet about forty-four feet in a single bound and clear an eleven-foot-high fence. They can move at forty miles per hour and will travel up to two hundred miles in dry seasons searching for grass and water.

* * * * *

2. How To Get (Some) More Money

The next best time to raise money is when the business first becomes profitable.

Put another way, you can sell the steak as well as the sizzle.

But there is a catch: Paper profits are not worth anything.

We agreed on that back at the end of *Chapter 5*. Remember? But we never did get to explaining what paper profits were, did we? Well, you had to be warned about Mr. Murphy first, or you would probably never get near a profit, paper or otherwise.

The point, to resume our discussion, is that you might not have made a profit yet. Not a real one, anyway, but you might well have paper profits, which are what most businesses have before they get to visit the bank each week with leftover cash.

Paper profits are profits that cannot be spent, as they are usually the result of accounting treatments. Depreciation of equipment, for example, creates paper profits. Why? Because the cost of the piece of equipment may be spread over five years, even though you may have paid for it all at once. On your P&L statement, this accounting treatment might translate into profits, but not any real profits that can be deposited, used to pay bills, or earmarked for expansion. **The Money**'s long gone and you do not get to spend what you do not have. So you will have to rely on your old friend, *externally generated capital*, to provide **More Money** until there are real profits.

Wherever the money comes from, it will now come in two flavors: **debt** or **equity**. Up until now, it is likely that most entrepreneurs have not been able to get into *real debt*, large amounts of money that will have to be paid back over a long time period (three to five years). However, it may now be time, since those wonderful private investors that helped you launch your business are likely to be anxious and ready to get their money back. They are probably not anxious about buying any more shares of your stock, however. They have probably crossed the line by now, moving from fear to greed. Those supportive, unconditionally loving people who helped you get started are waiting to get the bang for their already-advanced bucks. They are no longer afraid of losing what they have already invested but are instead calculating how much money they are going to make, not how much more they have to risk.

There are only three possible things that would excite private investors enough to sink some **More Money** into your business, especially if it is still an unprofitable business: *Growth*, *More Growth* and, of course, *A Lot More Growth*! Some of your early investors might, in other words, add to their investments if revenues are increasing. That, at least, says to them that the plan is coming together well enough for the company to eventually become self-supporting and profitable. But that is the exception rather than the rule, though that was exactly what happened at HEARx and at MetPath (*noted back in Chapter 3, if you remember*).

Entrepreneurs have a little attitude adjustment of their own to make when they think about raising money from their stable of private investors for a second time. They must be willing to go through the arduous task again. It was probably not easy to approach every friend and relative that you have ever known since nursery school for **The Money** in the first place. It is harder to go back to them a second or a third time. But if you are going to raise expansion capital through private investors, you really have no choice, unless you want to try beating the bushes to find a new crop of private investors. Most entrepreneurs have to approach their existing investor group and hope that a *white knight* will surface who can provide introductions to other investors. Like my friend Joe, one of the original investors in MetPath that hung on and made a lot of money. He invested in HEARx, too, and each time HEARx has had to go out and raise money, he has been a source of names.

If you find a Joe and can raise enough **More Money** from private investors, the advantages remain the same as in the start-up mode: Each buys small enough pieces so that it is easier for the entrepreneur to stay in control and they will invest at a much higher value than venture capitalists would. Still, private investors are a very big "if" when you are talking about expansion capital. Most people do not reinvest, and it gets harder and harder for the entrepreneur to beat the bushes for new ones. Private investors, at any rate, are probably not going to be a steady source of a large amount of new capital. You may get a little bit from a few each time around, but that is not how you are going to finance the survival or expansion of your business.

Do not panic! This does not mean that you have to run off and raise money from a venture capitalist, if you are not ready. You may *want* to, which is an option that will be considered a bit later in this chapter. For now, just take a moment to recall what was said all the way back in *Chapter 1* about "need" and "greed." When a business is ready to expand, for whatever reason, this is one of the times where the needs of the business and the entrepreneur's greed can cause fearful and impatient decisions that can have negative results, like bad timing, bad investments, and bad partnerships. Not all money is "good" money, remember. I still shudder to think of what might have happened if I had taken Frank on as a partner in MetPath.

But it is the entrepreneur's need and investors' greed that really come into play when a company is hunting for **More Money**. The balancing of the two, begun during the start-up phase, now becomes an essential skill if the entrepreneur is going to remain in control of the business—a critical issue now made even more critical if the entrepreneur has already let go of a good percentage of equity. You may already have given up as much as 40 percent (the absolute maximum in my book), hopefully spread among as many investors as possible to keep any one investor from having too much say in your business. The shareholders will not throw out management (i.e., *you*) when things are going well. But at the first sign of trouble, even your best friend may vote against you. Be sure you do not give up financial control of the company to a single large investor or investor group until you have to, which should only be when the company becomes profitable.

Entrepreneurs can try to avoid giving up too much equity to greedy investors by selling debt rather than equity, despite debt's basic drawback, to wit: As soon as you get **The Money**, you have to start paying it back, which eats into the cash you need to expand your business—yet another Catch-22 of the business jungle. Investors only get paid if you make a profit. The main advantage with debt instruments is that you generally do not have to give up a significant amount of equity to get your money, although there will always be greedy exceptions.

There are several places for businesses seeking new capital to get debt or equity when private investment avenues are closed or temporarily inaccessible, beginning with **banks**. Although still the last place to look to find **The Money** for a start-up, banks might now be a good place to seek **More Money**. They have not changed, of course; bankers still will not want to take any risks and will still demand a whole lot of hoop-jumping from the entrepreneur seeking a loan. What has changed, however, is that the entrepreneur probably has some of either or most likely both of the things that bankers like to see: a positive cash flow and collateral.

If your business is showing a *positive* cash flow—when your accountant can show the bank that you are spending less money each month than you are being paid by your customers—and you need ***More Money***, then **banks will probably give you a loan**. If your business has sufficient *hard assets*—receivables or other assets such as furniture, fixtures, and equipment (FF&E), or property, plant, and equipment (PP&E)—they might loan you money against them. But not a lot. Your FF&E might fetch only ten to twenty cents on the dollar.

If your business has enough *liquid assets*, like a growing bank account, some certificates of deposit, investments in commercial paper or government securities, bankers might free up some funds for your business. They might even give you a loan if you can show enough personal liquidity to secure the loan. As always, bankers need to be convinced that they are taking the least possible risk, which to bankers means never getting very far away from ***The Money*** they loan you. The bottom line for bankers is not what you can put up for security, but how fast it can be turned into cash. That is why paper profits, generally, cannot be taken to the bank.

Accounts receivable financing is usually an easy way to get money from banks, because banks hope they can convert that type of asset into cash faster than selling trucks, test tubes or whatever. Banks would prefer CDs, marketable securities, or other liquid assets, true; but since they are only giving you a small percentage of the value of your accounts receivable portfolio, banks are fairly confident of getting their money back.. Banks may give you a loan equal to about 80 percent of your receivables that are less than ninety days old, at an interest rate that might be two or three points over the prime lending rate. The rest of your receivables are not worth anything to a bank. You will need good statistics to show what kind of collection history you have and the "aging" of your receivables. Unless you can show the bank how much is currently owed to your business, by whom, and for how long—and not too long, mind you—then you are going to have a hard time doing receivables financing with a bank.

Arranging a loan against accounts receivable may seem an obvious way to raise ***More Money***. Surprisingly, it is not always obvious to everyone. A business consultant friend of mine met some entrepreneurs who were having trouble raising money. He agreed to analyze their business for a fee plus a small percentage of the company. These businessmen were desperate and could not find a way out on their own, so they agreed. My friend went in, expecting a long and complicated investigation, but in almost no time at all, he discovered that they had never borrowed against their receivables. What was even more surprising, they did not know anything about receivables financing. So he simply figured out which receivables they could borrow against, put in for a loan at their bank, and got the company financed to the tune of hundreds of thousands of dollars. The business did very well thereafter and he wound up with a piece of the profits—all for doing what the entrepreneurs should have been able to do themselves.

Accounts receivable financing through a bank is actually a pretty good deal for the entrepreneur. Besides, it is nice to have a relationship with a bank, if only because most businesses need a checking account, electronic funds transfer and other services that banks provide, as well as someplace safe to keep your cash besides the bottom drawer of their desks. Remember this, too: **If you never establish any credit by paying your loans back, you will never be able to establish any credit.** Definitely another Catch-22!

Unprofitable businesses with few assets and shaky accounts receivable need not apply. However, there are still **independent finance companies**. They are happy to step into the breach and buy your accounts receivable. They are seldom the first stop, however, because they are far more expensive than banks. Entrepreneurs usually wind up with these independents because they are in some kind of trouble and have gotten turned down by a bank—hardly an unusual scenario in the business jungle. The urgency brought on by hard times often drives an entrepreneur to seek new capital.

That same urgency for **More Money** can be felt when things are going well, sort of the way a bumpy cab ride in the middle of the night might induce labor in a pregnant woman. Independent finance companies can provide money to a business in trouble or to one in need of cash, but that is their only positive aspect. The amount usually will not be as much as could be gained from a bank, since independents tend to loan a lower percentage of the value of the receivables. Not only that, they charge a higher interest rate—probably anywhere from 12 to 15 percent if the prime rate is at 6, double or triple what the bank would charge—so you wind up paying more for less. Admittedly, they are taking a greater risk and, for that, they will try to nail you to the wall.

Yet there is another more important but less obvious potential cost that is associated with independent finance companies. Entrepreneurs actually sell their receivables to them and so lose control over collections. Bankers would rather give you **The Money** and trust you to collect the receivables to pay the bank back. Independents are not that trusting, and literally wind up with your customers—the good payers and the bad debts—in their hands. The danger is they can hardly be expected to be as diplomatic, understanding or even polite as you when they dun people for payment. Whereas if you borrow against your receivables from the bank, you still own the receivables and the bank will not hassle your client base. But give your receivables to an independent who screams and yells at your clients for payment and you may lose those clients. Start losing customers and the word likely will spread—and before you know it your (former) finance source and your (former) competitors will be the only ones talking to your (former) customers.

Another source of capital for a business hoping to survive or grow might be a **leasing company**, which could be your first or last stop for *More Money*. When you raise capital from a leasing company, its not unlike raising capital from an independent finance company. The only difference is, instead of accounts receivable, one or more of your fixed assets—anything already owned by the business or needed to run the business that is not intended for sale—secures the loan. We used a leasing company at MetPath to acquire our two Autochemists. (*Remember? Those were the machines we used to expand our lab production back in Chapter 6.*) The machines each cost $500,000 apiece and, since we definitely did not have a million dollars in cash laying around at the time (or the ability to borrow it), we went to an equipment leasing company.

We "bought" the equipment and "sold" it to a leasing company (on paper), which leased them back to us for five years. We made a monthly payment (i.e., principal plus interest, just like a home mortgage) at a high rate of interest (eight points over prime). At the end of the lease period, we could buy back the machines for $1 apiece, or re-lease them at the then fair-market value of the machines. All of this was part and parcel of an arrangement straightforwardly known as a sale-leaseback agreement.

Straightforward or not, leasing companies are also well aware that most entrepreneurs who show up on their doorstep with assets in hand, looking for expansion capital, are probably in trouble or at the very least unable to get *More Money* from other capital sources, or unable to make the connections. Just like their cousins over in the finance companies, leasing companies want to try and nail you to the wall too, but tend to use bigger nails. They figure they are taking a bigger risk from the outset, since fixed assets often are not as easy to "unload" as receivables, so the interest rate they charge the lessee will be higher than the independent finance companies.

On top of that, most leasing companies try to make a really big chunk of money through residual-value resale or re-leasing.

Chapter Seven: The Kangaroo

▲ ▲ ▲ ▲ ▲

Getting $100,000 from a five-year sale-and-leaseback agreement means you pay back the principal and as much as 15 percent interest every month for sixty months. Not great, but then again, not terrible, until the end of the term. If you have to buy the equipment at a $50,000 fair-market value or re-lease it for another five years at an equally high interest rate so you can keep operating, the cost of that original lease has skyrocketed.

Now for those "notable exceptions" we mentioned earlier, where debt and equity come together. Only those entrepreneurs and businesses in financial trouble need apply, since the healthier ones likely will not be anxious to be bled dry. When finance and leasing companies also start eating into an entrepreneur's equity, they get more exorbitantly expensive as a source for **More Money**. The more creative (greedy?) among them will not even consider loaning funds against receivables or fixed assets unless they are assured of getting a piece of the business for their trouble. That assurance often comes with what are often referred to as *equity kickers*—a term aptly borrowed from the poker table, where a "kicker" or additional ante is made to "sweeten the pot," i.e., make it more attractive for other players to gamble more of their money. The way I look at it, it's an equity kicker when the entrepreneur suggests the idea to the capital source; but when the capital source starts demanding such things, it is more like getting kicked in the equity.

Some leasing companies in my own experience—let's call them **venture leasing companies**—have been particularly predatory in demanding equity positions. One came to MetPath during the first couple of years we were in Hackensack. We were, not unusually, in deep trouble. We had no money and few avenues of capital open to us, and we needed something like $10,000 for a weekly payroll. We called a leasing company to look at an exhibit we had built that we took to shows. Two men arrived and I was in awe that their arms did not seem to fit naturally down by their sides. They wanted to see everything in the building and, after gingerly escorting their bulging underarms through the lab, I watched them get all excited. Then, one guy said to the other in his best B-movie-or-worse Newarkese:

"Hey, Pat! We could do a lot of leasing here, right?"

"Absolutely, Lou!"

"Hey, Doc! What do you want to lease? Equipment, furniture, wastebaskets—whatever you want, we'll lease it for you. And we can get you a lot more than just $10,000."

I was sure that they could, recalling "Frank" and his green-lined desk drawer. I was also quite sure that, as part of the contract, I would have to put my foot size next to my signature, so they would know how big to make the cement overshoes should I not be able to pay them back—and maybe even if I did pay them!

But that was only the half of it. They also wanted an equity kicker in the form of a *warrant*, which would effectively have amounted to giving them about 10 percent of the company at a bargain price within a few years because they were loaning me money against my equipment. A warrant is a **stock option**, giving somebody the right to buy a fixed number of shares of *common stock* at a fixed price at some future date, usually within two to five years.

"Right! But what is **common stock**?"

I do not know who just asked that question, but everyone should be glad someone did. Certainly, explanation of the concept of stock itself is warranted before traveling any further into the business jungle. To begin with, a share of common stock represents a share of equity in a company, whether the company is public or private. Many people think that stock only has to do with public companies trading their stock on the stock market, but that is not true. Stock is just another way of describing the ownership of a company.

A couple of simple concepts must be grasped here. **Authorized shares** (or authorized stock) are all the shares of common stock that can be issued by a company, the maximum number of shares a company may distribute or sell. It is an arbitrary number, defined by the entrepreneur and/or the company's financial management and board of directors. The number of **outstanding shares**, meanwhile, is a real number, the actual number of shares of common stock in the hands of the shareholders, which is all the stock that is generally available for sale. Once stock is on the market (available for sale), every outstanding share of common stock has the same value as every other outstanding share. All authorized stock is not necessarily for sale all the time; when stock is not for sale, it is not outstanding. Since a warrant reserves a percentage of common stock for sale at a later date, for example, it is not yet in anyone's possession. Therefore, it is not for sale and, therefore, does not become outstanding until the warrant is actually exercised.

This knowledge is critical to understanding a concept that many people—entrepreneurs included—seem to have a very hard time understanding: *The relationship between stock ownership and value.* Entrepreneurs who want to maintain control of their companies need to be concerned about what percentage of those outstanding shares they own, since **the value of the company is simply the price per share of stock times the number of outstanding shares.** If you, the entrepreneur, own ten shares of stock that sell for $1,000 a share when your company has only twenty shares outstanding. That means you own 50 percent of the company. That is far better than owning ten shares of your company's stock that sell for $20 a share with 1,000 shares outstanding, since that means you only own 1 percent of your company. Please note that your company in both cases has a value of $20,000.

The value of your company can increase because the price per share of outstanding shares increases, or because the price remains the same and the number of outstanding shares increases. You can authorize and issue new stock as needed for sale in private placements or public offerings, which may increase the value of your company. Remember, though—especially if you want to maintain control of your company—that a greater number of outstanding shares means that your percentage of ownership will decrease unless you buy a proportionate number of shares of the new issue. A higher stock price, then, will be required to raise **More Money** without significantly affecting your ownership. And the only way to set a higher price is to increase the sizzle (sales growth, the promise of profitability) or the steak (profit).

What this means to entrepreneurs searching for **More Money** is that they can give away a greater percentage of their companies and not worry about losing control. Even so, that holds true only so long as things are going well. The risk is that, if things go sour, all those people you sold stock to might band together and start thinking they are smarter than you are ... and you could wind up on the outside looking in on your (former) company. Which is exactly where you were warned you might wind up during the start-up had you then decided to raise capital from **professional investors** (*venture capitalists*). So, if you have been unsuccessful or unwilling to raise money from banks, private investors or other financial sources, professional investors deserve a second look.

Professional investors, after all, are the most creative of all when it comes to figuring out how to raise money; maybe *too* creative, as they occasionally take over businesses themselves. The characteristics they exhibited back in *Chapter 3* certainly have not changed, but a couple of other things may have: either you are better equipped to deal with them or you are in greater need of them. Either way, if your roster of private investors will not take your phone calls and you cannot afford to go into the kind of debt it would take to continue to develop your business, you might want to call up that venture capitalist who gave you his card a few months (or years) ago. Professional investors may now be the way to raise that next round of capital.

The best thing about getting money from a venture capital firm is that you finally have somebody else organizing and looking for

The Money, while you pay attention to running your business. In the beginning, when you needed money to start the company, you went around and beat the bushes because you had nothing else to do. At this stage, you have a lot to do and you probably do not have a big management staff that allows you to take four-week vacations and disappear whenever you want to. You do not have enough time for fundraising, which can be a full-time activity, or close to it. I spent probably 75 percent of my time raising money for HEARx during the first nine years of its existence.

Venture capitalists put the meetings together, bring the investors in, put together the offering circular, and take care of all the details. Sure, you will spend some time working on a new business plan, but after that all you usually have to do is show up to make presentations that they arrange. You still have to hone your "parrot" skills—look nice and talk well, too—but the professionals help sell the deal, which takes off even more pressure.

Another benefit of raising funds through professional investors is that they are realistic and always go into deals knowing that **More Money** will be needed later on. A private investor might go into a deal saying something to himself, "Oh, I'm putting up $10,000 and I'm going to become a millionaire." Venture capitalists think a bit differently: "We're putting up $100,000 and will probably have to put up another $100,000, because the plan probably will not work out the way the entrepreneur thinks it will going to work out." So they are prepared when you come back the next time. The negative, of course, is that they are just as ready to take as much from you as they can when you do come back.

Remember, professional investors are looking at quintupling their investment over five years. It makes no difference to venture capitalists what eventually happens to your company as long as they make a return on their investment. All they are interested in is making money. They can do that whether you run the company or whether they sell it once you are pushed out of the picture. Never forget that the more they own of your company, the more they will try to control things. So if your business has just turned the corner, it may still be a good idea to stay away from professional investors until you make more of a profit so you will not be forced to give up too much of your company. There are other avenues open to you for **More Money**, anyway; see where they lead first. Better to wait until your company is making a good-sized profit, because your valuation will become a multiple of those earnings, rather than projections. (Remember, you are selling steak and it may be worth less than sizzle.) As with any investment, real profits come more from what price you paid for something, rather than what price you sell it.

Chapter Seven: The Kangaroo
▲ ▲ ▲ ▲ ▲

Professional investors, naturally enough, want to buy in as cheaply as possible and they will not value your company as highly as other capital sources would when it is not making any money either. Go to a venture capital firm for money when opportunity knocks and all they hear is opportunity knocking for them, and your business is it. So if you have sizzle to sell, turn up the heat and sell it as hard as you can! If you have not lived up to projections so far and your business is not yet making it ... watch out! The professional investor will try to take an arm and a leg. If you are growing faster than expected, then they will treat you a little bit better because they have no choice. Most of the time, though, they will take the biggest piece of your hide as fast as they can, no matter how well your company is doing.

When HEARx completed a $30 million private placement with a group of institutional investors, they said that they were *really* interested in our long-term game plan and strategy. But when they were confronted with the opportunity to make a 30 percent profit after only six months, almost every one of them sold their positions. If long-term means six months instead of five years, that's fine! We got what we needed and they got what they *really* wanted: a quick profit.

That taught me that everyone who gives you money may not have the same goal as you or even the goal *they* say they have.

That was not the end of my education, however. There seems no end to the predatory habits of professional investors.

You always have to pay attention.

Remember that!

*   *   *   *   *

Perhaps the briefness of a joey's birth is recompense to the mother for having to put up with each offspring as long as she does. Female roos are perennially pregnant, which makes it all the more surprising that joeys are allowed to live in their pouches for as long as they do. It is five months or so before the joey first peeks over the lip of the pouch. At age six months, weighing about four and one-half pounds, it is ready to come out and try its legs. But it quickly goes back after these brief initial excursions, diving in and somersaulting head-over-heels to get its head outside the pouch—coming to rest heels-over-head, its oversized feet jutting out above its ears. While the pouch expands to accommodate these timid youngsters, they can no longer fit when they get to about fourteen or fifteen pounds. Still, those joeys that survive stick around mom for quite some time—males for about a year, females for as long as two—for safety and tutoring.

* * * * *

3. How To Get The (Most) More Money

Corporate partners, in my estimation, are among the best sources for **More Money**. They should not be classified simply as **corporate investors**, which is a very important distinction. Corporate investors, such as a pension fund or the investment division of a conglomerate, are not at all different from any other group of sophisticated investors out there in the business jungle. Like professional investors or venture leasing companies, corporate investors are not putting money in your company because they like you. They might never even meet you! They do it because they want to make money. The major difference between corporate investors and other investor types is that they are harder to find. Professional investors who make a living raising money may be able to locate and tap into a corporation for the dollars you need, but entrepreneurs would have a hard time getting near them.

Corporate partners are even harder to find. Your business can be growing like crazy and even be profitable. You can approach them and send them a business plan. But most of the time they are not even interested. The reason is that corporate partners have other priorities besides money when they seek to invest in a company. They may not be looking just to make money on their investment, nor to take over your company, like other investor types. In fact, they are likely to give you **More Money** and take less equity than any other group of investors, shy of a public offering of your shares on Wall Street. The last thing they want to do is run your company; they want you to run it for them, which means you also get to keep operational control.

Corporate partners do not see money as their primary goal. Although they certainly are not looking to lose any money, they have other axes to grind. If they are players in the same market your business is in, for example, they might invest in your company with the idea of acquiring it some time in the future or to expand market share for one of their subsidiaries or divisions. Potential corporate partners might see the purchase of an entrepreneurial company as a relatively inexpensive way to enter what they believe to be a growing market. Very often, the primary reason is to test their products and/or their advertising. They have a "little problem" they want solved and that is where you and your company come in. Can you help test and improve their products? Can you help define the market?

Whatever is on their mind, corporate partners are not as greedy as any other investors because they have other reasons for making their investments. The most important thing for an entrepreneur to have is patience when dealing with potential corporate partners, since corporations are glacially slow when it comes to making decisions. You will need all of that patience when you encounter their "what do we need you for?" attitude. But that is simply the way it is! Since they have a lot of money and are obviously more successful than you, they automatically think they have more talent in every area. **Corporate partners are bigger, so they believe they are better.** Yet it is their size and reach, their fiscal and operational prowess, which make big businesses attractive to an entrepreneur looking for a corporate sponsor.

On the surface, it appeared that when Corning invested in MetPath, they became our "corporate partner." The deal was done very quickly, within sixty days from the time we first started talking. But the reality was that it was the end of an already long search for Corning. They had made the decision that they needed a clinical lab long before they came to us, after looking at three other companies. All had ethical or legal problems and Corning actually had given up their search. They had concluded that there was no one to invest in that had the right strategy and operations or who could meet their standards of ethics. Then, over a period of a few months, a major banking institution, a competitor and a leading headhunter for scientific personnel all suggested to Corning that they go take a look at MetPath. We were only doing about $4 million annually in sales at that time and, of course, losing money. But we had a lot of sizzle; Corning was aware of our sales growth and interested in the efforts we had already initiated to help clean up the clinical laboratory industry.

The deal might have come about rapidly after that, except for the negotiations. Corning wanted to invest $1 million in the company in a stock deal. MetPath stock was trading for $5 a share at the time. Even though we had no money, I automatically felt that a better price was in order, since there was a buyer before there was a seller. They knew that and I knew that, but I must admit that I got a bit carried away. But then, I was only twenty-nine years old with delusions of grandeur and had already turned down a lot of money from venture capitalists (*back in Chapter 3, if you remember*), after I saw they would have taken over the company at the drop of a hat. I was determined not to make it easy for anyone else.

"Well, it's very simple, guys," I told the Corning executive and his entourage who were involved in the negotiations. "I will sell you one share of common stock for five dollars, because that's what you can buy on the open market. But the more you want to buy, the more you have to pay."

"You want to run that by us again?"

"Sure," I pressed on. "If you go into the open market to buy my stock, the more you want to buy, the more you will have to pay. So that's how we'll work it for this deal. I'll sell you $1 million worth of stock at eight dollars a share."

"What? That's ridiculous! Your stock's only trading at five dollars," they came back. After a lengthy discussion, they offered me seven dollars a share.

"No, no, no," I said. "Eight dollars, or no deal!"

We argued over that dollar until I finally walked out of the meeting. The headhunter that put us together called me up later that day.

"I don't believe that, for one lousy dollar," he roared at me, "you walked out on Corning as a corporate partner. MetPath is flat on its back, desperately in need of capital, and you refuse to take their money because you want more. What's wrong with seven dollars a share?"

"They'll be back," I said confidently. Despite the financial pressure, I stuck to my guns. (My attorney was very supportive of this, by the way, and came up with an interesting way of defining such negotiations when we developed our strategies to sell the business—which you will hear all about in *Chapter 9*.) The wait for Corning's response was tough, but I survived it. Finally, the headhunter called back.

"Look," he began quietly. "You want to get a higher price, they've got to save face." He explained to me that buying into a five dollars a share company at eight dollars a share was too embarrassing. "So why don't you do the deal at $7.50, using preferred stock instead of common stock? Then they save face and you split the difference with them on the price of the stock." So I said okay and everything got put back on track, for a little while, anyway.

The deal was very simple using common stock, but doing a **preferred stock** deal complicated things. Preferred stock involves special rights concerning liquidity, preferences (in case your company goes out of business) and often dividends. A **convertible preferred stock** deal, for example, allows conversion of preferred stock into common stock based on some formula, e.g., one share of preferred stock might pay a dividend, but it can be converted to common stock at any time.

You can easily imagine that, once the lawyers got into drafting the papers, the deal got more and more complicated each day until things were at an impasse all over again. Finally, a Corning executive called me and we agreed instead to a common stock deal at $7.50 a share. As soon as we announced that Corning had bought in at $7.50, the stock immediately went up to that price on the market and never traded below that. That negotiation was the exception rather than the rule, however. If the entrepreneur pursues the corporate investor, things work a bit differently.

When HEARx pursued 3M as its corporate partner, we found out what a slow decision-making process really was. Aside from the fact that they were not looking for us, 3M is a much larger company than Corning. We had to talk to them for more than six months before they showed any interest in us at all, and then it took another six months before they agreed to make their first investment. 3M, unlike Corning, was willing to invest only at a price below the market value of the stock (although still above the *real* value of a company that was not making any profit.) Even though 3M's investment in HEARx was being made for essentially the same reasons as Corning's investment in MetPath, Corning only took 10 percent of MetPath, while 3M started with about 17 percent of HEARx and until late 1997 owned about 11 percent. Corning wanted an arms-length relationship with MetPath, since it already had sizable medical lab-related businesses it wanted to expand. 3M's relationship with HEARx was to be more arms-around, to help their start-up hearing-care business.

The important thing, for both MetPath and HEARx, was that they had **the right corporate partners at the right time.** Differences and negotiating strategies notwithstanding, they each wanted to make the investment as much as I wanted them to. The great thing about most corporate investor relationships is that everybody wins. 3M learned how to make a better product and develop a better marketing program by working with HEARx, and made a significant profit when it sold its shares. HEARx increased its market share and its revenues while working with 3M. That is part of the payoff for patience. There are many long-term potential benefits that come with a corporate partner and must be considered in making any deal, whether the terms are absolutely in the entrepreneur's favor at the beginning or not. Relatively easy access to future funds, as well as to corporate, financial, marketing, product development and organizational expertise, are important advantages that could accrue to the entrepreneur.

Those are future considerations, however. There is no way of telling who, if anyone, will come along and show an interest in your humble company. The primary focus for the entrepreneur in the initial stages of any relationship with a corporate partner should remain gaining needed expansion capital. Once the right one does come along, however, it can become a long, steady and mutually beneficial relationship in many areas. Corporate partners typically wind up to be the most loyal supporters an entrepreneur can have, but they are not without their faults. They may even seem very fickle and can change their minds in an instant—like when 3M decided to sell their hearing-aid business, which was the reason they made the investment in HEARx in the first place. Major corporations operate on such a large scale that some global trend, all but invisible to you, might alter their strategy.

On top of that, you must adapt to a corporate partner's decision-making process—long, long, long! You may have to wait months while executives overcome the paralysis of over-analysis that can strike them at any time. Large corporations seem to have a hard time just figuring out what is on their collective mind before they can begin to take a long time to make up that mind to do anything. This characteristic, one of their least attractive traits, persists long after they have put money into your company.

Once, when I asked 3M to make a loan instead of an investment with funds previously approved by the corporation, I was told that would make things more difficult. The reason? A loan would require the approval of a loan committee since the funds had been approved for an equity investment only. Further along in our relationship, I waited and waited for 3M to approve a particular advertisement I had proposed. My instinct told me it would work. It was tough enough waiting for the approval; but when the campaign finally got the go ahead and indeed proved successful, it was exceptionally frustrating that we had wasted so much time when there was money to be made.

Remember, what makes you an entrepreneur is that you often shoot from the hip and sometimes miss the target. Corporate partners often do not want to even draw the gun until absolutely sure they will hit the target—and even then, they miss! But that is just the way things are. It is not that corporate partners are not capable of making a decision quickly, it is just not in their culture. That does not mean it cannot happen, though: 3M actually decided on a $1 million additional investment in a four-day time span. I think we are both still in shock!

That could well be the major reason why relationships with corporate partners last so long; if they did not, there would never be time enough for them to make a decision! Perhaps their plodding reticence can be understood, since they have to contend with constantly shifting business goals and strategies, internal politics, financial concerns and executive agendas. My view is that it has a lot to do with management structure. Decisions can be delayed for months as you run the gauntlet of committees at corporate,

departmental, and/or divisional levels. These are most often composed of people who are most interested in avoiding blame if the
deal goes wrong. A score or more of *decision influencers* and *super-
decision influencers* must be satisfied before you even get close to
the real decision-makers—and you may never meet them, even if
things go in your favor!

Though many steps removed from the deal, these are the realities that an impatient entrepreneur will never be able to handle—
unless you happen to be a prophet and a mind reader, too. You
never know how things are going to work out. The bottom line for
Corning came ten years later when they bought MetPath for nearly $140 million, closed their other two businesses, and wound up
with a clinical testing business and other testing entities that grew
to almost $2 billion before getting spun off to Corning sharehold-
ers as Quest Diagnostics.

Whatever happens, a true corporate partner is just as interested in having your business succeed as you are and is willing to
help. They can even come to share your vision of the future and
can actually help make your business succeed. Unlike professional investors, they are not just looking to make a quick buck and
get out; likewise, entrepreneurs cannot look for corporate partners
with the idea of just getting bailed out of financial trouble. Too
many other things have to fit for them to make the investment.
But if you can find a corporate partner that wants to invest in your
business, you will be extremely well off. If you underestimated
your need, they can live with that. Growing faster than expected?
That's great! Want capital to expand? That's super! They are looking at you as a long-term strategic investment, not as a short-term
gain. Most other investors, by comparison, are looking at you as a
ticket to win the lottery.

Which brings us to **public offerings**, the ultimate way to raise
More Money for your business. They are better than the lottery,
but considerably more costly. We have already spoken quite a bit
about the initial public offering and public offerings in general.
From there, the way into the Promised Land of public offerings
goes through the door of Wall Street **brokerage firms (investment
bankers)** and eventually reaches the stock market investor.

Brokerage houses, it must be understood, do not care very
much about your company. They want a successful stock offering
because that leads to the next stock offering, which they hope to
sell to the same investors and collect on that deal, too. If you can
remember all the way back to *Chapter 3*, we called venture capitalists greedy cowards. If that is true, then most everyone on Wall
Street is just plain greedy. Brokers, of course, have to pick winners more often than losers in order to build a reputation and

attract investors so they must consider how your company looks on paper. But it is *all* paper, as far as they are concerned, and that is the way it looks to a lot of investors, too.

What is of utmost concern, however, is your *story* and how it will look and sound to an investor reading the prospectus or listening to you talk. **The better the story, the *More Money* brokers will be able to raise.** The more they raise for you, the more they make, since they get a percentage of the deal as a commission. They also get an equity kicker, usually consisting of five-year warrants to purchase common stock equivalent to 10 percent of the shares they sold, all at the original offering price.

Everyone on Wall Street particularly likes a story with a **black box** (something coming in the future but not quantifiable now). The possibility of a future breakthrough creates the thought in investors' minds that they could make a whole lot *More Money* than they expect—maybe even *Big Money*! A black box has a lot of sizzle but little substance. HEARx, for example, had been negotiating for a contract with a major university for rights to a drug under development that would stop tinnitus, commonly known as ringing in the ear. There are 36 million people with tinnitus who would gladly pay a dollar a day to get rid of it. That works out to potential annual sales of $11 billion. Now that is what I call a black box!

Since the idea or prototype has not been fully realized, you never let anyone see what is in the black box. What happens with most black boxes, as you might imagine, is that when the product comes out of the box, it does not work. One of the big black boxes we had with MetPath was a test for cancer. We worked two years on developing it, but we never could really get it to work. So we nailed the box shut, threw it in the ocean, and went looking for a new black box. But for a while it was a real possibility, which helped create and sustain investor interest in MetPath.

So, if you want the best value for your company, head for Wall Street. You will raise *The Most Money* while giving up the least percentage of your company. Your investment banker will get you whatever the market will bear. Such a high-powered, fast-paced environment demands that you know your numbers, but the numbers that really count are not necessarily in your business projections. What Wall Street is figuring is how much money they are going to make, not how much your business will. Remember, small investors believe in you, the entrepreneur; professional investors and venture capitalists believe in financial projections; banks definitely believe in collateral; while corporate partners believe in themselves. Wall Street investors, on the other hand, believe what their brokers tell them, for the most part... which is often baloney.

Obviously, **brokers believe in commissions**. Let me give you an idea of just how firmly they believe in commissions. MetPath at one point had a deal with a brokerage house to do a **firm underwriting**, in which the price of the stock and the commission rate are not set until the day before you sell the stock. It turns out that there is nothing firm in a firm underwriting. The least solid item in your offering will be the price that the shares will be sold at—which will be just about as firm as Jell-O. The letter of intent for an underwriting from the investment banker may state a proposed price, but that letter and a dollar bill might get you a cup of coffee. The brokers pre-sell the issue based on that expected price and it gets scheduled to be sold on the day of the sale—the day following final approval of the documents from the SEC (Securities and Exchange Commission). But even then, you have to wait five days before you get any money, barring a *force majeure*, a cataclysmic event that would cancel the deal.

On one of MetPath's public offerings (we had about six), when we sent out the **red herring**—the red-bordered offering statement prepared for investors prior to SEC approval—MetPath stock was trading at seventeen dollars in this particular deal. The brokers went on the street with it, lining up the investors, getting them ready to put their money down. But just as we were about to get our SEC approval the stock fell to twelve dollars, which meant that the deal would not bring in as much money as originally planned.

Now, I was not a Wall Street professional, privy to all the reasons why stocks go up and down. When the broker gave me this big speech that it was natural, I put my naive hat on and decided that I was being screwed. There was more to it than just the question of commission. Depending on the size of the offering, the printing, accounting, and legal costs can easily run to $150,000, to say nothing about the management time and expense to put on the road show—traveling around from city to city, trying to sell investors on the deal. To this must be added the underwriter's expenses for legal, travel, and miscellaneous, plus of course, their commissions. So, the cost of having a public offering can range from 15 percent to 20 percent of the amount to be raised.

I got a little heated. Since the stock had gone down five points because of market conditions, I figured it was not a good time to raise money. I tore up the deal and walked out. A year later we were back with them for another offering. This time, however, I added a much better known brokerage house as a co-underwriter. I did that because I felt I needed their clout. Both brokerage houses were reputable enough to assure a successful offering. I felt more comfortable having two investment bankers handling the deal, considering what had happened the year before. I was no longer naive and I was not taking any chances. But when we sat down to negotiate the stock price and their commission on the deal (at the pricing meeting), after receiving our SEC approval to go effective, the head of the brokerage did not waste any time.

"Paul …," he began, not looking at me, leaving a small silence at the end of my name for dramatic effect.

Why, I wondered to myself in that moment, *do so many of these discussions start off with someone calling me by my first name, and then pausing?*

"… we remember the way you tore up our underwriting and threw it away last year." Then he looked at me and smiled. "I'm glad that the stock didn't drop the precipitous way it did last time."

I just sat there and chuckled. *Here it comes!*

"But," he pressed on quickly, "we're going to have to charge you 6.75 percent to do this deal. It's been a much harder deal to sell."

I just sat there, still smiling, not saying a word. He must have gauged my response positively, so he went ahead and delivered what he probably imagined would be the *coup de grace*:

"As a matter of fact, it isn't all sold, Paul!

Oops! He's calling my name again.

Leaning back in his leather-bound swivel chair, he nonchalantly added, "So we'll have to trim a quarter of a point off the price and increase the brokers' commission."

I kept smiling. "Jack …," I began, and immediately got his attention. "… that's just terrible!"

His eyes darted from side to side before looking at me quizzically, but I did not give him a chance to interrupt.

"Why," I pressed on, "don't we make everybody happy? Instead of trying to close on 450,000 shares tomorrow morning, let's go with the 350,000 that are already sold. That way, there's no problem, and you don't have to worry about selling those other 100,000 shares!"

And that is exactly what we wound up doing.

Now, the uninitiated might think me daring, even—God forbid!—lucky. Not so! What could he do? It was my company, my shares, and I could sell as much or as little as I wanted. Though he was losing a commission on 100,000 shares, there were still 350,000 shares to sell—a figure that no broker could walk away from. After that, for some reason, I never again had any problems doing my deals on Wall Street.

There have been other times when a firm underwriting with large brokerage houses would have been a disaster. Years later, when I cut the deal for the HEARx IPO (that stands for "initial public offering," in case you have forgotten) of $3.3 million in October of 1987, I made it a **best efforts underwriting**. That means the price of the stock and the broker's commission get set months in advance. The price was fixed at ten dollars a unit (there were shares and warrants) and the commission was set at 10 percent. There was nothing to negotiate further; either the deal was going to go or it was not. But that is not the only advantage to a best efforts deal; with it, you get an automatic time extension to complete the offering if you fail to close the first time. As things turned out, we needed every advantage we could get.

I used a small broker, because I wanted whoever sold the IPO to be aggressive. I did not need the clout of a big-name broker, since I already had my own reputation on Wall Street. The combination proved to be the right one: a tremendous effort resulted in over $7 million worth of indications for orders of our stock by Thursday, October 15. We were all ready to go, but the practice on Wall Street is not to do a sale on Friday, since investors tend to back out of deals when they have a weekend to think about it. So we waited until Monday, October 19, 1987—better known as "Black Monday," the day the stock market fell through the floor. When the market opened at 10 a.m. that day, our $7 million of potential orders went to zero and there was no deal.

What saved us was that it was a best efforts underwriting, and we were able to use the time extension to do the deal. We all worked to sell it—me included! Finally, on February 5, 1988, the entire $3.3 million offering was concluded, with a third of the new shares going to MetPath employees, one-third going to previous shareholders and the remainder going to new shareholders. Timing (need we say it?) is everything in the stock market, as it is in the Business Jungle.

If I had gone with a major investment banker and had a firm underwriting (they do not do best efforts deals) for the HEARx IPO, I would have gotten the same kind of treatment I received when I took MetPath public in 1970. That deal started out as a firm underwriting for an estimated eight dollars a share on an offering of 125,000 shares, but we wound up selling 150,000 shares at six dollars a share instead. The investment bankers convinced me that, in order to do the deal, I would have to personally add 25,000 shares of my own so that they could complete the offering. The deal got done, although I had to give up more of the company than I wanted to at the time, but it all worked out for the best in the end. Just look what I eventually made on my original $500 investment: $10 million after taxes! So it was a good thing I gave in. Timing (need we say it, *again*?) is everything on the stock market, as it is in the business jungle.

There are only a few things you really need to know how to use if you are looking to fill your pouch with **More Money**. We have already talked about all of them. You do not have to be an expert in any of them. If you need an expert, you hire one. You just need to know what these things are and how they work. They are the basic tools for financial survival for the entrepreneur, the building blocks of what might be called "advanced finance." Whether your company is public or private, making a profit or not, growing or standing still, if you need **More Money**, you now possess all you need to know to get it.

Once you have filled your pouch with **More Money**, you have to get back to work.

You have a company to build, remember?

So, what are you going to do with all that money?

Perhaps you should go buy something ...

$ECRET$ OF THE KANGAROO

*Too Much Money can delay success
as much as too little money can.*

---

*Giving up control of your company
before profitability is reached
may also mean giving up your job.*

---

*Different types of investors should be used
for The Money at different stages
of your company's growth.*

Satisfying Your Appetite

Chapter Eight
The Tiger: Satisfying Your Appetite

▲ ▲ ▲ ▲ ▲

Tiger (Panthera tigris) is a four-legged catlike beast rivaled only by the lion in size, strength and ferocity. The tiger is of the same genus (carnivora) as the lion, but native only to Asia. However, various breeds range over most of that huge territory, as far north as Siberia and northern China; to the islands of Sumatra, Java, and Bali in the Indian Ocean to the south; east to the island of Sakhalin off the Russian coast in the Sea of Okhotsk; and as far west as Turkish Georgia. Tigers favor grassy plains and jungle swamps, yet they are also fond of forests and seem to like living in and near old ruins. They normally do not climb tress, but will when pressed; they also take to water and are good swimmers. Their adaptability to various environments and conditions leaves few places safe for their prey.

*　　*　　*　　*　　*

Acquisition hunger was strong at MetPath in the mid to late '70s, once the company began making a profit. The grand scheme, envisioned years before when Metropolitan Pathology Laboratory opened in that two-room apartment across the street from Columbia Presbyterian Hospital in New York, had become more of a possibility than a pipe dream. Expansion through acquisition was the key to its fulfillment. We had become big enough to be taken seriously, and had sufficient resources in terms of real profits and access to capital to back up our intentions.

But we never knew what we were going to encounter, once we started hunting potential acquirees, nor how the chase would turn out. Sometimes the kill was swift and easy; other times long, drawn-out battles ensued between prey and predator, the outcome in doubt to the very end. Acquisition is a risky business, after all, even when the hunted walks right up to the hunter, begging to be eaten.

Take Grace & Company's laboratory division—please! That was just about what one of their executives said when he called us at our New Jersey headquarters in 1978, telling us that Grace had decided to sell off its lab division.

"Are you interested in purchasing the division?"

"Well, yes, we might be," I answered cagily.

"Good," came the matter-of-fact reply. "We'll have our corporate plane pick you up at Teterboro Airport and fly you here to Cincinnati. You may bring your attorney with you; just don't tell anyone where you are going. We're not telling anyone else about this." And that included anyone else in their own company; we were not going to be allowed to look inside any of Grace's lab facilities or talk to other personnel.

So intent were they on getting it done quietly that we met, not at the lab's headquarters but in a Cincinnati hotel room, to begin negotiations. The Grace people wanted $10 million for the lab division. We had no way of knowing for sure if the balance sheet and sales figures were for real, and we told them we had a problem with that.

"No problem," the main Grace negotiator replied. "We will legally represent the figures as true and warranty everything."

Which was really another way for him to say the following:

"Look, we want out of this business as quickly and cleanly as possible. Here are our numbers: Our accounts receivable total $3.6 million. If you don't collect that much, we'll make up the difference. We owe $2.2 million to our creditors. If it turns out we owe more than that, we'll make up the difference. We think the business is worth $10 million. We will make it up to you if anything we say is not the truth." We settled at about $8 million, and all the contracts were written, signed, and delivered in ten days.

The deal was so clean and quick that it required little more negotiating prowess than staying awake and on our feet. But that is the exception and not the rule; things usually are slower and messier—sometimes a lot slower and a lot messier. A few years earlier, nearly the exact opposite of the Grace deal occurred when MetPath became interested in buying what was at the time Bristol-Meyers' laboratory subsidiary, Biomedical Procedures, in California. They wanted nearly $8 million for that business when we showed up and started talking to them in the mid '70s.

Although Bristol-Meyers, like Grace, wanted to keep the deal quiet, they were willing to let us tour the laboratory facility. They warned us sternly not to tell anyone they were selling. I agreed without hesitation. Then, when they told us it was okay to come out and look at the lab, the Bristol-Meyers negotiating team wanted an added precaution: They did not want to tell anyone who I was. I agreed to that too, but it really did not matter. As it turned out, their carefully executed plan was doomed from the start.

When we got to the lab they introduced me as "Dr. Bennett" to the chief pathologist there. My "cover" was that I was a pathologist from a New York hospital who wanted to see how the lab ran, as I was supposedly thinking of doing business with them. Small talk purposely was kept to a minimum as we tooled around the lab, but I was able to ask many questions that more than satisfied my real need for information. Their plan for secrecy was holding up fine until we got about halfway through the tour.

"Paul! Why, Paul Brown," someone called out as we passed one of the testing stations. "What are you doing here?"

"What ... !?!"

"Who ... !?!"

"How ... !?!"

Exclamations began popping out of everyone's mouth as the entourage came to a dead halt. I turned to see a smiling lab technician coming towards me, hand outstretched in greeting.

"It's so good to see you, Paul," he said, vigorously shaking my hand. "How are you?"

"I'm just fine," I said quickly. The unexpected greeting came from a former MetPath employee from New Jersey who had moved to California several years before and wound up working for Bristol Meyers. I fielded his exuberant questions as well as I could, while one of the Bristol-Meyers negotiators quietly tried to explain the situation to the obviously perplexed chief pathologist. His expression changed from surprised to embarrassed to indignant, as I meanwhile brought the unexpected interview to as quick a conclusion as possible. We regrouped, but it was too late. The cat was out of the bag.

As the tour moved away from his station, we all could hear the technician unconsciously adding insult to injury as he innocently told another technician:

"Do you know who that was? That's Paul Brown, the man who founded MetPath!"

Despite the *faux pas*, negotiations continued without the cover of secrecy that they had hoped to maintain. There were a few other secrets Bristol-Meyers was trying to keep, as well; secrets much more serious as far as MetPath was concerned. The negotiators gave us all their numbers, showing they had put approximately $5 million into the division, built a $5 million facility and had lost $5 million each year for a couple of years. So they were into it for about $20 million, with annual sales of close to $10 million.

MetPath had just started to make money and was not all that big yet, but was in good position for initial expansion. This was our first big hunt and we were very excited—almost too excited. We thought we had been given a good view of the quarry but a financial trap had been laid that we nearly missed. The pitfall was hidden in their sales figures. A good portion of the strong sales growth they showed on paper was from a recent promotion that gave doctors lab tests at a discount if they bought a coupon book. A doctor would pre-pay perhaps $100 for a coupon book with ten blood-sugar test coupons in it, each coupon representing, say, a 50 percent savings over the regular price of those tests. The coupon was sent instead of money whenever a test was ordered and the doctor's account would be credited.

It was simple enough: discounts and coupons are perfectly good promotional tools. They seemed to offer no impediment to the deal, so we wrote the contracts, and everything was ready. Then, at what was supposed to be our final meeting, I asked what proved to be an all-important question:

"How many coupons have you sold, by the way?"

"What do you mean," they responded defensively, "how many coupons have we sold?"

"Well," I pressed on, more than a little surprised, "you show sales increasing every month. Don't you know how many of the sales you've recorded are coupon sales?"

"That's not important," they replied.

"Excuse me, but it's very important," I said. "Those tests that haven't been done yet will have to be done in the future, after you sell the division and I own it. So I need to know how many coupons you have outstanding because that is a liability for me. If I acquire the business, I'll have to do those tests for free because you already have gotten the money."

"Well," they answered, a little *too* quickly, "we have no idea how many coupons we sold. We have no numbers on that."

"Well, I think you're going to have to find some, just to protect yourself," I suggested, "since you're going to have to pay me for every coupon that comes in. I'll honor the coupons, but it is only fair that I am paid for them. You've already gotten your dollar, but haven't done any work. *I'll* be doing the work." It sounded reasonable to me but they would not hear of it, refusing again to tell me how many coupon sales there were. Several voices were raised simultaneously from both sides of the table as the disagreement became a little heated.

"STOP!" Their chief negotiator shouted down the din, then added in his most reasonable tones, "Why don't we just stop all this fencing? Either you want the deal, or you don't."

"We're not fencing," I replied. "I want those figures."

"LOOK!" One of their more exasperated negotiators called out. "How much could the risk be? We have only been selling coupons for a little while."

"I need to know how many," I came back sharply, "or there is no deal!" That pronouncement brought another healthy chorus of raised voices.

"LISTEN, Paul," the chief negotiator broke in loudly, silencing the room once again. "Why don't we just *stop* all this. *Look*, the papers are all ready to sign! *Listen* to me and finish the deal!"

"No, I can't do that right now. I'll call you," I said, leaving them at the conference table. But I did call them at 5 p.m. the next day, as I was driving to what was supposed to be the closing. Everyone was in New York with the lawyers, ready to make the $7.8 million deal, but I said, "No thanks, I've decided not to do it. It's too risky."

They continued to try to sell the division but no one else would bite. After I had turned them down, potential purchasers became very cautious when they pursued the deal. They went over the same ground I did, saw the same things, and likewise turned away from the chase. One year later, Bristol-Meyers had exhausted all other avenues before they came back and spoke with me again.

That was when I bought the division, but the price was now $1.8 million instead of $7.8 million.

Which just goes to show ...

It ain't over until it's over!

*   *   *   *   *

Although superficially distinct, lions and tigers are very closely allied both anatomically and physiologically. They have been known to mate under certain conditions; the offspring are called "tigons" or "ligers," depending on their paternity. A tigress may have litters of as many as six cubs, but three is the common number. Smaller and more lightly colored than her mate, she is a dutiful mother, and will defend her cubs with courage and energy—although she may desert her offspring and might even eat them in times of famine. Normally, however, she kills meat for the cubs as she teaches them to hunt small animals. She trains and protects the cubs until they are about two years old, or until they are able to kill food for themselves.

*   *   *   *   *

1. *What's A Buyer To Buy?*

Children in city neighborhoods often played a game called "Truth, Dares, Consequences, Remembrances or Repeats." One was asked to tell the truth, to perform a feat, to recall some fact, to imitate a tongue twister—or suffer a consequence. Usually, that was something dreadful to a ten-year-old boy or girl, such as the former being made to give the latter a kiss or the latter suffered to pick up something squirmy by the former.

Growth-minded entrepreneurs—and which ones are not?—play a modified edition of the same game when looking to make acquisitions. If they refuse to take a chance, ask the wrong questions, forget an important fact, or miss a misstatement, there will be consequences. Only they will be quite a bit more serious than those endured in the childhood version of the game.

The possible penalties of the game still require that participants possess at least a little bit of honesty, plus two other important attributes: courage and knowledge. Surely, it takes courage to kiss a girl or to pick up a frog, as difficult as those things might be. Worse yet, however, would be to pick up a frog and kiss it, expecting it to turn into royalty. The trick is to know which frogs are enchanted and which ones are not.

Now, courage and honesty, like the entrepreneurial spirit, cannot be learned. Either you have them or you don't. But knowledge—ah, that is something else again. And all you need to know how to succeed at the entrepreneurial edition of the game are three things:

DR. BROWN'S ACQUISITION PRESCRIPTION

1. *Focus on what will be gained from the acquisition.*

2. *Find out why the seller is selling.*

3. *Figure out what it is worth and how to pay for it.*

Not by accident, these three points make up the three sections of this chapter and are the closest thing to rules that acquisitive entrepreneurs will come by. There are no "Rules of Acquisition," because each deal is different. Only the specific details and your own business knowledge and experience will tell you what or what not to buy, or how to negotiate the purchase. No one can tell you how much to pay for someone else's business either, since there are so many constantly shifting market, money and management forces that affect the value of a deal. What should not be shifting, however, is the picture of what you intend to buy in order to grow your business.

Entrepreneurs need to focus on specific acquisition targets. If you do not know how to choose them, pay close attention to this chapter. But first, go back to your business plan. The path for your growth should already have been decided. Never mind that getting to this point has taken you twice as long and cost you twice as much as you expected! But somewhere in that plan should be a description of the type(s) of business(es) you hope to get into. If they are not there, then you need to fire your advisors, hire some new ones and write a plan that includes exactly for what it is you are looking.

Whatever your planning horizons, **there are only three types of businesses or companies that entrepreneurs can buy.**

1. *Something that*

   E   X   P   A   N   D   S

   your base business.

2. *Something that V*
                  E
   INTEGRATES with your base business.
                  T
                  I
                  C
                  A
                  L
                  L
                  Y

3. *Something that is*

                         COMPLETELY UNRELATED

   to your base business.

You may eventually buy all three types of companies in your business life, but you can only buy them one at a time—unless you have unlimited access to capital and do not care if you lose everything because of a bad decision. One step at a time, one company at a time, is the best way to play the acquisition game; otherwise, your attention divided, you will make a mistake that will have to be paid for, sooner or later.

The most common and most obvious acquisitions are **companies that expand the base business**. If you are in the clinical lab business, then it would make sense to acquire another clinical lab. If you are in the retail hearing-care business, then another retail operation is a likely next step. Expansion most often means gaining additional facilities, a higher market share, an increased revenue base and more profit potential in your own and/or other geographic marketplaces—all related directly to your base.

Acquisition is not the only path to expansion, by the way. HEARx, at this writing, has a 20 percent share of the retail hearing-care market in Palm Beach, Dade, and Broward counties in south Florida. Were we to acquire more centers, we obviously could increase our market share. But we could also increase our market share by spending more money on marketing or by opening more retail centers ourselves.

Each situation will be different. The decision of how to expand your presence or increase penetration in a given market must be based on any number of current business realities. Every businessman, of course, would like to have 100 percent of a market. You can, but there is one condition: The government does not allow you to buy an entire market by going around and acquiring all of your competitors. But if you gain 100 percent of a market by way of marketing prowess, there is no law against that.

The second potential acquisition group involves **companies that enhance your base business, allowing vertical integration**. As opposed to expansion, the idea here is to buy something that will help your base business be more profitable, which is the whole point of vertical integration. The focus must remain there, and not turn into a mere exercise in collecting companies.

HEARx bought a hearing diagnostic equipment distribution company in Georgia. Why? Because we were already buying diagnostic equipment and owning a distributor meant we could buy at a discount. Certainly, there was a potential opportunity to make money with the distributor from the sale of equipment to others and there is nothing wrong with that. But the focus of the acquisition was on vertical integration, the opportunity to benefit our base business by saving money on equipment purchases.

Now, in case you have missed the obvious point here, let me drive it home with a subsequent revelation. We later divested ourselves of that distributor when the general U.S. economic climate and governmental scrutiny of dubious practices in the hearing aid industry (two things we had no control over) made things tough for the retail hearing aid industry.

HEARx has survived not because we are marketing geniuses or know some fiscal wizards, or even because we stand on the side of right. Those things are important, of course! But the basic reason for our survival was the ability to change our strategy and be flexible; for example, divesting ourselves of the equipment distributor when times got hard. If we could not let go of the distributorship (which we sold to its employees, by the way), then our base business would have been in jeopardy.

The third possible group of acquisition targets are those **companies that enlarge the concept of your base business**. This means going into a whole new field, something brand new that is completely unrelated to your current base business. Now, that is not to say your existing customers will not be interested in the new product or service that you offer them; ideally, they should be. But the acquired business itself will not add profitability to what you are already doing.

A perfect example is that HEARx once looked at an opportunity to acquire a product line that removes wax from the ear. Now, ear wax is a problem for the hearing-impaired, which is our customer base, and also for the non-hearing impaired. If we acquire the product, it is something that we can sell to our existing customer base and to everyone else. We could distribute it exclusively through HEARx stores or through other retail outlets. Either way, we could probably make money with it, but it is unlikely to add a dime to our base business.

Some entrepreneurs, possessed perhaps with more guts than good sense, take this option to an extreme. "The company I buy doesn't have to have anything to do with my customer base," one might say. "I'm just really smart and I have a fantastic management team. We can run anything. We'll just do it all over again and run our other business besides." History shows us that success in conglomerate-building is a rare occurrence, indeed. Back in the '60s people would buy anything, but most of those conglomerates choked and never made it to the '90s.

That last note brings to mind another important caveat that holds true no matter what type of business you buy: **Exactly what you want could be more than you can handle.** When MetPath acquired the W.R. Grace clinical laboratory division, for example, we unwittingly bought a business that almost choked us to death. The price was right, we did the deal quickly and cleanly, but our eyes almost proved bigger than our stomachs. It was too big for us to acquire at the time and we barely survived the digestive process, which took almost a year. Your company just cannot swallow a thousand new employees in one weekend!

The point is that if you are going to go buy something with your profits or, more likely, the capital just raised in Chapter 7, be as sure as you can that it is the right something. Look at a lot of somethings and then look at everything to do with those somethings. Weigh them all, look at them from every conceivable angle, and pray you make the correct choice before you actively pursue the several deals that might be out there.

I learned an important lesson from the man who was one of Bristol-Meyers' lawyers during our negotiations, who eventually became its president. The second time through, after we had agreed to buy the division, he took me aside and said:

"Paul, always try to do deals that fit your strategy. Don't change the strategy to fit the deal; change the deal to fit the strategy. Walk away if it's not a good fit. Don't do deals just for the sake of doing deals."

I agree. If my strategy is to concentrate on building a retail hearing-care business in Florida, then that is what I should be following. If someone offers me an opportunity to buy another network in Texas and I take it just because it is there, that changes my strategy. Just because someone wants to sell you something, you do not have to buy it, which was the case in our negotiations with Bristol-Meyers.

But there is one thing that always bothered me about that lawyer's advice.

I have never known for sure if he was congratulating me for not buying the Bristol-Meyers company the first time or whether he was warning me to watch out for such things in the future.

Which proved to be another important lesson:

People may really mean what they say in the business jungle.

But you may never figure out what they really mean.

*   *   *   *   *

The largest Bengal tiger may exceed the lion in length; specimens ten feet from the tip of the nose to the end of the tail are not unusual. Adult males average 5½ to 6½ feet from nose to the root of the tail, which continues for another three feet. Tigers are predominantly colored a rufous fawn or tawny yellow, beautifully marked with dark, almost black, transverse stripes. Black and white specimens have been recorded, but they are extremely rare. Tigers of hotter climes have shorter and smoother hair, and are more richly colored and distinctly striped. Their northerly cousins tend to have longer, softer fur with lighter colors. Wherever they live and whatever their physical makeup, these powerful beasts are made doubly dangerous as hunters by their natural camouflage.

*　　*　　*　　*　　*

2. What Is Truth?

There were a couple of old TV game shows called *To Tell the Truth* and *What's My Line?* that acquisitive entrepreneurs might find instructive. Both featured panels of celebrities asking questions of various guests to discover their true identity and/or occupation. If the panelists failed, the contestants won a sum of money.

One presented its panel with three guests, all claiming to be the same person. Each panelist asked numerous questions in turn and all three contestants had to answer everything put to them. Two were liars who could invent any plausible fabrication to fool the panel. A similar panel on the other show had to interrogate a single guest who would only give yes or no answers. This was a more intense battle of wits, minus the multiple choice, especially since the contestant had to tell the truth.

The trick was for the panelists to come up with the right questions, in either case. When they did, they deduced the right answer; when they did not, they were reduced to guessing. Sometimes they guessed right, but just as often they guessed wrong. Unless the panelists asked pithy and precisely targeted questions, they would likely be left to explain their ineptitude while their antagonists walked off with the cash.

The same thing could happen when an entrepreneur gets an opportunity to acquire another company. Quite a few questions need answering to **discover the real reasons why someone wants to sell a business.** If somebody is willing to sell, in my experience there are only three (most often well-hidden) reasons.

SSSHHHH! (SELLERS' SECRETS)

(They know something about the business that you do not.)

(They have decided they want to do something else, or at least to not do whatever it is they have been doing.)

(They may want to be part of something more grandiose than their current business.)

The most potentially damaging reason to a buyer is that **the seller knows something about the business that the buyer does not.** Obviously, that secret is not going to be that windfall profits are about to descend on the business. What often drives a company to sell out are problems, anything from crimes and misdemeanors to the potential of financial trouble on the horizon. Rest assured that, whatever it is, the seller is hoping to keep the buyer in the dark until after the deal is done.

MetPath was a potential buyer of a private Belgian clinical laboratory doing maybe $10 million a year. We wanted it very badly because it would get us into the whole of Europe.

"I want $20 million in cash for my lab," the owner said.

"My friend," I said, "I don't mind paying you $20 million. Your lab is worth $20 million if it keeps earning money at the present rate. But it isn't worth $20 million in one check, at one time."

"Well, that's what I want."

"Tell you what I'll do. I will give you $5 million in cash on the closing. Then, for each year for the next three or four years that the level of sales from your customers stays the same or improves, I will give you another $5 million."

"Oh, no," he replied emphatically. "No, no! My accountant said I should take all of the money, all at once."

"My accountants would tell me the same thing," I rejoined. "But I don't think you will find anyone who is going to give you $20 million in one shot for your lab."

"Yes, I will," he said ... and he did!

The Belgian later sold his company to a huge German chemical company that wanted to get into the clinical lab business very badly, so they paid him his $20 million in cash. And that was a full $20 million, since there were no taxes involved. Europeans commonly use bearer bonds or unregistered stock certificates with no name on them. Whoever holds those owns the company. The chemical company wrote him a check for $20 million and he gave them his certificates. Since the deal was between companies in two separate countries and the certificates had no name on them, there was nothing on which to base any tax.

The seller promptly moved to the Bahamas with his newfound wealth. Six months later, the Belgian government reduced the reimbursement rates for lab tests by about one-third. In all fairness, the Belgian government might have decided not to take the action it did and, just maybe, the lab owner had no advance notice of the pending change. He may have had other reasons for wanting out of the business too, so this could just be chalked up to shrewd negotiating. (I leave it to you to decide, but I have my own opinion on the subject!)

Regardless, the acquired clinical lab went from a very profitable business to one that was losing money. The last I heard, it lost money for about three or four years before the chemical company closed it down. The buyer paid a premium for the business but apparently had gone on the acquisition hunt without doing his homework and studying the market.

Both buyers and sellers often hire search firms, consultants or other middlemen (the usual complement of attorneys, bankers, accountants, et al.) to avoid such pitfalls. They can be worth the money they earn to help qualify potential deals. How the deal arrives is going to make a difference in negotiations, by the way. Acquisition opportunities come only one of two ways: buyers find sellers, or vice versa. If buyers show up first, they will most likely pay more than if the seller comes looking for them.

Then there are times when the secrets surrounding an acquisition are flagrantly fraudulent, but so well-hidden that no one would know about them. Some are even to the point of being institutionalized. MetPath had a deal going in Italy, one that we had initiated. We toured the lab and asked what their revenues were.

"Just a second," said one of the principals, bringing out his books. "We're doing $1.5 million."

"Really? Well, I've heard through the grapevine that you were much bigger than that," I said. "And if I multiply out the number of specimens that your lab people said you do each month, times your average charge you gave me, that doesn't add up."

"Oh, of course," he replied, smiling broadly. "I forgot, you are an American. The figure I gave you is only for the government. Mario! Bring in the black book!" And in came Mario with a black book, which revealed a much higher and more believable figure.

I learned later on that it is a not uncommon practice in Italy for companies to keep several sets of books, usually three: One "real" set of books for the owners, another one for the government, and a third one for their wives. Whether that is true or not, two sets were enough to send me packing. There was no way I was going to buy into a business where I could never be sure just what it was I was buying until after I had bought it!

Two stories told to me by auditors from a CPA firm reveal the extent to which some will go. The accountants went into a junkyard to do an audit, and the owner had nine piles of scrap steel, each maybe twenty feet high and twenty feet in diameter. The owner claimed each pile was worth $100,000. The auditors had him move one of the piles, and discovered it was composed of a single layer of scrap over a huge mound of sand.

Then there was a haberdashery company, whose warehouse was filled with boxes of hats. All were neatly aligned on shelves, all properly marked by size and style, row after row after row. The auditors selected a row and asked the owners to open the boxes and, of course, most of the boxes were empty. Hard to believe? Perhaps a bit audacious, but not as uncommon as you might think; and it often takes an auditing firm to expose these and lesser frauds.

Certified audits by CPA firms can give buyers some level of comfort in physical and financial fact-finding efforts. Accountants can verify the existence of assets, the extent of liabilities, and the relative veracity of a profit and loss statement far better than most entrepreneurs. A certified accounting statement from a CPA, covering at least the past two years, is about the only way you can be sure that an acquisition target is as advertised. As sure as you can be, at any rate.

The other plus is that you have someone to sue when they turn out to be wrong. Even CPAs can miss the hanky-panky. Entrepreneurs must structure a deal to protect themselves. Always keep in mind that the person selling a business has a reason to sell, which you may or may not be able to figure out. Go into every deal as if you do not know the reason, as if the seller is holding something back.

I nearly got burned in a deal with a man who had a soap company; a genius. He had figured out ways of putting logos in glycerin soap so that as you used it, the last thing to disappear was the logo in the middle. He told me he was already doing $2 million selling the soap. Well, I got really excited. I spent a lot of time with him and was pleased to learn that one of the big accounting firms had already completed a certified audit for the past three years. I was ready to help him find an underwriter to take the company public. Things seemed to be going along nicely, until one day I got a call. He wanted to see me and talk some things over. There, sitting in my library, he said:

"Look, Paul .... " Since he started off with my first name, I immediately knew I was not going to like what followed.

"You have been very honest and helpful to me, and I've really enjoyed working with you. I appreciate all you have done. But I think I better tell you something."

"What's that?" I was hoping as I asked that it was nothing serious, but I was afraid that I knew better.

"Well, we have an error in the books."

"How can that be? You have three years of certified numbers."

"Well, the accounting firm made an error," he admitted. "I saw it but I didn't correct it."

"What do you mean? What kind of an error?"

"Well, there's a $400,000 error in revenues," he explained.

"Wait a minute," I said, motioning him to stop. "If there's a $400,000 error in revenues, then there has to be a $200,000 inventory error."

"Yeah, that's right."

"And those would create a $200,000 error in the P&L statement, as well."

"Yeah," he said, looking very contrite. "I just couldn't have you go up to New York and make the presentation to someone to take us public. Eventually, someone's going to find the mistake."

He had the right idea, even if he had it too late and for the wrong reasons. If you fail to **tell the truth all the time**, it will come back and get you. This is the real world version of *Truth or Consequences*. As it was, I just dropped the deal before I wound up with my reputation soiled while he cleaned up. The erstwhile soap baron eventually went out of business and probably went on to some other slippery venture.

Even honest businessmen want **to move on and do something else**, which is a perfectly valid reason for selling a business. Some just want to quit working and retire, while others want to stop doing what they are doing and go into something entirely different. MetPath acquired a lab from a chemist in Switzerland who wanted to go into the ministry. The purchase was something of a miracle to him, since we came along at just the right time. He was making money but he did not want to be running a lab anymore and he did not know how he was ever going to get rid of it. The acquisition provided him with an income for the rest of his life and gave him the opportunity to go off and get a doctorate in theology, realizing his dream of becoming a minister.

But so-called "classic" entrepreneurs do not stay with the businesses they create either. What most people think of as entrepreneurs, in fact, are really just inventors with a little bit of business sense. They might start a business but they soon tire of it and want to move on. The general motivation of the man with the soap company, honest or not, was to sell everything he created. He just kept inventing one type of soap after another, designing new products all the time.

He had many, many projects. One was a shampoo with green and gold stripes in a clear bottle that came out in a swirl. It looked very rich. Then he invented a unique shampoo carrier for the tub, and on, and on, but not one of his products had been properly marketed. He just kept taking any money that came in from his projects and dumping it right back into developing another. He never got to market with anything. When we parted company, all his soap was sitting in a trailer.

Such people do not have the patience to grow with and build a business; they just take the money and run onto the next thing. They are more opportunists than entrepreneurs. True entrepreneurship in my book means starting a business and building it from nothing into something special, like MetPath. Or, on a much larger scale, the way Bill Gates stuck with MicroSoft and turned it into a multi-billion-dollar enterprise.

The allure of such grandiose success may be enough reason

for someone to sell a business. Obviously, if you are buying a business from a large company, they are not interested in becoming a part of your company. They just want to get rid of what they have, for whatever reasons. Small, privately held companies, however, are particularly prone to this attraction. They often see being acquired as a way to get rid of their financial risks, realize a financial reward, and still have career potential.

You have to consider these things in an acquisition; sometimes they work out and sometimes not. When HEARx just got started, we found a twenty-five-year-old family-owned hearing-aid retailer in Atlanta that had about $2 million a year in sales. It was run by two brothers and their mother, the father long since deceased. Once we explained to them what we hoped to accomplish, they were very excited about becoming involved in a big business.

They got their chance when we bought their operation. Mom wound up in a secure retirement, but the brothers did not end up with long-term careers. We gave them multi-year contracts, and one of them stayed on until his ran out, then left to go do something else—which is probably what he wanted to do in the first place. The other we had to let go; we bought out his contract.

Buyers should understand that getting even one good management person in an acquisition is a plus, even in large-scale acquisitions. MetPath wound up with a good vice president of marketing in the Bristol-Meyers deal and one management person from W.R. Grace stayed with us. When Corning bought MetPath, the change of operating style and corporate philosophy created terrific culture shock. Eventually, most of my management people left or Corning got rid of them, though there still are one or two left.

When it comes to the owners of acquired companies, the offer of a consultancy might be the key that turns the lock on a deal, as long as it fits both the buyers' and the sellers' designs. An executive of a chemical company I know of received a call from a Ph.D. chemist who wanted to sell his company. The call was well-received, but there was one sticking point: The chemical company wanted the owner to stay on for five years after the buyout. The chemist only wanted to stay for three. The telephone conversation continued, and there seemed to be no other serious impediments to a deal. Finally, the chemical company executive offhandedly asked the chemist:

"By the way, doctor, how old are you?"

"Me? I'm ninety-two."

He got his three-year contract.

Perhaps the most important consideration for buyers to remember when negotiating an acquisition is that sellers do not like to think they are being acquired. They always want to talk about "the merger" and how they are "putting their company together" with yours. They want to imply that they are still important. Psychologically it feels better to merge as opposed to being acquired. Sometimes their pride is salvaged when they are kept on for awhile.

Such pride can create problems for buyers negotiating an acquisition. Greed creates even more problems. MetPath was ready to buy a clinical lab in Paris and I flew over with a check for $3.5 million to close the deal. The contracts were done and we sat at the table. I had the check in my inside coat pocket and we were all in good spirits. Then one of the partners who owned the lab, the one who refused to speak English (although he could), said in French:

"I have some good news and bad news." The interpreter began to translate, but I had gotten the gist.

"Well, let's have the good news first," I replied easily, thinking that he was starting to tell a joke.

"We just got a new contract for another 450,000 francs."

"Wonderful!" I replied. "Now, what's the bad news?"

"We have decided we want another $500,000 for the lab."

"You what?" I listened intently as the interpreter regurgitated his words.

"We want another half a million dollars," he repeated. Some joke! I could hardly believe what I was hearing but I could see that he was serious.

"Jacques," I began purposefully, "I've got some good news and bad news, as well. The bad news is that I'm only prepared to pay $3.5 million for your lab. The good news is that you get to keep your lab and all that new business. Congratulations!"

And with that I took the $3.5 million check out of my pocket, tore off my signature, slid the check across the conference table to them, and left the room without another word.

I wanted him to know that his greed had lost him $3.5 million dollars. His loss actually was much greater than that: At the time, the French franc was trading at 3.6 francs to the dollar, but there were signs that was going to change, and it did; within eighteen months, it was trading at nearly six francs to the dollar. If he had not tried to squeeze me, he could have made at least a couple of million more on the currency exchange.

Which just goes to show: sometimes, when it's over, it definitely *is* over.

Now, a question for our panelists: What was the name of the TV game show discussed at the beginning of this section, where the contestants had to tell the truth?

My apologies to those who guessed "To Tell the Truth."

The correct answer is "What's My Line?"

▲ ▲ ▲ ▲ ▲

*   *   *   *   *

Tigers are, of course, carnivorous predators; the principal food of the Bengal tiger in India, for example, includes cattle, deer, wild hog, fowl, and occasionally human beings. The "man-eater" is usually an old tiger, long past its prime, with worn and defective teeth. It finds humans easier prey than wild game and so is likely to haunt a village. When attacking a large animal, such as a bullock, a tiger seizes the nape of the neck with its teeth, holds the victim firm with its sharp claws, and dislocates the vertebrae with a powerful wrench.

*   *   *   *   *

3. Paying the Price

The lady, or the tiger?

The question was first posed in the nineteenth century by fabulist Frank Richard Stockton in his story of a hero confronted with a choice. Two closed doors stand before him. Behind one is a beautiful woman; behind the other, a ferocious man-eating tiger. Which one, we wonder, will he choose? And we go on wondering, because Stockton never told us how things turn out.

Entrepreneurs play the same game of business jungle roulette when they acquire a company without doing their homework and asking the right questions. Once they make the choice, however, there will be no question about how things turn out. Either they will have gotten what they expected, or not; and if they made a really bad choice, well, better to leave that to your imagination.

But as has been pointed out, it is not always apparent if an acquisition target is everything it seems to be. Much may be hidden behind closed doors that could make the difference between a successful courtship and getting torn to pieces in the business jungle. Since the rule really is that you get what you pay for, it is worth taking some time up front to consider how to pay for what you will be paying, so you do not wind up paying the consequences later on.

The discussion here, importantly, is not about *how much* to pay for an acquisition. Of course, buyers want to pay as little as possible for as much as they can get, while sellers are interested in getting as much as they can for whatever they have, no matter how little it is. Buyers should be forewarned that most sellers want to get at least a million dollars after taxes for their businesses so they can call themselves millionaires.

Regardless of those considerations, how much a buyer should spend on an acquisition should be no more than a business is worth. Ah! But how do you figure out how much a business is worth? Simple: The value or worth of a business to a buyer depends on exactly what is being acquired. What is important, then, is that the buyer take a good look at the makeup of his acquisition target.

There are, generally speaking, only five things in a business that can be acquired:

FIVE INCREASINGLY DIFFICULT PIECES

Net Worth (Assets minus Liabilities)
Sales
Earnings
Market Considerations
Reputation

Any or all of these can be part of an acquisition but it gets more difficult to establish the value of the pieces as you go down the list. Notice, too, that the pieces become increasingly intangible and therefore potentially more expensive to a buyer as well. The cost of someone's reputation, relatively speaking, is going to be higher than the cost of a widget.

Widgets, other **hard assets** like furniture, fixtures and equipment (*see Chapter 7*), and cash on hand are the most tangible and therefore the easiest to identify and value, even if someone tries to sell you a pile of sand or empty boxes. They are worth what they are worth and that is what a buyer pays for them. **Liabilities** sometimes come with the purchase but, although unwanted, they are usually easy to identify. As long as the seller guarantees and verifies the extent of the liabilities, no problem. If the seller will not warrantee them, then ... buyer beware!

Sales are pretty easy to identify too. Since sales come from customers, buying a customer list hopefully will turn out to be the same thing as buying sales. But no matter what it is called, what a buyer really wants to buy is a positive stream of cash flow for years to come. The hard part is figuring out how many customers will still be swimming in the revenue stream of cash flow after the acquisition, over time.

Things get even more complicated if **accounts receivable** (*see Chapter 7*) are figured into the purchase price. They are sales, strictly speaking, although they have not been collected yet. Obviously, the inability to collect accounts receivables will affect what sales really were and, therefore, the real value of the company.

Earnings can be even more elusive figures to pin down, as should be obvious from earlier discussions (*see Chapter 5 and Chapter 7*). If buyers are interested in acquiring a company for its earnings, then another stream must be looked at, which could be called the *earnings flow.* If earnings are trending upwards over time for a company, then an acquisition will cost a buyer more; if trending down, a lower price will be in order. The price paid, in any event, will be figured as a multiple of earnings, just the way potential investors looked at your financial projections (*see Chapter 3*).

Then there are **market considerations** and **reputation**, the next two items that a buyer might buy. These are more intangible and there is no way either can be guaranteed. A good location, a market opportunity, cross-licensing agreements, a positive image—all these may cost a buyer a premium. But that prime spot could become a bad one in a few months and markets that seem attractive one day can seem unattractive the next. Buy a business dependent on locations in major cities and urban renewal or a zoning change could destroy your business in short order. A good reputation in an industry or a marketplace may come along with an acquisition or it may leave with the former owner.

Not only does the immediate impact of these elements affect a sale but their longer-term effects can be problematic as well. If buyers do not know the truth, then what they do not know can definitely hurt them financially, both in terms of the cost of the acquisition as well as their income over time. Play the game, pay the price. You may have to pay more than you would like if you show up first to the deal; if the seller arrives first, you may pay less. The point is to grow your business by making a good deal and, in that regard, **how you pay to acquire a business can be more important than how much you pay**.

Whatever amount you pay, there are lots of ways for buyers to finance a deal, as noted in *Chapter 7*. But there are only three ways to pay for it.

PAYMENT PLANS

1. *Pay a fixed price, all at once.*
2. *Pay a fixed price in regular installments.*
3. *Pay an adjustable price over time, based on performance.*

Number one can be a beastly choice, unless you have plenty of money and are absolutely certain about what it is you are buying. Even if the plan is simply to acquire a business, lock, stock and barrel, to put it out of business and reduce your competition, this payment plan is definitely the riskiest way to go. Whether the payout is in cash or stock or some combination, it is not contingent on anything, with no futures for the seller—and with no recourse to the buyer.

Such "walkaway" deals are fine if you are buying from a large corporation that will guarantee and warranty everything. If they hold anything back, watch out. Likewise, when you buy an independent business from an individual or a family, you have no idea what they may have in their desk drawers, although you can be pretty sure it is not bundles of money. There might be a whole bunch of bills the owner never bothered bringing across the hall to his bookkeeper because he knew the company could not afford to pay them.

Here is an imaginary but not unlikely scenario: I buy a company for cash. Some time after I hand over the check for the entire amount, I discover some past-due bills. I call up the former owner, but he has no idea of what I am taking about:

"Hello, Doctor Smith?"

"Yes, this is Doctor Smith."

"Doctor, I'm having a little trouble hearing you. Is the weather bad there in Hawaii?"

"No, but I have been having trouble with this car phone I just had installed in my new Bentley. Who is this, anyway?"

"This is Doctor Brown. I was the one who bought your company last month, remember?"

"Oh yes, Doctor Brown. What can I do for you?"

"I had a heck of a time tracking you down. I found these bills in your file cabinet that have not been paid."

"What? You say you found some pills in your bile samples that have decayed?"

"No. Bills in your files, not paid."

"I *am* sorry, I simply cannot hear you. If you can hear me, I'll call you in a few months after I get back from my around-the-world cruise. We can talk about your bile samples then."

Such experiences are like inhaling a poison dart from a blowgun—it leaves a bad taste in your mouth and can be fatal. Still, buyers get sucked in regularly that way.

The second payment possibility, also based on a fixed amount, has the advantage of being paid off in installments. The buyer at least has some leverage if any undisclosed hanky-panky is uncovered after an acquisition. These deals usually involve **giving the seller only a percentage of the purchase price up front**. The remainder is paid off over the course of time, usually in annual installments. This gives the buyer some time to pay and, depending on the terms of the contract, something of a safety margin. But a deal is a deal and, if things do not work out, the buyer may still have to pay the full price.

The third choice, to my mind the best one as a buyer, is to **negotiate a deal based on the performance of the acquired business**. Like number two, there is some cash or stock paid up front (because nobody sells anything without a down payment), and the remainder of the purchase price is paid off in annual installments. The difference is that those installments can vary depending on how well or how poorly the acquired business does in its new incarnation.

There are two types of performance-based buyouts: **earnouts** and **revenue-outs**, as I call them. **An earnout depends on the profitability of the acquired company.** Annual payments are made to the seller for a number of years, based on the earnings generated by his business. A buyer might agree to pay $1.2 million for a company, shelling out $200,000 up front and then $200,000 each year for the next five years, but only if the acquired company keeps earnings up to some agreed upon level. If that does not happen, then the buyer does not pay a penny, or perhaps pays only as much as earnings would allow. There are any number of possible formulas. A seller (unless somewhat deranged) is not taking that kind of a deal without remaining in charge. No one would leave the determination of profit to strangers, even if the numbers are certified at the end of each year.

That is still risky business for the seller, but not for the buyer. I will buy businesses with earnouts all day long. I'm protected: If the company makes money, I give the seller some money; if not, not. The only major concession I may have to make as a buyer is to let the seller stay on for at least a few years, however long the payout formula lasts.

I believe **a revenue-out is the fairest deal for everyone concerned**. The annual payment to the seller in a revenue-out is based on how much of the acquired company's sales are maintained over time. It is much more equitable than an earnout, because there are too many factors which could influence a company's profitability that have nothing to do with the deal. There may be no profits—any percentage of nothing is nothing—and as the new owner, I would control the profitmaking. But there should always be sales, unless a company folds.

My method was simply to acquire customer lists and locations only, not the entire business, and pay the seller. That way, my risk was reduced as much as possible. I had no concern over how much money was owed or due the business. Since I did not buy the company, I would not own the seller's liabilities, so I did not have to worry about whether or not the seller was a crook. That last consideration was very important with MetPath, since kickbacks were rife in the clinical lab business. One of our big concerns, especially when buying smaller labs, was that the former owner had been paying off customers to keep them loyal. To reduce that risk, we did most of our acquisitions by paying about 20 percent of the prior year's sales volume as a down payment. Then we agreed to give the sellers annually something like twenty cents per dollar of sales volume that their customers generated for us over a certain number of years. The higher the sales, the more money they would get. So they could end up getting 100 cents on the dollar during a five-year period.

This approach paid off more than once. We bought a lab from a doctor in New York City this way and we did not lose one of his clients for the first two months after the acquisition. This was extraordinary, so we were really excited. Then we started getting phone calls.

"Ah, Doctor Brown? Dr. Ripoff here. I didn't get my envelope."

"What do you mean, Doctor? What are you talking about?"

"I sent the blood in and I didn't get an envelope back."

"Dr. Ripoff, we operate on an overnight basis. If you sent blood in, you should have gotten the report back the next morning."

"Ah, I'm not talking about the report, Doctor. I'm talking about the envelope!"

"What envelope is that, Dr. Ripoff?"

"You know! The envelope! With all the green!"

"Doctor! I'm getting nervous about this. We don't send out any envelopes with green in them. We only have envelopes with blue lab reports in them."

"Well! I used to get back 20 percent of the amount my old lab billed Medicare. If you're not going to give me the envelope the way my friend Doctor Payoff did, there's no reason for me using your lab!"

"That's a decision you will have to make for yourself. We believe we're delivering quality care and service. That is the reason we are in business."

"Not with me you're not!"

This was a fairly typical conversation over the next ninety days, wherein we lost all but about 20 percent of the business, which is about all we wound up paying for through the revenue-out approach. Such self-protective formulas, however, only work in certain situations. Most often, financial savvy and negotiating prowess are the tools that buyers must rely on in acquisitions.

Especially when the wall is black.

That was what we dubbed the negotiating strategy used by Milan Panic, chairman of the board for International Chemical Nuclear (ICN) Pharmaceuticals, when MetPath was trying to buy its United Medical Laboratories subsidiary. (This is the same Milan Panic who recently tried to gain political control of

Yugoslavia and help move it toward a democratic government when Communism failed.)

His political aspirations fell short and so did his negotiating strategy for selling United Medical. He had been trying to sell the business for years and MetPath had been trying to buy it for years. He would bring it to market and show everybody the revenue base and how revenues were continuing to rise slowly, year after year. ICN almost got acquired several times by conglomerates that were not in the clinical lab business. They did not understand the business, and for one reason or another those deals never went through. Perhaps they all discovered what those of us in the lab business already knew: The most important thing to look at in the lab business is specimen volume, not dollar volume. You could lose 5 percent of your business and then raise prices 10 percent to hide the loss.

We went into negotiations knowing what to look for and ran totals of the number of specimens processed for the last several years. It was easy to see the direction the business was heading and it was not heading up. Regardless, Milan wanted $10 million, which was his annual revenue at that time. It did not make any difference how I structured the deal, it had to come out to $10 million. Put another way, *the wall was black.* It did not matter what color the wall was or what color you wanted to paint it, to Milan it was black.

"Milan, it's not worth $10 million," I once complained. "I'll give you $5 million cash and a $3 million earnout."

"I have to get $10 million," he replied.

"You keep saying that, but the figures don't work out at $10 million," I replied. "Listen, how about $6 million cash and $2 million on an earnout?"

"That's still not $10 million. Like I said, I've got to have $10 million."

This went on for years. I was slow. Finally, I got the message: The wall was black.

"Milan, tell you what. You're doing $10 million a year, according to your numbers. Is that right?"

"Absolutely!"

"Do you think we will keep 80 percent of the business after we buy it?"

"Absolutely!"

"Then here's what I'm going to do. I'm going to give you $5 million in cash for your company at the closing. And if, at the end of your first year, your revenues are at least $8 million, you'll get another $2.5 million. And I will give you another $2.5 million at the end of each of the second and third years, if revenues stay at that level."

"Now we're talking! That means I'll get $12.5 million, because there's no way you're going to lose 20 percent of my business!"

So he went to his board and told them he was selling the lab for $12.5 million, and therefore they approved the deal.

In the long run, he got $5 million.

Absolutely not a penny more.

Which just goes to show ...

Things are never as black as they seem.

$ECRET$ OF THE TIGER

*Be sure and discover the real reason why
the seller wants to sell, or you could become
one very disappointed buyer!*

――――――――――

Never change your strategy to fit an acquisition.

――――――――――

*Always value the worth of an acquisition
before you have bought and improved it.*

The Hunter or the Hunted

Chapter Nine
Foxes and Hounds:
The Hunter or the Hunted

▲ ▲ ▲ ▲ ▲

Fox, the common name for several species of the car-nivorous mammalian genera **Vulpes, Fennecus, Urocyon, Alopex,** *and* **Otocyon,** *representing all of the dog family* (Canidae). *The common red (***Vulpes,*** or "true") fox enjoys a wide geographic distribution:* **V. vulpes** *occurs over most of Europe, temperate Asia, and Africa north of the Sahara;* **V. fulva** *ranges over most of North America. Its preferred habitat is mixed farm-lands and woodlots, especially weedy, brushy fence rows bordering fields. Foxes exhibit little variation in behavior, whatever their genera. The American gray fox (***Urocyon cinereoargenteus),*** for example, is a grizzled gray animal of shier, more retiring disposition. Lacking the craftiness of its red cousin, it prefers living in swamps, dense thickets and underbrush, and usually avoids pursuers by hiding. It seldom stores food and is the only fox that climbs trees, but otherwise its behav-ior and general habits resemble those of the red fox.*

*   *   *   *   *

The second year that I was full owner of Metropolitan Pathology Laboratory, Inc. *(see Chapter 1)* was an unprof-itable one in which the company saw only $210,000 in sales. But we had high hopes.

Guy Seay, vice president of finance for the company that we by then were calling MetPath, arrived shortly after we opened our first full-fledged, six thousand-square-foot, state of the art labora-tory in Teaneck, New Jersey, just across the Hudson River from Manhattan. One of his first tasks was to prepare five-year projec-tions. They anticipated that we would be profitable before very long. We were definitely *not* anticipating that it would take seven more years to get out of the red ink! Still, even without showing a profit and only modest revenues, MetPath was bigger and showed more promise than almost any other clinical pathology laboratory in business at that time.

So I was only a little surprised when, only two weeks after we had opened our doors, someone named Ben called to arrange a lunch meeting. He was a vice president of the U.S. Vitamin Corporation, a subsidiary of the giant Revlon Corporation, which had just gotten into the laboratory business with the acquisition of a laboratory in Long Island City, New York, just across the East River from Manhattan.

We rolled out the only carpet we had when Ben arrived at our plant in Teaneck, N.J. Ben was suitably impressed with our facility, easily the most impressive in the area at the time—built, of course, in anticipation of great things to come. After touring the lab, the three of us went across the street to lunch at the Red Robin Restaurant, an establishment that fit well in the commercial area where our lab was situated. We crowded into a well-worn red-leatherette booth and all ordered hamburgers of the lowest grade. When lunch was served, Ben had gotten down to business:

"I don't know if you're aware of it, but Revlon has decided to go into the laboratory business," he began. "We're acquiring laboratories and we're interested in MetPath. "How much do you want for the company?"

"What do you think?" I asked Guy, swallowing hard but hiding it well. I could hardly believe what I was hearing.

Guy seemed to be straining for words too. It took a while for him to answer, twirling the hair at the back of his head and staring off into space as he often did when thinking. Ben, seriously awaiting Guy's reply, gently prodded him after nearly a full minute of silence.

"Guy? You still with us?"

"Well, Ben," Guy finally offered, not missing a beat. "I've been working on our projections for a few months and based on what I see now, I figure the business is worth ... well, now, I'll tell you ... I suspect we would take about $100 million for the company."

Now it was Ben's turn to be silent. My only thought was that Guy was joking. Ben looked at me and grimaced, letting out a little laugh. He held up well enough, considering the shock, but the conversation died shortly thereafter. Guy and I let Ben pick up the check.Two weeks later, back Ben came to meet with us—much too early to be invited back to the Red Robin for lunch, I might add. This time, he had a big entourage in tow, including a controller and numerous corporate types for whom we again rolled out our carpet for a tour of the lab. Soon we all crowded into my office. A little small talk, and Ben was right back on the scent.

"Paul, we're serious," he began. "We've talked it over and we want to buy your company. How much do you *really* want?"

"Well," I responded slowly, looking to Guy. "If you're *really* serious, Ben, then I think we can probably make a deal for $50 million." At that, Ben smiled and turned to his controller, laughing:

"Now we're *really* getting someplace! I think we can get this for less, probably for $25 million. Paul's already come down 50 percent from his original price in just two weeks!"

Everybody else laughed too, but there was no deal that day. When they came back a year later, there was no deal—and no laughter either. But once each year for the next nine, they came back with a hunting party and offered us what I had asked for the year before. We evaded them every time.

There were other reasons why I never made a deal with Revlon, reasons not so obvious but much more serious in nature. Not only was their Long Island City laboratory on the other side of Manhattan from ours, their intentions were far to the other side of good will.

I will never forget the remarks that the controller made to me during that first attempt to buy MetPath. He called me aside and the two of us went into my office. After he closed the door behind us, he said: "You know, you should sell."

"Why do you say that?" I answered, expecting a new overture.

"Think about this," he suggested. "You've been doing this for two years, and you've got a lot invested in it. You could go out and get run over by a truck. I'd hate to see your family wind up with nothing if something like that happens. You should seriously consider our offer."

The vaguely threatening and downright sinister implications of his remarks settled the question for me. Aside from having economic, ethical and entrepreneurial differences with them of the highest order, I would never, *ever* expose my company to management like that. Still, I kept listening to their overtures year after year, as much out of curiosity and for an ego boost as anything else. On my last visit to their offices, I was sitting with a covey of Revlon executives in their fancy mahogany dining room after a lunch with silver service on fine china, nursing an after dinner glass of red wine. I told them that I had a problem selling my company to them because of their unethical and illegal activities.

"Once you get rid of those," I said, "I'd be glad to seriously consider you as a candidate."

"Illegal? We're not doing anything illegal!"

"Well, you do have a lab in Detroit called Check Lab, and I know for a fact that you kick back about a third of all the Medicare money you get to the referring doctors. Isn't that illegal?" Michele Bergerac, who was then the chairman, turned to one of his laboratory executives and asked, point blank:

"Hey! Is that what we do?"

"Well, we are only doing that until we get back the cost of the acquisition," came the answer. "Then we're going to stop."

That was my last trip to Revlon's New York headquarters.

That was the end of the mahogany, the silver service and the red wine.

That was the end of their yearly hunting parties ...

and my pretending that I was interested.

Basically, it was one less mistake to make.

*   *   *   *   *

The fox should be an endangered species, given the odds against it, yet it is not. It enjoys the reputation of being a wily and sagacious animal, skilled in deceiving pursuing hounds and in avoiding traps. The fox is adept at avoiding detection and capture, but its cleverness is probably as much due to its keen senses as to its intelligence. It needs every bit of its cleverness and instinct, too, given the characteristics of its chief adversaries. Hunting hounds have keen scent and are at least seven or eight times as large as the fox, are equally speedy, and are possessed of much greater endurance and strength.

*   *   *   *   *

1. Get Ready . . .

One of the oldest truisms is that the greatest lessons are learned from one's mistakes. An entrepreneur was probably the first one to say it. As this book attests, building a business most often resembles a state of constant damage control. At least there never seems to be a lack of mistakes to learn from.

When you are ready to put your business up for sale, all of your mistakes need to be far in the future, especially if you started up your company just to sell it to make a quick profit. Otherwise, if you have been at it any length of time; your mistakes need to be well behind you. You simply cannot afford any mistakes to show at all when you are selling your business. Being ready to sell your company to a large degree means being able to minimize your mistakes and maximize your potential to prospective buyers.

Let's assume that you have built a successful business and things have been running (relatively) smoothly for awhile. The company you started, however many years ago, is now a big company. All the people and systems needed to operate the business are in place and Mr. Murphy has not been heard from in some time. You have made all the right acquisitions to build the business up. Your company is making money and the market is growing right along with your financial projections, which makes both you and your investors very happy. You personally have a job with a nice salary, good benefits and what seems like stability. You have enough income to live on plus stock in a company with a real value. Things, in fact, hardly could be better and you are even able to enjoy some of the fruits of your labor.

Now, all that sounds wonderful—unless you are an entrepreneur, of course. Instead of finding contentment in your success, you may find yourself often feeling bored and restless. The edge seems to be slipping. Your enthusiasm for accomplishing daily tasks is slipping and, while there is still plenty to do, daydreaming becomes an integral part of your workday. A vague sense of emptiness may start creeping in on you and you might try filling it with anything from living the high life to immersing yourself in community service projects. But the thrill is gone; something is missing and you cannot for the life of you figure out what. Finally, you begin to think that the time has come to sell your business.

Before you think about that, think about this ...

Are you ready to sell your business?

You are if you can pass . . .

DR. BROWN'S BUSINESS FINAL

1. *Why do I want to sell my business?*
2. *Who is going to buy my business?*
3. *How do I sell my business?*

This is an essay test, by the way, and you must answer all questions completely. The answer to the first question is by far the most important: Why, indeed, should you sell your business? Fortunately, readers of this book already have the inside track on the answer from the last chapter. Remember those three secrets that buyers are dying to find out about sellers? *(See Chapter 8.)* Well, those are also the three reasons why most businessmen would want to sell their companies.

Selling your company, in fact, can best be explained as buying someone else's business turned inside out, and vice versa. So go back and re-read *Chapter 8*. When you are selling your company, many things are exactly the opposite of what happens when you acquire a company. It is almost a mirror image. What has changed is perspective; as the seller, you are now on the inside looking out for yourself, not the buyer on the outside looking in, wanting to build your company.

Let's review those three reasons for acquiring a company and look at them from the perspective of selling your company. The first reason why you might sell your business is because **you know something that the buyer does not.** Such secrets can be either *business* or *personal* and will always be negatives rather than positives from the point of view of either the buyer or the seller.

Our notions of morality, fair play, and integrity would make it difficult for most of us to knowingly sell someone a pig in a poke. It is my own philosophy that both sides should come away feeling they have made a good deal. Some, however, might be driven by fear, greed, or pride (among the more notable drivers) to a different place. Instead of cutting their losses as best as they can and starting over, they try to unload their company on an unsuspecting buyer. Even though the seller knows that something at least unfavorable if not downright disastrous is going to happen to the business (like the Belgian lab owner in *Chapter 8*), they neglect to tell the buyer.

This is a very poor choice. For starters, there is probably no more sure-fire way to ruin your business reputation. Besides that, it is only a 50-50 proposition at best that your business secret will not get found out. Save yourself the embarrassment. The rule *caveat emptor (Let the buyer beware!)* remains uppermost in the Business Jungle and buyers will be making diligent efforts to discover everything there is to know about your business anyway.

It is also worth considering, on the other hand, just how potentially damaging your little secret actually is in terms of the deal that is being negotiated. A potential buyer may have an agenda in buying your company that might not even be impacted by your secret. You might *believe* that your business has peaked, that the economy is terrible, that politics are spoiling your opportunities, whatever. The buyer may believe something else entirely or not even care about it, which could make your secrets not as important as you think.

There is one area, however, where secrets are both reasonable and often necessary. You will have *personal reasons* for selling a business, some of them secrets that no one else needs to know about, especially family and health matters. A potential buyer for your business does not need to know anything about your personal life and you should not volunteer any information of that type. Just as importantly, do not for a minute think that you can use any sort of personal "hard luck" story as leverage in negotiations, hoping perhaps for the buyer's sympathy and good will. It would be an unusual entrepreneurial animal that would not try to take your personal problems and somehow turn them to his own advantage. This is, after all, the Business Jungle.

The allure of being part of something bigger is the second reason for selling your business. This is a strong motivator for many entrepreneurs who want to run a bigger business but lack the skills, vision, or confidence to move in that direction. This is a great reason for selling a business, but it may not work out. *(More about that later in this chapter.)*

That leaves only one other reason for selling your business: **When you are motivated to do something else, or are at least no longer motivated to do what you have been doing.** That also happens to be the *best reason of all* for selling your business.

You may have another business idea or want to retire, or you may want to do something entirely different with your life. Whatever the reason you have for selling off your business, there are two things that you must be absolutely sure of before you start negotiating. You need to be in **financial control** of your business and you need to **know what you want** out of the deal. Just as when you started up your business, when you decide to get of it, *you need a good plan with a well-defined goal.* Otherwise, you more than likely will be courting trouble.

When Revlon came calling at the start-up of MetPath, they were in an acquisition mode but we were not in a selling mode, at that point primarily because they could not give me what I wanted. I told them that I wanted $10 million after taxes and, if they could come up with a deal to accomplish that, then I would sell the company to them. All it would have taken in the beginning was about $25 million. Twelve years later, when MetPath was purchased by Corning for $140 million, I got exactly what I had wanted all along: My share was $15 million and that, less taxes, came to about $10 million. I knew what I wanted and I had financial control of the company, so I could easily rebuff Revlon's advances then and each year afterward.

The second time the potential sale of Metpath came up was a little more difficult to deal with, since it was an attempted takeover and sellout of the company that was secretly engineered by several of the original investors! This may shock those of you who are new to the entrepreneurial ranks but such situations are not uncommon. It happens time and time again that a company's founder may have a strategic conflict with some of the investors, or a personality conflict, or a results conflict, i.e., the results are not turning out the way the investors think they ought to. The next thing the founder knows is that the investors are looking to take over, sellout, or, if possible, get rid of the founder.

Chapter Nine: Foxes and Hounds
▲ ▲ ▲ ▲ ▲

When that almost happened to me at age twenty-nine, it was a very rude awakening. Here were all these very big supporters of mine, all my friends who had put up $250,000 to start up MetPath. But as they were calling me, all excited about the company, they were having secret meetings with the competition to get out and line their own pockets. Like their cousins the venture capitalists, they were talking long-term to me while planning to make a short-term killing. Just like the institutional investors that put $30 million into HEARx, for whom long-term turned out to be about six months (*see Chapter 7*), as soon as they saw an opportunity to make a quick buck, they took it. It just took longer.

What saved me, again, was that I had financial control of MetPath and I knew what I wanted. I was able to head them off at the pass, even though they had a head start. Part of the reason they were able to gather momentum was that I had been drafted ninety days after we had opened the lab and I was running the company over a long-distance telephone line. The other part of the reason was that MetPath had gone public very early on in its existence and the stock was trading for about $8 a share within the course of a year and a half. The original shareholders, who had paid eighty cents a share long before we went public, had made ten times on their money (at least on paper).

That started one of the major shareholders thinking and he decided that enough was not quite enough. His reasoning ran something like this:

"Paul is in the Navy. Who will run the company? Let's get rid of it while we can and sell it off. We can make ten times on our money and Paul will be happy because he will make money too."

He and the other investors went behind my back and trotted off to Damon Corp., another large company in an acquisition mode, to discuss the sale of MetPath. They eventually got an offer from Damon for between three dollars and four dollars a share up front in Damon's stock and, if MetPath's earnings developed according to plan, the shareholders would get another three dollars to four dollars per share, again paid in Damon stock. All the stock was restricted, in any event, and would have to be held for two years before it could be sold.

Only after they had organized and structured this whole package did the investors tell me they had this deal. By then, however, it had been cut in half, since Damon had withdrawn the earnout portion of the deal. I voted against the deal because the investors, besides making a bad deal, had made the wrong deal.

Damon was a competitor with a strategy totally different from ours. Damon was making one acquisition after another with their stock in order to keep their stock price up. I sensed there might be a total collapse of the stock. In fact, I was out telling everyone their strategy was wrong and that investors should be buying MetPath stock, not Damon stock. I suppose I might have done the deal for cash, but Damon's stock was being hyped and I was not interested in taking Damon's paper, even though I stood to make a profit of some significance as owner of 70 percent of the stock.

Time has proven out my strategy in two ways. First of all, MetPath did not show a profit for six more years, so we never would have benefitted from any earnout deal. Second, and even more significant for the shareholders, Damon stock went from somewhere in the $60 per-share range to about $3 per-share in less than two years. If we had accepted the deal, we would have received practically nothing. My investors would have been barely able to get their original investment back!

What finally happened, twenty years later and long after I had left, was that MetPath bought Damon after Damon had gone through a bankruptcy and a restructuring. But had I been careless when I started my company and given up more than 30 percent of the company for the initial $250,000 investment, my company would have been gone twenty years ago and I would have wound up with nothing to show for it. I would have been history, and so would have my investors' profits. Instead, I got a chance to make everyone a lot of money.

Just remember that **a decision to sell your company may not turn out to be yours**. Unless you have financial control and know what you want out of any deal, the sale of your company may be determined by a few major shareholders—which goes back to how well you spread out the investments—or even by a prospective buyer. The result of letting someone else control the timing, pricing or any other element of the sale of your company is the same as letting someone else control the elements of your product or service business—you can be sure you will not have very much say in the outcome (*see Chapter 3*) and you definitely will end up poorer for your trouble.

Money, or the opportunity for money, makes some people do strange things.

Even your friends and supporters might even turn on you.

Just another reason why they call it the Business Jungle ... Make no mistake!

*   *   *   *   *

The red fox is a small mammal, averaging nearly three and one-half feet in length, including about fourteen inches of fluffy, white-tipped tail. It stands sixteen inches high at the shoulders and weighs only five to ten pounds. An inquisitive animal that behaves in the wild like a shy but friendly dog, the red fox is a solitary hunter, never seen in packs like dogs and wolves. It relies on keen ears, eyes and nose to detect prey, ending a highly skillful and patient stalk with a lightning-quick pounce. Although sometimes a pest because of its storied hen house raids, it is valuable in controlling rodents. Mice and rabbits are staple elements of the fox's diet; but domestic fowl, as well as eggs and fruits, are accepted avidly. The red fox seldom kills animals larger than a rabbit, although occasionally a fawn will be brought down.

*   *   *   *   *

2. Get Set . . .

The world is a very small place.

A French friend of mine happened one day to be in the U.S. on business and got on a crowded elevator in an large office building. He squeezed in and almost immediately heard two people talking in French. He could not help listening to their conversation, which they were probably sure no one could understand. Before long, he realized they were talking about what an idiot their boss's son was. Imagine his surprise when he realized that the father and son they were talking about were friends of his!

Then there was the time that MetPath was trying to buy a lab in Paris (*see Chapter 8*). Several weeks before the deal-breaking, the principals of the lab and I had (successfully, I thought) negotiated a deal. The negotiations were to be our little secret. We went to dinner at one of those small, intimate Paris restaurants to celebrate our deal-making. I spoke some broken French and they spoke some broken English, although we stuck to French for the most part.

We were having a grand time, laughing at my grammatical blunders and nearly oblivious of the other diners more or less sitting on top of one another in the crowded cafe. All of a sudden, one of the two men sitting at the table next to us said in English:

"Pardon me. I don't speak French very well," he ventured. "But I thought I overheard you talking about a laboratory. Is that a medical lab, by any chance?"

"Oh, yes! Oui! But of course! I run the biggest medical testing lab here in Paris," replied one of the Frenchmen in heavily accented English. "And now I'm getting very rich and selling it here to my friend, Dr. Paul Brown, from MetPath."

"Paul Brown? You're Paul Brown?"

"Yes," I said, surprised. "You know me?"

"Well, I've heard about you," he admitted.

"And you are . . . ?"

"Oh! Me? Hah! Heh-heh! I'm Bill Williams . . . from Revlon."

There we were, celebrating a secret acquisition of a company with a competitor literally right next to me! He may not have been very good in French, but managed to pick up a couple of words, enough to make our secret deal a non-secret, in short order. And, as you already know, the deal fell through. I do not believe that Revlon ever made them an offer. But short of a formal introduction, I could not have given them any better *entree*.

Experiences like the two above taught me an important rule of the business jungle: *Never speak French in an elevator or at the dinner table.*

Just kidding, of course! (You should be used to that by now.) Seriously, do not talk business in an elevator unless you are alone. But then, if you are alone in an elevator, there is no point in talking. The point is this: **Watch how you say what to whom, and when and where you say it. And you better have a good reason why you say anything at all.**

You need to be as cagey as a fox when looking to make a deal to sell your company. Make too much noise and your prey will escape and no one will make a killing. What you say in public or in private can kill your deal, no matter how secure you think things are ... just ask my wife Cynthia.

She was sitting in the lobby of the hotel in which the Swedish manufacturers and I were hammering out the deal for the two Autochemist testing machines that MetPath needed. She had arrived early, was waiting patiently for me to finish the meeting so that we could go and have lunch together. Meanwhile, the Swedes and I had come to an impasse over one part of the contract. I wanted them to pay the import duty on the machines, a not-insubstantial sum since the machines cost about $1 million for the pair. They wanted me to pay it and we were at loggerheads on the issue.

They finally excused themselves, saying that they wanted to go and call their home office to get the "official" position about the duty. I stayed in the meeting room while they went off into the main lobby to make their call. But before they got to the phones, the entourage stopped right there in the lobby and commandeered several chairs for an impromptu meeting to talk about the import duty—right next to Cynthia. They did not know who she was, so they openly discussed what they thought of me, the deal and what they were going to do next. Then they all went off to find a phone.

I emerged from the meeting room moments later to stretch my legs and saw Cynthia sitting there. She got up and met me.

"Paul, you'll never believe what just happened," she said.

"Don't tell me, let me guess," I said. "You were nearly trampled by a herd of Swedes."

"Well, you're close," she laughed, and in a few moments explained to my incredulous ears the Swedes' entire negotiating strategy concerning the import duty, which, by the way, they agreed to pay within minutes of their return.

You never know who is listening! So when you even get the idea to sell your company, contain the inside discussions to only a few people, making sure everyone understands the necessity of secrecy. And of course, keep as quiet as possible in public.

"But how do you sell your company," the most perceptive readers will ask, *"unless you let people know that you want to sell your company?"*

At last, a good question!

The answer is: Build it, and they will come.

This is no *Field of Dreams* movie scenario but a hard-headed business philosophy that can pay big dividends. If the business you built has **value**, someone will buy it, whether a buyer comes to you or (less happily) if you have to look for a buyer. No matter which path you take, however, you have to analyze who sees the value in your business and who has enough money to buy it. There is no sense in even talking about selling your company unless there is someone out there who wants to buy it. Worse yet, talking to someone who wants to buy it but cannot afford it wastes everyone's time and energy. If there is no fit, then you at least can get back to building your business. But if you do find a fit, it most likely will be with one of three types of companies.

The first type that may fit are **competitors**. More than a few of them would be interested in getting rid of you, the competition that has been giving them fits in the marketplace. Some would be more than willing to buy your business just to accomplish that and to make their businesses grow bigger. Look at the competitors who are most likely to benefit from such a strategy and, more importantly, who have the financial resources. It is highly unlikely that you could sell your business to someone that's only a fraction of your size.

The next possible fit are **companies interested in vertical integration**. They want to grow by adding different elements. Here, the product or service you are selling fits into a potential buyer's larger scheme. The first place to look for this type of company is among those customers that buy your products or utilize your service on a large scale or among suppliers that sell to you.

The last fit might be **companies who want access to your customer base**. This can take several forms. One part of our customer base at HEARx, for example, is made of consumers of hearing-care products and services, which includes a large number of elderly people. Companies that would want to buy HEARx might want to sell some other, perhaps unrelated product or service to such a customer base. Another part of the HEARx customer base includes managed-care companies who use us to provide hearing care to their customers. A vision-care company wanting to get into the managed-care business might see buying HEARx as the way to accomplish that.

However, building a company with enough value to attract buyers of any description usually takes time. It may be a while, maybe a long while, before anyone is even interested in looking at your company. MetPath, for example, went from one buyout offer and one sellout attempt early on, to zero offers to buy the company (not counting the annual Revlon gambit) for the next nine years.

I really had no particular interest in selling the company during that time either. But that began to change when MetPath found itself in the middle of an expansion program with a huge new laboratory facility under construction in Chicago. Interest rates, meanwhile, were climbing and the stock market was falling. Given those circumstances, senior management and I began getting nervous. The sale of the company became more and more a topic of conversation and I began actively entertaining the idea. Our concern was that we had taken on a much-too-major liability with the Chicago facility, a 200,000-square-foot, $22 million monster that could choke us. We were going to have to ride it through until the expansion proved itself out, which probably would take years. We decided that the time had come to sell the company, so we began to **position the company appropriately to help maximize the potential for the sale of the company.**

One of the first things we had to tackle, for example, was the makeup of our management. After hearing over and over again that the company was completely dependent on me, it became obvious that if anyone was ever going to buy the company we would have to **bring in professional management**. I hired a new president from IBM and other top executives from Johnson & Johnson and General Electric, giving MetPath what anyone would perceive as professional management. Our public relations team made it a point to emphasize the changes we were undertaking and the positive things we were doing, making the company appear as attractive and successful as possible on a regular basis. It certainly did not hurt that our earnings had increased significantly either, which was another thing that could be trumpeted without calling attention to the fact that we were interested in selling the company.

We positioned ourselves and waited to see what would happen. Before long our patience was rewarded. MetPath ended up in negotiations with three major companies who were interested in the clinical lab/health-care business—Nestle, Boehringer-Ingleheim, and Corning—without once going out and trying to sell the company. Boehringer came to us through one of our vendors; Corning was already a partner in the business *(see Chapter 7)*; and Nestle came to us through a finder.

They were all attracted to MetPath. No one had to be hired to put the company on the market. When I came to the point where I was ready to walk out the door, I knew that we would have to attract buyers the same way that we attracted investors in the beginning or during expansion.

"I get it," I hear someone saying. *"You promoted the sale of the company, just like you promoted MetPath to investors when you started up the business."*

Did you say *promote*?

When you are ready to sell your company, **there is a huge difference between keeping a potential buyer's attention and promoting a sale**. Promote the sale of your business to a prospective buyer and one of two things will happen: No sale, because you have come on too strong; or the buyer will be getting a bargain basement deal. Promotion creates an aura of urgency and need, which is exactly the image you need to project when you are trying to start up your company, but not when you are trying to sell it. Instead, you should be doing everything you can to put yourself in a position that will allow you to negotiate from a position of strength. Otherwise, you wind up in the same position that you would be in if you had to sell your company or if you hired a finder to sell it for you. Either way, you will wind up getting the *least* amount of money for your company.

The rule is attraction, not promotion. Remember, if a buyer comes to you, either directly or through a finder that they hired, you are going to get the *most* money for your company. Make your company look as good as you can in as many ways as you can, but stop short of actively pursuing a buyer. The trick to getting a man to marry, I have heard some women advise, is to "chase him until he catches you." That's the idea! Just make your company so attractive in so many ways that when the right suitor comes along, he will be irresistibly drawn to buying you out.

But once he shows up, the challenge becomes how to keep him interested. That is why, when you are ready to sell your business, it is time to learn how to do:

THE THREE Rs

Reflection
Refocus
Reformation

Reflection begins with a look at your track record and see just how far the company has come since you started up the business. **Your view of your company's past** will include many things. There will be successes and failures, people and situations, some high drama, and at least a little low comedy. Whatever your specific memories include, it is worthwhile to end the retrospective with a few positive conclusions, forming **your view of your company's present**. Your vision is now a reality that has been accepted by the investors and employees who have helped you build the company, by the stock market and by sundry others, including your family. Your financial projections are now backed up by financial accomplishments. You have built a successful company on a product or service that was only an idea when the company started out.

Buyers have been attracted to your company by that track record, by great public relations, terrific products, and your growing profit picture, and you need to remember all of it. Not only will all of that serve to help prepare you emotionally and intellectually for the at least difficult and sometimes grueling ordeal of selling your company, but it also opens the door to your next immediate concern: *How do you keep potential buyers interested?* Your company's track record only gets the buyer in the door. Whatever brought them, you need to keep their attention, and to do that you need to focus them on something that they have not seen yet: **Your view of your company's future**. But before you show it to them, it would be a good idea to make sure that you know what it is yourself.

Do you remember International Medical Services? That was the name for my private scheme for the future of Metropolitan Pathology Laboratory, Inc., way back in the planning stages of the business (*see Chapter 2*). It was to include three separate areas of business: a laboratory services division; a medical products division; and a financial services division. MetPath was only the laboratory services component, one-third of the grand delusion that ultimately sold Corning on buying MetPath.

I had planned it all out and written it all down back then, but could hardly have shared the idea with anyone, since no one would have believed the ravings of a twenty-nine-year-old clinical pathologist with no track record in business whatsoever. But when I was ready to sell MetPath, I was *believable.* I was a forty-something success story who had built a successful international business. That was the time to reveal the full extent of my delusion, since I had already proven that one part could work.

If you are now considering the sale of your business, you will have come full cycle too, and you must take the time to *refocus* upon your delusions of grandeur. Your original delusions more than likely have changed a little and become more or less grandiose. Some of your other delusions may not have developed until years after you started up your company. Like me, you may have seen only one or two of your delusions of grandeur become reality. Whatever your situation, make sure you have a good focus on where you believe the company could grow to from wherever you are.

Once you have gone through all this reflection and refocusing, you are ready for the last and most important step in this cumulative process. As soon as you know exactly where your company has been, where it is now, and where you would like to go with it, you are ready for *reformation.* It is not very far from what you did back when you were seeking funds from investors to expand your company (*see Chapter 7*). The major differences are that you are not looking for investors but buyers of one form or another and your personal future will not be tied in with the future of the company (*at least not for very long, as you will see in Chapter 10*). But the principles you must follow are essentially the same. Whoever or whatever the target, the things that you needed to attract investors to your company are exactly what you need to attract buyers to your company.

You have to go back and cook up a new recipe for buyers of **promised products or services, your particular vision and some fantastic financial projections**. They will be different than the ones you used before, of course, but they need to be just as good as those that kept investors drooling. It's like preparing a meal and presenting it to buyers.

Something like this:

YOUR ULTIMATE BUSINESS DINING EXPERIENCE

**Start off with Appetizing and
Well-prepared Facts of Company**

**Enjoy Our Excellent Entree,
(At Market Prices)**

**A Track Record of Profitability,
with
Your Choice of Successful Products
and
Well-baked New Ideas.**

**Finish it off with
A Collection of Colorful Pie-charts,
Sweet Financial Projections,
and
Promises of More to Come . . .**

**All Prepared by a Dedicated
Staff of Cordon Bleu Chefs
Who Could Have Prepared the Entire Menu,
Even if the Head Chef Were Absent.**

*(Generous gratuities expected. No credit cards.
Cash and/or stock along with valuable stock options only.)*

The meal is prepared. The important thing now is presentation. If you want to get a buyer's attention here at the send-off, you will need once again to serve it sizzling with anticipation and complete with all the trimmings. In other words, **maximize your products or services, your people, and your profits when you are ready to sell your company**.

Now you need new *products or services* on the drawing board, more "black boxes" (*see Chapter 7*) to enhance the value of your company and whet the appetite of the potential buyers. You have to be able to show them specifically what your view of the future includes in terms of new products, new services, new concepts . . . new everything.

Once the Chicago laboratory opened, for example, MetPath's profits were going to be shredded. The best time to sell the business was before the Chicago lab opened and, had I known beforehand that I was going to sell the company, I never would have bothered building it at all. It would have been much better to just have talked about building a lab in Chicago, with intimations of market expansion, and let the buyer and their pencil-pushers put their pencils to it.

". . . and, by the way, we are going to have another facility that is going to be capable of doing $50-$70 million dollars."

"Really?"

"Yes. We're looking at Chicago, because of its central location."

"Well, that makes sense for a national lab."

"Yes. And the expansion fits right in with our projections of market growth."

"No kidding!"

"Yes. Here, let me show you the figures ... ."

You will also need to convince potential buyers that you have the *people* in place who can run the company, whether you are there or not. Big corporations and sometimes competitors that are looking to buy your business ultimately will not care, of course, because they think they are smarter than you and your people anyway. But that does not matter at this point, since you have no idea who will come forward to buy your company. The big corporate buyers want to be assured that the business has been and will be in good hands with or without you, at least until they get their hands on it. Potential buyers that have no experience in your business area or market segment are different animals, however. They might walk away from a deal if they think that the company would implode if something happened to you as soon as they bought the company. Buyers worry that if they give you all this money, you might say, "Thanks! Now, I'm going to go play a lot of golf." They want to be assured that if something happens to you, there is someone capable left to run the business.

When we brought new management into MetPath, buyers had the additional comfort zone of knowing that there were new people on board who would not necessarily be loyal to the old ownership (me), but who could at least be expected to transfer loyalty fairly easily to the new owners (them). However, since you do not know when a sale is going to be consummated, continue to relate to your employees—new and old—as you always have. Keep in mind that you may not be able to sell the company. Deals fall through. Do not stop feeding your management with your vision of the future until the day the papers are signed.

Maximizing your profits when selling your company is the goal. There is no point strategically in positioning yourself to increase market share down the road (as MetPath did by building with the Chicago lab), if your plan is to sell the company. So everything you do, every decision you make, should be shifted to reduce costs and maximize profits. There are many ways of doing that—some good and some ... well, you be the judge. A hearing-aid manufacturer named Dahlberg, for example, the maker of Miracle-Ear products, had been doing a lot of television advertising before putting the company on the market. After deciding to sell the company, it decreased television advertising. The net result was that the company made more money over the short-term and, therefore, looked more attractive to the buyer while the deal was being put together.

Such strategies may survive the sale of the business.

Then again, they could be mistakes.

Caveat emptor!

*   *   *   *   *

Man is the chief enemy of the red fox and the foxhound its nemesis. Few other creatures bother the fox and they continue to flourish, even in areas which have large human and canine populations, where they are constantly harassed, trapped for their fur and hunted for sport. A foxhunt can involve a pack of as many as twenty-five to forty hounds that try to find and flush out a fox in an area where the fox has its earth, or den. When a fox is found and starts to run, the whole hunt follows it in full cry across the country. Those who are present when the fox is caught by the hounds are said to be "at the death."

*   *   *   *   *

3. *Leave!*

After you have prepared and presented your company for sale to all those buyers you attracted, then you have got only one thing left to do: **Close the sale.**

Which means, translated into the language of The Business Jungle: **You have to take the position that you do not *really* want to sell your business, so that you can maximize what you are going to get when you finally do sell it.**

This requires an art of **negotiation** that I call *The Br'er Rabbit Routine.* If my memory of Walt Disney's *Uncle Remus* is correct, Br'er Rabbit avoids being eaten by Br'er Fox by begging not to be thrown into the brier patch—which was exactly where he wanted to get to, the only place he could go to escape. When the greedy Br'er Fox throws him in, he unwittingly allows the crafty Br'er Rabbit to save his skin.

"Oh, please, please, *please* don't buy my business," Brother Entrepreneur says, when the opportunistic Brother Buyer tries to seize the opportunity. "What was that figure again?"

"No, please, I don't want to sell my company. ... How much did you say you would pay?"

"Well, that's nice, but I really have no interest in selling my company. ... How much will I be getting?"

And so on. The routine is a necessary self-protective mechanism. When you are selling your company, you are very much alone. Just like a fox hunt, you are the fox that the hounds would love to tear apart. Your objective, once the hunt begins, is to get to a place of safety. No matter that you get treed, since you want to get "caught." You just want to get out of it with your skin intact.

Put another way, negotiating with a potential buyer is about as safe as getting into a bathtub with a barracuda. (*That is the "interesting" way of defining such negotiations that my lawyer came up with back in Chapter 7. Told you we would get around to it!*) The fact is that whoever is trying to buy your company will be difficult to handle and more than likely is going to think they are a lot smarter than you are, if only for the simple reason they are a lot bigger and stronger and have more senior staff than you have.

My negotiations with Nestle showed me what "big" really meant. When they asked if I was interested in selling MetPath my answer was yes, provided the price was right. Near the end of our negotiations, they said they would take it up at committee and decide if they wanted to go forward. I could not imagine how they could go and make a decision in a little committee about spending $140 million. Then I sat down and figured out that $140 million to them was only about one percent of Nestle's annual sales, which at that time were about $14 billion. When I compared MetPath's annual sales of $78 million and took one percent of that, I realized it represented the cost of a piece of automated lab equipment that we once decided on buying in a committee meeting. All of a sudden, I understood that they operated in a context quite different from mine.

The deal did not go forward for other reasons, one mine and one theirs. My reason was that they wanted it to be a cash transaction. I did not want that because it would have been taxable income for our shareholders. But their reason was the real reason. Nestle was concerned that if they made an offer, our corporate partner would simply match it, since Corning had the right of first refusal. Nestle did not want to wind up in a bidding war with Corning. That would have been great for MetPath, had we not (unknowingly) shot ourselves in the foot by not putting any time limit on that right of first refusal when, years before, Corning became our corporate partner. We never should have done that; in fact, I have since made it a rule to **never give away any rights without a time limit**. Otherwise, shareholders could stand to lose millions.

MetPath almost wound up in another bidding war when Boehringer-Ingleheim expressed an interest in buying MetPath because it was the largest lab in the U.S. A vendor of ours asked me to fly over to Germany for lunch and talk to them, which I did. They remained interested and before long were visiting us in New Jersey. One meeting, in fact, found Boehringer-Ingleheim in my office and Corning in my boardroom. I was shuttling back and forth between the two of them, discussing the structure of the potential deals and moving them both forward. But Boehringer, like Nestle, could only pay cash, so there was little hope for that deal to work out.

Corning, for its part, had not made an offer through all of these negotiation. It finally came while Cynthia and I were visiting Palm Beach on a weekend—over the phone! The substance of the conversation was that, since MetPath's stock was trading at fourteen dollars a share, Corning would pay twenty dollars a share, which amounted to $140 million in a tax-free deal. Basically, it was a take it or leave it deal, and I took it. I did very well in getting the price I did with Corning and so did my shareholders.

The value I placed on MetPath was even higher, of course. I had invested thirteen years of my life in MetPath, gave up many things and put off many others to realize my dream. My delusions of grandeur, the same ones that brought me to start a business with $500, dreaming that I could build it into a big business, would not let me settle for a low-ball bid. Corning's bid was hardly that, although I would have liked a higher offer. But given the state of the economy at the time and the question mark posed by the new Chicago lab, it seemed prudent to accept a bid over the phone that would bring me $15 million personally before taxes. My shareholders, who had only greed to sustain them, and the stock analysts who had their opinions, probably would have settled for much less.

But that was not the end of it. It took another two and a half months to work out all the details of the acquisition. There is a lot more to negotiating the close of the sale of your business than just **settling on a price.** That is only a third of the negotiating process when you are selling your company. More or less simultaneously, you must also come to an agreement with the buyer about **how you are going to get paid** and what kind of **employment contract** you are going to wind up with.

"Didn't we just hear about that in Chapter 8?"

Yes, but I refuse to repeat myself. Simply turn back a few pages yourself and turn the rules there around to the seller's perspective. What the buyer is going to pay, for example, obviously becomes what you are going to get. But the questions generated by that fact are a bit different. Are you getting paid in cash, stock, or a combination of the two? Can you sell the stock immediately or do you have to wait? Are you getting paid a fixed price up front? Or will the payment be based on the future performance of your company within the buyer's corporation, or on the corporation's performance as a whole?

Those considerations all tie in directly with your personal situation. (*Remember? We also discussed that in the preceding chapter.*) If you opt for the *walkaway*, they will pay you off and you leave, which means you will not have a job, will not be involved with the new owners, and will have nothing more to do with your business. Or you can have an *earnout* deal (a share in the earnings) or, better yet, a *revenue-out* deal (a share in the revenues), where you are going to be running the business for the new owners for a time. Or you might opt for structuring the deal so that you wind up with an *employment contract* that does not tie your income to the future fortunes of the company or its new owners. Perhaps you might favor a small payment up front and a long-term, no-cut *consulting* arrangement.

As a buyer, I get excited about someone who wants to be part of something bigger. There is nothing I would like better than buy your business because you want to become part of my business and you want to make it work. I will work with you and we will try to make it work. If it does not work out, which is true more often than not, then it did not work out. HEARx acquired a family owned hearing-aid dealer that was doing a reasonable amount of business in New York. He was an audiologist and he got cash, stock, and a note for his business. But the most important thing he got was to be the manager for the whole New York market. He went from having a small business selling twenty hearing aids a month, to being responsible for fifteen stores in two states. But things did not work out and he lasted about six months.

When you are selling your company, the buyer wants to think that things will work out. Most of the people, however, will not stick around. We kept perhaps five people out of twenty acquisitions at MetPath, people who could grow with the company. So **be careful about the kind of employment contract you choose**. If you negotiate an employment contract and your income is not somehow tied to the performance of your company within the new corporate structure, then your employment there will very likely be short-lived.

On the other hand, you may get a three or five year employment contract easily enough, but holding onto it might be a lot tougher. At first, everyone will be happy with you and they will pick your brain and they will do all these nice things for you in return. Then they will begin putting in their own people and become concerned that the management people you hired were loyal to you, not to them. And so, slowly but surely, the new owners put in their players. You begin to be left out of meetings and, one way and another, you get the message. Next thing you know, they are buying out your employment contract and you are history.

Or perhaps you end up being "vice president of special projects," which entails reading the *Wall Street Journal* every morning and waiting for somebody to call you. Finally, you go to them and say, "Look, maybe I shouldn't stay here." There are five years on your employment contract and they buy you out at three. It finally becomes a question of who wants out first. If they can bore you to death, then you will go to them and they will make a token payment to get rid of you. If they want to get rid of you, they will come to you and make a larger payment. (*Sound familiar?*)

The likelihood is that, if you sell your business with the idea that you are going to be a part of something bigger, you will not be part of it for very long. A new broom definitely sweeps clean in corporate life. Very few people get to have their cake and eat it too. A friend of mine, the founder of Charles River Breeding Labs in Boston, sold his company to Bausch & Lomb for a tremendous amount of stock and he is still running his company, years after the transaction. But that is highly unusual, in my experience.

Therefore, as you are signing your employment contract, keep in mind that at the end you may be unemployed. **You can be**

wealthy and unemployed at the same time, you know. In my case, I took the money and negotiated a five-year employment contract and, a year later, the contract was renewed for another five years. Sounds wonderful, on paper. But ... need I say it? Things are seldom what they seem in The Business Jungle. A year or so after that, I was out the door.

The final deal will not be like the handshake. Be prepared that things are not going to happen as initially agreed. Few deals, if any at all, go smoothly, even with a super-positive business situation and the most anxious buyers in the world. The reason, of course, is that it is all about *money* and *money* does not pass hands easily. There are going to be bumps in the road in the writing of the agreements or in the investigation of your business or in negotiating your employment contract. There will be snags and stops, fits and starts, and many variations.

But you, on the other hand, only have one opportunity to get what is most important to you, even for a potentially wealthy unemployed person, and that is health benefits. When I sold MetPath, I negotiated ten-year coverage for my family. I am only sorry I did not negotiate lifetime health benefits, considering what has happened to the health care system. Another very important item is whether or not to sign a non-compete clause, for how long and what territory it will cover. Some agree to it for a year or two, some for five years. In my case, I agreed to stay out of the business in the U.S. and Europe for two years after my employment contract expired, whenever it expired.

Remember: You do not get to negotiate any further with the buyers afterwards. Once the deal is done and signed, it is a done deal, unless *they* agree to something different and they will only do that if they can see a benefit for themselves.

"Oh, you know, I really would like to ....,"

"Sorry," comes the most likely reply. "The deal's over."

You simply have got to get as much as you can into your employment contract or into the deal the first time through.

Especially since this is the last time around.

$ECRET$ OF THE FOX

You will get more for your business
if someone wants to buy it
before you want to sell it.

When you have decided to sell your company and
you want to increase its value,
keep your strategic planning short-term and
your vision long-term.

No matter what your employment contract says
(if you get one)
you will probably be employed for a very short time.

Sleep on It

Chapter Ten
The Bear: Sleep on It

▲ ▲ ▲ ▲ ▲

Bear, *any of the large mammals of the family* Ursidae, *order* Carnivora, *are grouped along with the dog, rac-coon, and weasel families in the super-family* Canoidea. *Known the world over, all bears are covered with coarse, shaggy fur that may be colored various shades of black, brown, cinnamon, yellow, or white, depending on their species. The six living bear genera—* Ursus, Tremarctos, Selenarctos, Thalarctos, Melursus *and* Helarctos—*come in all sizes. The largest living land carnivore, the giant grizzly (*Ursus horribilis*) of Alaska's Kodiak Island, can grow to over nine feet tall and weigh more than 1,500 pounds, about fifteen times the weight of its littlest relative, the hundred-pound, three-foot tall Malay bear (*Helarctos malayensis*).*

*　　*　　*　　*　　*

My son Mark filled out a college application not long after I had sold MetPath. He did not know what to write down in the space provided for "Father's Occupation," so he put down that I was "unemployed."

Had I been there, I could have told him to put down "physician" or even "retired businessman." Either would have been accurate. But his confusion over who I was put my status (or the lack of it, more precisely) in clear focus for me for the first time.

I was, in fact, unemployed.

And that is the way it is when you sell your business. No matter how big or profitable or interesting or satisfying or ego-gratifying your company is, there will come the day in your business life when you will have to leave your company or your company will have to leave you.

That's right, I said *leave* ... sooner or later.

Chapter Ten: The Bear
▲ ▲ ▲ ▲ ▲

You *sold* your company, but you have not left it yet. You know what you *want* to do, since your exit revolves around the reasons why you sold your business in the first place: because *you wanted to go and do something else*; because *you wanted to become part of something bigger*; or because *you knew about something that no one else knew about*.

And at least two things should have already been accomplished: You should have sold your business for a good price and you should have taken the money and run, or worked out a decent employment contract.

The papers are signed, sealed and delivered.

The debts are paid off.

The keys are in the hands of the new owners.

No more sleepless nights for you! No more emergency forty-minute drives to the plant at midnight. No more problems with employees, suppliers, or your executive staff. No more, no more, no more! Everything is, literally, finished.

But—need we say it again?—this is The Business Jungle, where **selling your company is one thing and leaving it is quite another**. The situation is summed up neatly in a single question that, consciously or unconsciously, every entrepreneur who sells a business will ask: *"What in the world is going to happen now that I'm gone?"*

Psychologists tell us that divorce, job changes, and moving to a new home are at the top of the list for most people in terms of stress. If that is so, then the entrepreneur's stress level when selling his business is off the charts. The hunt for a buyer and then the haggling over terms and price produce worry and stress sufficient for anyone's lifetime.

But, wait! There's more!

That kind of stress is only part of the picture. Once you sell your business, you not only have to leave it but you have got to *deal* with leaving it, which creates a different level of stress.

Experience says you probably will be unable emotionally or intellectually to let go of your company for some time, even if you just took the money and ran and chose not to work out an employment contract. Meanwhile, although you may know exactly what it is that you plan to do next, you still have to go out and do it. Truth is, most of us are *willing* and *able* to leave but very few of us are really *ready* to leave and face the next challenge immediately after we sell our businesses.

So, get ready! Wherever, whenever and however you land, the personal and professional challenges you are going to meet will be—like everything else in The Business Jungle—unlike anything you have ever before faced.

Even before you sell, you will be the only one who does not know that you are already gone. When word of the sale of the business comes out, everyone else will be thinking that you left the day before yesterday.

SINCE YOU'VE BEEN GONE

- *The (new) owner will be looking forward to all the things that he can do without you.*

- *Your (former) business friends and associates will begin speaking about you in the past tense.*

- *Your (surviving) ex-employees will have written you off as soon as they hear about the deal.*

- *Your (loyal) spouse will be looking forward to all the things that you will be able to do or buy together now that you have left your company.*

All of these things are natural enough, but that does not make them any less uncomfortable. If you accidentally overhear something like, "Yeah, if Doctor Brown was still around..." and you *are* still around, trust me, it bothers you, more than you can imagine. Unless you have experienced leaving your successful business, you have no idea of what it feels like or how hard it is to let go—especially a business you have eaten, drank, and dreamed about for years. I gave MetPath and the people involved with it thirteen years of my life and, as these words are being written, it has been another fourteen years since I sold MetPath. There are some things I *still* have not been able to let go. (More about that shortly.)

The fact is, however, that no matter how well you ran things, you are *not* running things anymore. It may be easy enough to *admit* that (maybe not in public), but it will be some time before you can actually *accept* the fact (even in private). If you are anything like me, you will probably go running off into *action* (again) to try something else before allowing all the dust to settle and wind up paying a financial penalty as a result.

There are at least a couple of closely linked reasons why an entrepreneur acts that way. The first is a sense of **proprietorship**. *I* may have transferred **ownership** to someone else, but it is still *my* company. It does not matter to me who *owns* it, it is still *mine*, every last part of it, from top to bottom. The second reason is that any entrepreneur worth the name is congenitally incapable of accepting reality in the first place. It is a necessary attitude for building a business. But now, with the grand delusions realized, the vision complete, the race run, and the difficulties overcome, the end has finally arrived. There is just no altering that reality. No bulldog mentality can overcome it. Yet, like a child on a roller coaster, the entrepreneur just cannot accept the fact that the ride, so long anticipated and so heartily enjoyed, has ended so incredibly soon.

But, as you have read so often on these pages, *don't worry!* You will accept things sooner or later. And if you negotiated an employment contract, you will have plenty of help learning how to accept reality from the new owners of your company.

Excuse me ... your *ex-company*. (Although that is not what the new owners call it; they just call it *their* company.)

They also want you out of the way as soon as possible, no matter what they or that ironclad employment contract may say. The hardest thing to accept is that you will have very little, if anything at all, to say about it.

The proof is in the procedure.

POWER DRAIN

Titles change.
Responsibilities change.
The power structure of the company changes.

These thing may take some time, as the new owners may still have some use for you. But they will happen.

When I sold MetPath, for example, I took the money and negotiated a five-year employment contract as chairman of the board **AND** chief executive officer. I had an office with a balcony, nice display cabinets, a fish tank, and a bathroom. A year or so later, the contract was renewed for another five years, if I would give up the position of CEO, allowing Corning to put in one of its executives as the president **AND** CEO of the company. It did not seem like much of a concession at the time, considering all that I was getting in return. Plus, I got to stay on as chairman in my nice office, while the new "president **AND** CEO" had a smaller office.

But that small matter was the first tangible proof that I was really no longer there. Sure enough, a year later the new "president **AND** CEO" wanted my office, so Corning bought out the rest of my contract. As far as I know, I am the only person who sold his company and then sold his office two and a half years later. The funny thing is that the only thing Corning kept with my name on it was my office door. The only reason they kept it was because my name was engraved right into the wood—they could not take it out unless they replaced the whole door! So they kept the door but finally turned my office into a library.

So whether or not you negotiate yourself back into your office after the sale of your business, the change in your title is really the first step out the door, because **once your title changes, your responsibilities change** as well. More accurately, just about everything you ever did at the company gets taken away from you or done differently or done without you. Your relationships with your staff change (not to mention your staff) and your relationship with the new owners begins to change. This is also where things start to get hard to accept, even if (or maybe especially because) the changes are inevitable.

A seminar that I attended years ago brought out three pertinent points that help explain some of the changes that occur after you sell your company. A major brokerage firm invited four entrepreneurs and representatives of four major corporations who had bought entrepreneurial companies, put all eight on a panel, and asked them each what happened after the sale.

The first point that came out was that when the companies were run by the entrepreneurs, strategic planning really translated into getting market share. The focus was growth, growth, growth—all entrepreneurs ever want to do is get bigger and bigger and bigger. Once they sold their companies to the large corporations, however, strategic planning was driven by the new owners, and became the next quarter's profitability. What large corporations care about is how much money will be made and when.

The second thing they pointed out was that successful entrepreneurs are able to effectively motivate their employees (*see Chapter 4*) and get everyone working toward the success of the company. But if you take the entrepreneur out of the game, then there is no one to be the cheerleader. There is no one who cares as deeply as the entrepreneur about the company, or about the people that make up the company, which is why entrepreneurs are so good at motivating employees and generating a "we're all in this together" attitude. It is also highly unlikely that corporate owners who have no personal stake or connection with your ex-company can become cheerleaders for strangers that they probably do not even want to get to know.

The third thing that came out of the seminar was that it was probably better for the corporation to buy a majority but not all of a company, thereby leaving some ownership in the hands of the original owners, management and employees. That leaves some continuing incentive for management and the entrepreneur stays on as the cheerleader for the business. However, I have not seen too many buyouts done that way. It certainly was not what Corning did with me. Corning wanted me out of MetPath. They did not want me at meetings or participating in the decisions. They did not want me wandering through the lab talking to the managers and employees because they wanted *their* people wandering through the lab. They wanted to change things and they did. Big changes, not small changes, that wound up costing them in the same proportions. As a matter of fact, in the twelve years since I sold the company, the new owners have paid out more in fines for Medicare fraud than they originally paid for the company. No one seemed to know or even care about what was going on. Only profits counted!

Finally, *the power structure within the business changes.* All the decision-makers change and with them the philosophy and concepts upon which you built the business. This is the part that is really hard to watch, made worse by the fact that you have to watch it mainly in silence. The new owners of your ex-company begin to put in their own people, players and programs. So, when you stay, you have to stay through a period in which the power changes hands and the decision-making process changes, while your opinions become less valid, even if proved right later.

When Corning bought out my second five-year contract only thirty months from the signing of the first one, I finally came to the point where I knew that I was gone. They bought me out with the proviso that I never show up again. "We'll call you, don't call us, and don't come in the building until we call you," was more or less what they told me.

I wish they would have called. Maybe then we could have saved my ex-company some of those Medicare fraud fines.

The end result? Although their acquisition became about a $2 billion business not long ago, Corning began losing as much money each year as they paid for the company. Now, *not making money* when you are starting up a business is one thing—(obviously something with which I and countless other entrepreneurs are well-acquainted. But *losing* money after acquiring a profitable business is something else entirely. They recently gave the entire laboratory business to the Corning shareholders. What a gift!

Corning destroyed the concept on which MetPath was built because they thought they were smarter than I was. But, as we already know, that is the way large corporations are. They think they are smarter because they are bigger. Once a corporation buys you out, they really do not want to hear from you anymore. When you sell your company, your strategy likely will no longer be the company's strategy and you will not be involved in the decision-making process any longer.

As hard as that is, you just have to live with it.

But that's okay.

That is just the way things are.

Besides, you have a few other decisions to make.

And these are much more important decisions . . .

Now that you're gone.

*   *   *   *   *

Bears that live in cold climates become fat with the onset of cold weather. They go into hibernation, rousing at irregular intervals but spending most of the winter asleep. The extremely isolated polar bear (Thalarctos maritimus), which lives on ice floes in the open ocean and wanders great distances in search of food, is the exception.

*   *   *   *   *

1. Hibernate

Aside from being "gone," the day you sell your business you have two things that, the day before, you did not have.

Those two things are **money** and **time**.

You also have a need, a need that began growing the day you decided to sell your business.

That need is to **plan what you are going to do with your money and your time, in that order**.

You *think* you have a plan of what you would *like* to do. But that is all you have—an *idea* about what you *think* you would like to do next. Be honest. Have you really planned your retirement or your next venture?

When I graduated from college, my goals were to become a millionaire, to get a black belt in karate, and to learn French well enough to speak socially. Well, I now have a second-degree black belt in karate and I became a multi-millionaire when I sold MetPath. I sort of lost interest in learning to speak French and that is probably not something that I would like to spend the rest of my life doing anyway.

So ... what's next? And when?

When you made the decision to sell your company, you probably had a wish list of the things you would like to do when you were on your own. Perhaps your all-consuming passions were beckoning for you to become a world-class chef, do charitable work, or get on the PGA tour. Maybe that other business you had been eyeing was starting to look very attractive. You might have been spurred further and made a few inquiries into these opportunities. Maybe you went as far as starting to consider some of the things you would need to do once you sold your company in order to realize those possibilities. But that is probably as far as you got.

Let's face it: Running your company and trying to sell it at the same time made any real planning impossible.

That wish list may have gotten shortened somewhat after negotiations were completed too. Maybe you did not get as much money for your ex-company as you anticipated and moving to the French Riviera for an extended vacation is no longer an option. It may have taken you so long to build and sell your company that you are now better suited for an Arizona retirement community rather than the French Riviera. Your physician might even have something to say about what it is you will be doing for the next phase of your life, as well.

Suddenly, however, the day comes when you sell your business and you have all this money! And it really is *sudden*, you know. One day you have a company. The next day you sign your name and, next thing you know, you are wealthy! You might not have it all, given the terms of the sale, but you probably have more than you have ever had before at any single moment in your life ... certainly enough to get you started in whatever it is you want to do next. Even with an employment contract or some form of consultancy, you also have all the time in the world to do some of that planning—right now, today, immediately!

What exhilaration! Makes you feel absolutely euphoric ...

Except that when you stop and try to figure out what to do with it all, you discover that if you had to begin doing whatever it is you want to do, you would probably crash and burn as quickly as you climbed to this rarefied altitude. Not that you shouldn't feel like you are on top of the world. Just avoid the trap of mistaking feelings for facts! And the facts are that, feelings aside, you really need to take control of your new situation and not let it take control of you.

So, given the abundance of your two new resources, which one do you think you should you take care of first?

PLEASE CHECK ONE:

☐ *Money*   ☐ Time

Good choice! The first thing to do is **take control of your personal finances**. Here are a few places to start:

QUESTIONS, QUESTIONS ...

- *If you have no golden parachute, what about insurance?*
- *How do you plan to provide for your retirement?*
- *What are you doing for your children, short- and long-term?*
- *Are you going to set up a foundation or some kind of trust?*
- *Since not all of us live forever, have you made out a will?*
- *What about a living will?*
- *Are you just going to give up a big chunk to the IRS?*
- *Will you be able to avoid the taxman later?*
- *Are you going to make any major purchases soon?*

Your own personal situation and knowledge will yield even more questions, but do not try working these things out on your own. First off, if you are married and do not already know your spouse's thinking on matters financial, you had better get in touch with that. And before you start trying to answer any of these questions or figure out what you are going to do with all your money, get some professionals involved to help you decide—even if you are a financial whiz. As far I know, most barbers do not regularly cut their own hair.

Your banker or some other financial advisor that you have developed a relationship with will be most helpful. Your accountant can help, too, and perhaps your attorney. Look to people you know you can trust—do not leave out your parents, friends, or some close relative—especially those who have been down this road before, if you can find them. This involves some care, so *avoid anyone who might want you to get involved in a new business venture or some stock deal*. Such things can wait. It is much too soon to be making any moves in those directions. The idea here is to get your whole personal financial house in order, period; for now, nothing else matters.

Once you have answered most of the questions and think you know what you want to do with your money, divide it up into three piles. The first pile to make is a medium-term "peace of mind" pile. Make sure that you put at least two years' worth of living expenses in this pile, enough to sustain you and your family at the level to which they have grown accustomed. This is the "no matter what happens we'll be okay" pile—which translates in the near term as the "just in case my consultancy or multi-year employment contract doesn't last too long" pile. This has nothing to do with the compensation you may be getting from other sources. It is strictly an emergency fund.

Include all current expenses you can think of, from charitable giving to food and clothing. Some things will be easy to recognize, like mortgage and home maintenance; children's school tuition and expenses; medical and life insurance premiums; debt service; taxes; automobile insurance and upkeep; and your cellular phone. But do not forget to make provision for things like visits to the veterinarian; dinner out once or twice a week; and those "special" things that crop up in your check register from time to time. Whatever, add it all up. Alternatively, you might simply look back over your tax records and take an average of your gross income over the last few years. However you arrive at your final figure, throw in a minimum of 10 percent more to cover the things you cannot foresee and put that whole pile into liquid investments. Then forget that it is even there. Let your bank manage it in high-grade U.S. government securities or some other zero-risk, easily accessible investment vehicle, so that if, heaven help you, you need your money you can have it.

The second pile includes most of the rest of your money. This is the long-term "nestegg" pile, which includes less liquid investments than the first pile such as blue chip stocks, bonds, real estate, IRAs, those sorts of things. This is also the pile from which you will draw the funds necessary to set up trusts for the children. This is the bulk of your fortune, so you want to have this pile spread out among places where you are least likely to lose it. Again, do not try to do this on your own. Get help and check your decisions thoroughly.

The third pile is one that you probably do not need any help with. This is the short-term "immediate gratification" spending pile. After all those years of delayed gratification, some indulgence is to be expected. This is the money to buy your new Jaguar, boat, or both; to give a special gift to your church, synagogue, or favorite charity; to use to play the stock market; to travel—to do or have whatever it is that money can afford. Try to settle on those things you would most like to have or do and set aside a chunk of money to accomplish those things. Then try not to exceed that amount. Just don't go crazy.

After you have taken care of your money, it is time to turn your attention to your time, your other great resource. This is where you **gain control of your personal life**. If it is true that you have to spend money to make money, it is also true that you have to spend time so that you will not spend your money—at least not all of it!

So take some time off. Not a ten-day cruise or a few weeks in Europe—I mean some *real* time off. We are talking about three months minimum here and six months or a year would be even better, if you could stand it! This is meant to be a complete break from where you have been and what you have been doing for however many years, free from everything and everyone, just you and your spouse and life after your ex-company. Get out of town, leave the country or—if you are reading this sometime in the third millennium A.D. and commercial space travel is an option (maybe from a company you built)—get off the planet!

How long and how far you can go on this trip in, around, or out of this world will depend, of course, on how much money you have to spend. So if you have put your financial house in order, you will know how much, won't you? Which goes back to why it is so important to figure out how much of your money is going to be spent before you start making decisions about how to spend your time. This may seem like an unnecessary point to make but, believe me, it is very necessary. The temptation is to let loose and go off somewhere with no plan at all or just the idea that you will take care of everything when you get back. But what if you never get back? No one lives forever and accidents do happen—even to people who have a lot of time and money. Your children and heirs might never forgive you for leaving them without making up a will; and the government, while not likely to think twice about it, will be very happy to take just as much of your money as it can get.

So settle your financial affairs first, then go out and live for a while. Sail around the world, if that's your thing. Go to all of those places you have always wanted to go to—and I mean *all* of them. Whatever you think you can afford in time and money, spend a little more. It will pay big dividends, especially if you leave as soon as you can. If you can depart immediately, do it!

I did not and I am sorry that no one advised me about taking a break when I sold MetPath. I did not even take a vacation after my employment contract was bought out. Anyone could have used some time off and I was certainly no exception, especially after spending thirty months experiencing a steady downgrade of responsibilities and activities. At the very least, I probably would not have had to move from New Jersey to Boston and finally to Florida to escape the phone calls. I had a terrible time with my ex-employees, who kept calling me up to tell me how bad things were since I left. "Did you hear what they did today?" I know that they were really being loyal, but they almost drove me crazy!

Aside from peace and quiet, getting away from it all and spending all this money and time *gives your head a chance to come back to normal size.* True, you have just spent years building something. You have been successful. You made it all happen. You have many worthy accomplishments to your credit. But, as you learned early on in The Business Jungle, you cannot survive very long on credit alone. You have spent an awful lot of yourself in pursuing your business. But when the business goes away, what becomes of you? Who are you now? A few (miserable) years with an employment contract, watching (helplessly) from the sidelines as your business continues to go (every which way but) up, only delays the inevitable; as soon as you slow down long enough to notice that you are no longer who you were, your realize your ego has been severely traumatized.

A good chunk of time off allows time for deep reflection. This is an opportunity to visit your own private little Shangri-La, far above the steamy business jungle. Here the cool light of reason reigns, rather than the glaring imperatives of performance. You can take a long, leisurely look at your experience, a kind of completely enjoyable adventure that has nothing but happy endings. (If you have lied, cheated and stolen in order to be successful, the endings might be miserable, so we will assume you have been *basically* honest down there in the jungle.) See what you have learned, who you have become, where you would like to go. What has made you successful? Where are your strengths and weaknesses now? How do you think other businessmen see you? Just try very hard to be honest when you answer yourself. Otherwise, you will be left with a flawed picture that will last only as long as you can sustain the lies you tell yourself.

The questions will come, don't worry. They seem a natural by-product of experience, as we all have this need to gauge our performance. They came to me, even though I never took a break. I have come through a little poorer but wiser for the experience. I made it through, but then I have tended to be the exception rather than the rule. I certainly would have preferred taking the quicker and less stressful road that I would have traveled had I taken some time off.

Still, I picked up some valuable insights along the way. Many of my discoveries were of a personal nature that would do no one but me any good. But many others seem to have broader applications that might even do *you* some good. One of the things I found is that *fame cuts both ways*. When you have it, you tend not to pay much attention to it and even try to downplay it. But when you lose it, you sure notice its absence. When you are successful and run a big company, you have fame of a sort and, like it or not, the impressions of others become part of your self-definition.

I had been featured in *Business Week* four times, *Fortune* twice and *Forbes*, as well as in the *Wall Street Journal.* I had testified before Congress. I was recognized as a leader in the clinical laboratory industry. Wall Street listened when I spoke. People knew who I was. I would go into New York restaurants and people would recognize my face. But when I sold MetPath, I became a non-persona. People stopped calling me. No one was asking me for my opinion of what was happening in a particular area. I was not going out to the restaurants as often either. There was no more Wall Street, no more testifying, no more articles in the newspaper.

I discovered that the lack of all that attention created a large hole that I needed to fill. But it was not as overwhelming a prospect for me as it could have been, partly because my entire self-image was not wrapped up with MetPath. Professionally, I always considered myself a physician. Whenever I fill out any form or application, for example, I put down that I am a physician. That is what I am and I will be that for all of my life. No one can take that away from me. Even more significantly, I am also a husband and a father. What my wife and my children think of me is very important. I did not, in fact, really think about who I was *ápres-* MetPath until Mark raised the issue on his college questionnaire.

Another discovery I made, albeit too late to make a difference, was that all my attempts to change a number of things in my life, including some investments, were ill-advised. Not that they were bad ideas; it was their *timing* that was wrong. The investments in oil-drilling and an office building in Houston might have been successful at another time, but not when I made them. The same was true for several small businesses I started up. I am convinced that, had I taken some time to get myself back on an even keel and then taken some time to better consider my next moves, I would have had much more positive and less expensive post-MetPath experiences. But I didn't, so I didn't. Instead, within a week of selling MetPath, I was investing in other ventures and have regretted it ever since. The $10 million I wound up with after taxes when I sold MetPath either disappeared or ended up invested in HEARx.

Given the current price of HEARx stock, I am still way ahead. But I wish I would have spent some time figuring out what to do with all my time and money. You may or may not go back to work or start another company. You may get involved in charities or sit on boards of directors. But you are going to be doing something and, if you are an entrepreneur, you will go crazy without something to do. In any event, you are going to have to decide what it is you are going to do.

All I can say is . . .

Do as I say, not as I did.

* * * * *

All bears are shy and retiring, sharing a proclivity for solitude. Most live in wilderness areas. Perhaps that is just as well. The bear family's main sensory drawback is relatively poor vision.

*   *   *   *   *

2. What (Not) To Do

Ah!

I see you have taken my suggestion to take some time and do some planning.

Good. The whole purpose for this book is to help keep you from making mistakes and, as has been said before, you can learn from other people's mistakes. If so, then there is a lot to learn in this chapter because here is where I made most of my mistakes. Again, I urge you to take that extended time-out to get your head screwed back on straight. Then, consider your next move in as much detail as possible. I know how important it is; I have been there and made just about every mistake there was to make.

Failure is important; ask anyone who has ever failed at anything and gone on to be successful. Most will tell you that their failures helped shape their successes. It is what you do with your failures that counts.

I actually published some of MetPath's failures and it had a terrific positive impact on our business. The Federal government had developed proficiency tests for laboratories and MetPath was required to take them. We got mostly As, but there were a few Ds and some Fs in there as well. We published the actual results in a booklet and gave it out as part of our promotional materials to the physicians we were trying to attract as lab customers. We published *all* of our grades and the physicians were shocked that we admitted that we had failed some of the tests.

Yet our failures helped create the reality of the company. No one else was going to put them in a booklet and publish them. Our credibility with the physicians came not so much because we had As, but because we put in the Ds and the Fs. Publishing those shortcomings gave the physicians a sense that MetPath was a company of integrity and honesty, and it did so in a way that a million dollars of advertising our strengths never could have accomplished in so short a time.

Likewise, I hope that no one who reads this book leaves with the message of "once successful, always successful" or anything like that. We are all pretty far from perfection and if you are left thinking that everything Dr. Brown did worked out, that would be a false image. This book was not written to tell you how wonderful my ideas are but to give you the benefit of my experience, both good and bad. It is up to you to make up your own mind whether or not to apply the principles found in this book to your own business—or your next business, for that matter, which brings us back to the topic at hand.

So, now that you have all this time and money, what do you think you will do ...

NEXT?

Do Nothing
Teach
Enter The Not-for-Profit World
Work For Someone Else
Consult
Start Up Another Business

Obviously, you could **do nothing**, now that you have the money and time. And if you have reached your goals—making a lot of money the primary one—then why go on? You can do just about anything you want, really, including nothing. Whatever you choose, of course, will be decided to some extent by your age, your health and your family situation. If you are eighty-five or seventy-five or sixty-five, it may make sense to do nothing. "That's it! I've worked all my life and now, at my age, I am going to quit. I have enough money, so I am going to travel, visit my kids, and give away some of my money to charity."

Then again, choosing to do nothing could be a big mistake in today's world. We now have about 57,000 people over the age of 100 in America, while more than 200 people a week pass the century mark. Over-eighty-five is the fastest growing segment of our population. So, if you are seventy years old and you sell your business, saying, "Hah! Why should I get involved in something else? How much time could I have left?" Well, you could have thirty years in which you could be a productive person.

Teaching certainly is an option for someone who has built a business. It can be very fulfilling, imparting your knowledge and experience to others, perhaps helping to mold tomorrow's leaders. If you have ever had an urge to write a book, the academic world might allow you the time. I had always been attracted to the idea of being a teacher and, not surprisingly, the idea of writing a book had occurred to me. I went so far as to have some discussions with Harvard Business School and the Columbia University School of Business after my employment was terminated. The schools thought it would be a great idea. But when they explained that I would only spend about two hours a week teaching and the rest of the time doing research, I realized that was not for me. I was not looking for a hobby and I did not want to write a book that much at the time. First and foremost, I wanted something to do.

I also considered **entering the not-for-profit world**. I

interviewed with one university, looking to take an administrative position. The president of the university listened to what I had to say and then I listened to him.

"This is not the place for you," he said, straight out.

"I don't understand," I replied. "I know it's an important position and the job is demanding but, believe me, I know about demanding. Don't you think I could do the job?"

"Well, let's go through a few things and then you tell me if you could do the job," he answered. "First of all, you come from the for-profit world. If you don't like the way one of your employees is doing their work, you get rid of them. We have a tenured environment and we thrive on mediocrity. You're going to go crazy with some of the people that are in the university that I have to put up with. But there's nothing I can do about it. Would you be able to handle that?"

"Well, I don't know," I replied, feeling a little uncertain.

"Okay, then think about this," he added. "In the for-profit world, when you wanted to do something, you made a decision and you did it. Our university has been here for well over 150 years. So, if something doesn't get done this year, big deal. The attitude essentially is that if we don't make a decision today, so what? We'll make it next year, or we'll put it off and make it up as part of a five-year plan, or whatever. Eventually the decision will be made and something will get done. You would go stark-raving mad waiting for the decision."

"Yes, I understand what you're saying," I replied. (I really did. I sat on the boards of directors of two museums and I almost did go crazy. I was looking for something to get involved in, something to give me back some sense of ego gratification. What I got instead were monthly board meetings attended by thirty people at which nothing ever seemed to happen.)

"Finally, you can come and go when you want when you own your own business," he continued. "If you want to come in late one day, because you're doing something else, that's fine. It's your business, after all. But in a university environment, if people come in and see your office empty, you're going to be looked at as a prima donna. Do you think you could handle all that?"

Frankly, I could not, so I stopped pressing my case in the not-for-profit world. Interestingly, at HEARx we recently hired a vice president of professional services who had been a member of our scientific advisory group. He left the university to join us. I am interested in watching how things work out for him. I suspect that the transition from the university into the for-profit world will work better than vice versa. But I *know* its going to be very different for him.

When I left MetPath, I thought I might be able to **work for somebody else** in the for-profit world, so I went to an outplacement guru. I had resumes written. I had done plenty of interviewing, but I had never interviewed for a job, so I had to learn how to interview from the other side of the desk. It did not work very well and, after two or three interviews, a pattern began to emerge. Every one of the companies who interviewed me asked why I would ever want to come back to work. They just could not believe that I was serious. The last one added another reason:

"You'll probably not do a thing we ask you to do," the interviewer said. "The first time we tell you there's a meeting in Chicago, you'll say you can't make it because you're taking your family on a cruise or you've got a tennis game that afternoon. You'll become a demoralizing factor on the company." So I stopped looking for a job.

Consulting attracted me then and it still seems attractive today, although I have yet to follow up on it. I particularly like the idea of helping somebody else like you, the reader, set up a business. After all, I wrote this book with that in mind. Since I already get to see a lot of business plans, either as an investor or as an advisor, I think the transition would be an easy one. You are really running your own business, although technically you are still working for someone else, whether for the principal of a company or the venture capitalists or whoever wants you to help set up a business, turn a company around, take it to the next level, whatever. The primary attraction of consulting is that a successful entrepreneur will still be fulfilling the role that business has prepared him for, that of the "chief strategic officer" (CSO).

A successful entrepreneur likely has worked at every operational and management level of his company, knows it backwards and forwards, and has grown into the role of the CSO. That role might be compared to painting by the numbers. The CSO does not necessarily like the painting part; instead, he wants to decide what the picture is and which numbers will be represented by which colors. Today, I am the chief strategic officer at HEARx; I plan the painting. Steve Hansbrough, the president of HEARx, does the painting. I am the outside man, he is the inside man. I am in charge of top line and concept, while he is in charge of bottom line and reality.

It is very difficult to go from being a CSO and then going to be anything but. Consulting at least gives you the chance to fill the same role you have always filled. The other reason why consulting appears to be a good choice for an entrepreneur who is so inclined is simply that you have been successful, which is exactly what all entrepreneurs would like to be. Dr. Michael Patipa, the man with whom I set up Permark, pointed out in a humorous way the value of having help from someone who has already been there when starting up a business. When I told him that I was writing this book, he said:

"So, you're writing a book on being an entrepreneur."

"That's right," I said proudly.

"Well, that's interesting, because I've been thinking about writing a book, too."

"No kidding," I responded. "What's it about?"

"Well, the title I'm working with is "My Famous Friends' Business Sayings," Dr. Patipa said. "I've got three other friends just like you who have been successful in business and they always keep telling me things like, 'Always negotiate from a position of strength.'"

"That one's mine," I said, smiling earnestly, still wondering if Dr. Patipa was serious about writing a book.

"That's right," he affirmed. "I've got a chapter just for your sayings; 'Brownisms' I call them."

"I am flattered," I replied. "But what gave you the idea to write a book?"

"Well, I keep quoting these things to other people," he told me. "So I figured I'd collect all the sayings in a book and that would save me a lot of time, at the very least. Instead of telling them all these things, I'd just sell them each a book and they'd have everything they ever needed to start up a business. I could get rich! No one would ever have to go to business school! They would just have to learn all these statements of my four friends."

We laughed, but Dr. Patipa's tongue-in-cheek pronouncement of his book-writing venture really pointed up the value of my own book. Most people need a successful guide through The Business Jungle. The truth is that you are not going to find most of the information in this book in a traditional business school text. If you are thinking about starting your own business and go to business school first, that's great. But read this book, too, and if you can afford one, hire an experienced guide who can help prevent you from making any fatal mistakes in the jungle. But you will never really learn anything unless you experience the business jungle firsthand. You will make your own mistakes and, once you have been successful, you can write a book and become a consultant.

If all of the above fail to fill in the blanks of your next step, perhaps the answer is, simply, *do it again!* **Go back into business**, start all over again. Well, not really *all* over again. You know who and what you are now; you have proved your entrepreneurial prowess in the marketplace. Plus, you have all this valuable experience. Seems a shame that it would all go to waste. So, go back to *Chapter 2* and begin once more. You become an owl again, looking for the opportunity. But do not for a minute think that just because you have been through it once before that your vision somehow has become sharper, more acute.

It has not. Trust me.

That is precisely why it is so important to re-establish your perspective. You need to take time to carefully consider your next step before you start trekking through The Business Jungle again. Before I finally went back to build HEARx, I had gone from one venture to another to another. I lost money on all four business ventures, one right after another. I had lost my perspective and nearly two and a half million dollars in those ill-advised attempts. Added to the $7 million I have invested in HEARx I went through all the money I made when I sold MetPath and then some. The money I have invested in HEARx has had a fantastic return, at least on paper, based on the price of the stock on the American Stock Exchange. But the money I lost in my four failures is another story.

Three of the four—Medex, Permark and Kinetix—have already been discussed in *Chapter 2* and *Chapter 5*. The fourth, SciMed Advances, is an example of how big mistakes can get. It was my first venture after leaving MetPath and was intended to be a public business development corporation that would fund medical research. Essentially a public stock offering that was going to be sold exclusively to physicians, I only wanted to do it if I had enough money to do it right. I raised $2 million from universities, but told them that if it did not work I would give them all their money back. They all invested on my guarantee. I had what I thought was a great idea, plus three Nobel laureates involved in it and my own successful track record on Wall Street. Everything indicated success, except for one thing: poor timing.

The ideal window of opportunity for SciMed Advances was about a decade away. When I came to the window, it was open only a crack. Few people were investing in biotech when SciMed began in 1982 and I was not willing to take the time it would take to convince them. So we were unable to get investors and I had to give back the original $2 million investment to the universities.

I had been ahead of my time one more time, a not unusual place for entrepreneurs to be. Both MetPath and HEARx, my business successes, were about ten years ahead of their time and my failures were no different. I learned much from those successes; but out of all those losses came some different lessons. I discovered that I could be deluded without having any grandeur and that my entrepreneurial spirit may be genetic but not foolproof. My bulldog mentality, so very important in my successes, obviously was not operating too well either. Until HEARx, I just did not have the sticking power, either constitutionally and financially, because I really did not have a good grasp of what I was getting myself into.

How easy it was to forget everything that I had learned about building a business! I failed in those four ventures because I did not follow the road that had brought me success with MetPath. I had no dream and no plan to get there. All I was doing was spending time, bouncing from one potential opportunity to another, grasping at anything that looked good enough to spend some money on. I needed instead to take some time and find a way to make some money, to shake off the past, and take a hard look at the probabilities. Without a plan, I was bound to fail; without a dream for the future, I was doomed to try to live off the phantom of my past success.

Nothing clouds the mind as much as success. There is life after your first company, but you must beware of the fact that your earlier success will affect your whole decision-making process as you try to move ahead. You think that just because you did it once, it's a piece of cake. I can give you example after example of the people who started one company and made a lot of money, then started another company and lost a lot of money, all because they lacked a coherent plan for the road ahead. I came very close to falling into that category myself.

If I had thought through what turned out to be my failures and not allowed my enthusiasm to rule, I probably would not have entered into several of them. If I had taken the time necessary for proper planning and investigation, at least that would have helped me reduce my losses in the ventures I did pursue, since they probably would have gone elsewhere for **The Money**.

All of which makes a very good argument for taking time out to plan your next steps after stepping out of your ex-company. And if your next step is heading back into The Business Jungle, at least you will go in fairly certain of what you do *not* want to do.

You might even know what it is you really want to do.

*   *   *   *   *

Whatever they lack in visual acuity, they more than make up for it with their prodigious strength and keen senses of smell and hearing—aside from being able to run at a surprising thirty miles an hour and to climb just about anything. Well-equipped hunters with broad, five-toed feet and nonretractile claws, even the largest bears are good swimmers. Most are omnivorous, although some are vegetarians. Regardless of diet, bears are addicted to sweets, making them one of the few kinds of wild animals that suffer from tooth cavities.

*   *   *   *   *

3. What To Do

When I finally got to the point where I was serious enough about really going into business for a second time, I found myself in a very uncomfortable place, having lost a considerable amount of money. But at least my ego was right-sized again, even if it had to be brought down to earth the hard way.

I began to dream about building a big company again. It was as if some dormant instinct was triggered in my entrepreneurial genetic code, something akin, perhaps, to the urge salmon have to head upstream to spawn in the waters where they were born. However, unlike the salmon, my code does not include a memory map. I could not just start out on my journey and expect to arrive safely. I had no automatic sense of how to get where I was going. Fortunately, God equipped me with a few other things that the salmon does not have—one of them a larger brain, which even works, on occasion. No sooner did I start dreaming big dreams but my wonderful mental apparatus kicked in and I heard:

"Go back to the beginning and start all over again."

Which, interestingly enough, is probably what the salmon hears! Anyway, already having exhausted quite a number of possibilities, I moved quickly into probability thinking. I sat down and wrote down a number of criteria that would make it possible for me to build a big business once again.

HEADING UPSTREAM

1. The business had to be in the health care industry. I did not just want to go back into business. I am a physician and I believe my success in the business world is a result of being a physician. **Play to your strengths.**
2. I wanted a giant business. I am not a niche investor. I would rather have a little piece of a giant business than a big piece of a small business. It is a lot easier to survive and have a viable business if you are only getting a little teeny piece of a giant market. **There is safety in numbers.**
3. I wanted a company with the potential for domestic and international business. Plus, I had fun running a company that was in multiple countries. **Do not limit yourself.**

4. I wanted a business that would grow due to external forces. I did not want to make it happen. I wanted somebody or something else to do that: legislation, the aging of the population, the environment, whatever. **Let someone else help develop your market.**

5. I wanted something that could benefit by being a public company because of the exposure it would get. If you are a crook, you should not have a public company; if you are not and do not mind people looking over your shoulder, then there is no reason not to. **Partners are fine, if you control the show.**

6. I wanted a non-cyclical business, not affected by every quirk of the weather or the economy. MetPath went up and down every time there was a snowstorm and always on Wednesdays, when doctors play golf. I wanted a business without those factors. HEARx, at least initially, was a seasonal business, when the "snowbirds" arrived in Florida. **Reduce potential problems.**

7. I wanted a business with higher gross profit margins than MetPath. We never made a lot of money in MetPath, although at 12 percent it was not bad for the lab business. But every time we had a bad quarter, Wall Street was ready to do an autopsy. Then when the stock went down investors called me, asking me if we were going out of business. I wanted something that was without those kinds of pressures. **Profits relieve all kinds of pressures.**

8. I wanted to do something that was socially significant. **Give something back to society.**

If you are going to try and do it again, recognize that you are now an educated, wealthy parrot *(see Chapter 3)*. You definitely will look as good as you sound to investors. It will be easy to raise money—from yourself, but not from them! They have not changed. You have. When investors look at your next project, they will be going back to square one and question your level of commitment.

You will probably have to start up your next business with at least some of the money you made on the first. Hopefully, it will not take **all of your money**. But the only way you will be likely to attract investors will be to be a major investor yourself, right at the outset. Then, when you need more money—because, as usual, everything will take twice as long and cost twice as much—do not be surprised when investors will want to know why you are not putting more of your own money into your business.

"If it's so good, why don't you put some more of your own money in?"

I heard that for nine years at HEARx and, no matter how much money I put into it, it was never enough money until sales topped

$10 million a year. Investors have very short memories, aside from being poor information gatherers. People made millions of dollars as a result of my efforts at MetPath, yet very few were willing to give me any money for HEARx. There were some who invested relatively early, of course, yet I am sure they would not have invested had I not been right there beside them with my own money until the company became profitable.

Be prepared to spend some or even a lot of your money. Timing, don't you know, is everything. Do it right and you may not have to spend all your money. Just be prepared to spend some of it, along with **all of your time**. That's right. *All* of your time, at least for a few years. The amount of your time it will take to start up a business remains constant, something that needs to be carefully considered. Are you willing to put in twelve to fourteen-hour days again? How much effort are you really prepared to put out? Are you just going to throw your hands up and walk away from the business when the going gets tough? Obviously, these are important issues that have to be decided before you ever head back into the business jungle, ideal items to consider during your time out after selling your ex-company.

And do not forget to consider the effects of spending as much as a year relaxing, resting, traveling and thinking about what you are going to do. It is going to be very different, going from doing nothing all day long except thinking and then suddenly having to go back to work again. Can you—do you really *want* to—go back to the grind? The investors want to know that! The investors who did not want to invest in HEARx in the beginning were primarily concerned with my commitment of time. Would I really get down to business or would I just go sailing and play tennis and bask in the Florida sun?

The point is that, second time around, you are going to want to know how much money and time you are going to commit, even if you are not planning on having any investors. If your plan is to buy a business or start something up on your own, you will of course have to settle on how much of your money you will commit. But you had better settle your commitment in time, too. You may have planned your work, but do not forget that you then have to go and work your plan. You are going have to spend a lot of your time, probably all of it, to get things off the ground.

It does not matter who you are or how much money you have; running a business requires your time and effort. No business runs itself. If one did, everyone would want to be in that business. But here in the real world, there are going to be all sorts of problems all over again—problems with money and people and adjusting the strategic plan; with suppliers and customers and banks and managers; and with production and service levels and quality control and computers and acquisitions and ...

Well, I am not going to repeat myself—except in being successful.

If that is what you want but have not been paying attention, go back and re-read the first nine chapters.

Everything you need is there.

Just make sure *you* are all there, all the time, if you plan to go through it again.

Good Hunting!

$ECRET$ OF THE BEAR

*Time spent doing nothing
will keep you from being left with nothing.*

---

*No amount of money is really enough
to make losses not matter.*

---

*One success in the Business Jungle only leaves
the faintest of trails to follow the next time!*

About the Authors
▲ ▲ ▲ ▲ ▲

Paul A. Brown, M.D., is a graduate of Harvard College and Tufts University School of Medicine. Although he had no formal business education, few have matched his feat of starting up a company with five hundred dollars and, in twelve years, building a world-wide organization with over one hundred million dollars in sales. MetPath, Inc. was among the first and easily the most successful among international clinical testing laboratories. Dr. Brown sold his brainchild to a major corporation in 1982 for one hundred and forty million dollars, personally netting ten million dollars after taxes. Along the way, he became a well-known and respected personality among his peers in the medical profession, within investment circles, and in the worlds of business and finance.

Dr. Brown's career has been extensively chronicled by *Fortune, Forbes, Venture,* the *Wall Street Journal,* the *New York Times,* the ABC show *Money and Medicine,* and other national and international media. His innovative strategies on Wall Street have become legendary, both during his association with MetPath and in later ventures. His bold style made news even when his moves were mistakes—such as the huge, two hundred and seventy- five million dollar offering that he attempted to float exclusively to medical doctors in 1984. That was credited by *Business Week* as the first ever, and easily the largest, attempt at raising capital for a new public company by selling stock only to a single type of investor.

Dr. Brown currently is the chairman and chief executive officer of another business called HEARx Ltd., a national chain of retail hearing care centers he started in 1986 which today trades on the American Stock Exchange. His twelve million shares in this venture have increased his net worth substantially.

Dr. Brown is a member of Tufts University's Board of Trustees and is also a past chairman of the Board of Overseers of Tufts University's School of Medicine. Dr. Brown also serves as a member of the Visiting Committee of Boston University's School of Medicine and is on the part-time faculty at Columbia University's College of Physicians and Surgeons. He holds a second-degree black belt in karate and resides in Palm Beach, Florida, with his wife, Cynthia, of thirty-six years.

Richard D. Hoffmann has enjoyed a successful professional writing career of nearly thirty years. A business journalist and editor for top New York business publishers such as Fairchild and CMP Publications for a dozen years, and later a freelance writer and editorial consultant, Mr. Hoffmann has published more than one thousand articles in a broad variety of newspapers and magazines ranging from *Information Week* to *Home Furnishings Daily* to *Popular Science*.

He moved to Florida in 1986 and, while on assignment there for *Venture* magazine, met Dr. Brown. The two soon after began a collaboration which resulted in *Success in the Business Jungle: Secrets of an Entrepreneurial Animal*, Mr. Hoffmann's third nonfiction book. He is currently at work on his fourth book, a biography of F. Lee Bailey. Mr. Hoffmann is married and resides in Palm Beach Gardens, Florida, with his wife, Susan, of twenty-five years.